Encountering Student

Encountering Student Texts

Interpretive Issues in
Reading Student Writing

Edited by

Bruce Lawson
University of Texas–El Paso

Susan Sterr Ryan
Santa Monica College

W. Ross Winterowd
University of Southern California–Los Angeles

National Council of Teachers of English
1111 Kenyon Road, Urbana, Illinois 61801

NCTE Editorial Board: Richard Abrahamson, Celia Genishi, Richard Lloyd-Jones, Raymond J. Rodrigues, Brooke Workman, Charles Suhor, *ex officio*, Michael Spooner, *ex officio*

Staff Editor: Robert A. Heister

Cover Design: Doug Burnett

Interior Book Design: Tom Kovacs for TGK Design

NCTE Stock Number 13400–3020

Library of Congress Cataloging in Publication Data

Encountering student texts : interpretive issues in reading student
   writing / edited by Bruce Lawson, Susan Sterr Ryan, W. Ross Winterowd.
      p.   cm.
   Includes bibliographical references.
   ISBN 0–8141–1340–0
   1. English language—Rhetoric—Study and teaching. 2. English
language—Rhetoric—Evaluation. 3. Grading and marking (Students)
4. College prose—Evaluation. I. Lawson, Bruce, 1947–   .
II. Ryan, Susan Sterr. III. Winterowd, W. Ross.
PE1404.E47 1990
808'.042'07—dc20   89-49574
                                           CIP

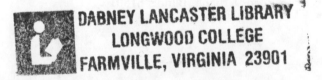

Contents

Introduction: Interpretive Issues in Student Writing

Bruce Lawson
University of Texas–El Paso

Susan Sterr Ryan
Santa Monica College

All chapters in this book were prepared in response to identical guidelines (see the appendix to this book) which were sent to writing education specialists around the country. How, we wanted to know, do writing teachers read student papers? Already there was a body of research about grading student writing. This research into evaluation practices had led compositionists to conduct further investigations about ways teachers respond to student papers. But it was the following question that spurred this volume: As writing teachers read papers, how do they interpret them? The question seemed to us fundamental to all analyses of evaluation and response.

The question was first asked some years ago by Louise Wetherbee Phelps and W. Ross Winterowd in the context of a graduate rhetoric seminar they were team-teaching at the University of Southern California. Phelps asked graduate students, most of whom were teaching freshman writing, to write phenomenological accounts of their reading processes of student papers. These accounts demonstrated that interpreting student writing involved important critical issues worth further exploration.

While teachers of literature have always had access to a massive body of theory concerning the interpretation and evaluation of prose fiction, poetry, and drama, teachers of composition have been without such a resource in regard to that other body of texts, the student writing that consumes so much time and energy in most secondary and post-secondary English departments. The 1986 *Longman Bibliography of Composition and Rhetoric* contains 113 items under "Evaluation of Students," but these sources do not address concerns represented by the sections of *Encountering Student Texts*: the ways teachers read

student writing, the conflicts they encounter between theory and
practice, the ethical responsibilities that weigh on them, and the
reflections they make on their own responses. A body of work on
student writing is, however, beginning to develop—for example, Hil-
gers's "Toward a Taxonomy of Beginning Writers' Evaluative Statements
on Written Compositions" (1984); Newkirk's "How Students Read
Student Essays: An Exploratory Study" (1984); and Porter's "The
Reasonable Reader: Knowledge and Inquiry in Freshman English"
(1987). Most recently, NCTE has published *Writing and Response*, edited
by Chris M. Anson (1988).

That writing teachers are only now beginning a critical study of
methods of interpretion is not, of course, surprising. Traditionally,
writing, like reading, was considered a linear, straightforward activity.
However, nearly two decades of scrutiny of the act of composition
have revealed the striking complexity of the writer's tasks. The "act"
of writing has become the "process" of writing, a process of inex-
haustible and unsettling richness, subtlety, and controversy. During
this period, the act of reading has also undergone linguistic, literary,
and philosophical scrutiny, which has shaken the very foundations of
our understanding of a reader's interaction with a text. The research
has resulted in a host of books and articles on reading theory. The
vast majority of these deal with the phenomenon of reading literary
texts. Considerable attention has also been paid to student writing as
text, but, to date, studies have focused on how teachers evaluate or
ought to respond to student papers.[1] Before teachers can evaluate or
respond to student writing, though, they must interpret it, and the
ways in which they interpret it are shaped by a multitude of assumptions and values—about language, about student writing, about their
students, and about their roles as readers. These are the issues that
the writers in this volume try to come to terms with as they reflect
on their own encounters with student texts.

It is our belief that student texts provide a unique intersection of
reading and composition theory. The uniqueness of student writing
and the peculiar writer-reader-text relationship that arises from teachers' interactions with students' essays are phenomena which have not
been adequately explored until this volume. Student writing not only
deserves critical attention because of its importance and ubiquity in
our society, but also because it is a fertile area in which to explore
and challenge our understanding of developments in reading and
composition theory.

Student papers create a rhetorical situation quite unlike that produced
by any other text. Special conditions are imposed upon all three

elements of the rhetorical triangle—the writer, the text, and the reader. Teachers must deal with these conditions every time they read their students' papers. For instance, they must contend with the strong and often negative forces created by the real and present student writer, by the peculiar nature of the text, and by their own particularly personal and ambivalent reader-relation to the text. In each of these areas, a multitude of problems unique to student writing must be addressed.

For example, student papers usually possess a texture which, among other things, contains various kinds of interference and miscues not usually encountered in other texts. Features such as spelling errors, structural defects, and solecisms make special demands upon a reader, demands that rarely need to be reckoned with in other texts.

Furthermore, student writing is unique in that few other reading situations allow the writer the degree of presence that he or she has in the student paper. The reader is acquainted with and personally accountable to the writer. The existence of this real and present writer—who must be responded to in terms of his or her writing—creates a morally and politically charged reading environment. The "real" writer puts a weight of responsibility on the reader which does not exist in other reading contexts.

No matter how humanitarian their concerns, teachers must, ultimately, bear the responsibility of evaluating their students' work. Not only must they evaluate and respond to papers, but often, as they guide students through assignments and make suggestions for revision, they even coauthor their students' writing. Naturally, this makes grading "objectively" difficult—in fact, impossible. Add to this complex situation the issue of teachers' attitudes—about their students (individually and as a group), about their jobs, about their role as readers. How many teachers, sitting up well past midnight reading student papers on a Sunday night, or carrying stacks of compositions with them on weekend vacations or holidays, have not known what it is to be the captive audience of their students, have not felt the responsibility of being perhaps the only audience on the authors' minds as they wrote?

Clearly, the relationships that teachers take for granted in other reading situations are distorted, or at least reordered, in the student writing context. H. P. Grice's "Cooperative Principle" (1967) identifies certain assumptions common to all normal discourse situations, including ordinary reading situations: the reader assumes that the text will provide enough information to get the point across and no more—that it will neither waste time nor leave the reader in a state of uncertainty; that the author will not deliberately write something that is false or lacks evidence; that everything in the text will be relevant to the subject at hand; that the author will have authority on the subject; that the text will be well-ordered and will avoid unnecessary obscurity and ambiguity.

These principles, which make sense in ordinary reading situations, are largely turned on their heads in the context of the writing class. How often, for example, do students make their points clearly and succinctly? To what extent do teachers trust the integrity of students and trust that they really believe what they write, or even that what they have written originated with them, since problems with plagiarism have made many instructors wary? In other words, when teachers read student papers, they inevitably read against the grain, subverting Grice's principles by approaching student writing with a skepticism quite unlike their approach to most other texts. The effect of such subversion cannot be minimized. The social and psychological forces created by having to discern weaknesses in the writing and then to confront the writer with these negative judgments certainly influence teachers as they interpret student texts.

Looking closely at the transaction that takes place between the teacher-reader and student writing may help to illuminate the teacher's role as reader-interpreter, deepen our understanding of the particularly problematic nature of student writing, and perhaps create empathy for the extraordinarily complex predicament of both the student writer and the evaluating teacher. When we examine the interaction between teachers and student text, we are necessarily inquiring into the very nature of text and textual interpretation. We are engaging in *hermeneutics*, the science of interpretation. The term, first applied to Biblical studies and exegesis, traditionally meant finding an author's meaning and explaining it to others. But, influenced by movements in philosophy and critical theory that have challenged definitions of text, author, reader, and meaning, hermeneutics has come to be understood as that enterprise which seeks to identify, understand, and illuminate issues of interpretation. Today the concepts of *determinacy* and *intentionality*, taken for granted by nearly all readers and writers, are highly problematic and provide the focus of critical perspectives. Increasingly, literary hermeneutics has shifted the spotlight of criticism from the text itself to the reader. This shift has had dramatic effects on the views of language and its relation to reality. And the implications for teachers of composition are significant.

More than thirty years ago, the New Critics upset classical notions of intentionality when they severed the author from the text. Before the advent of New Criticism, writing and reading seemed straightforward activities and attention focused on writers' authority. Writers began with meanings they intended to convey and which they conveyed in language. A reader's duty was to discover those intentions. But with their identification of the "intentional fallacy," Wimsatt and Beardsley (1954) challenged this traditional view. Once authors publish their texts, these critics claimed, the works took on lives of their own, independent of authors' intentions. What works writers had loosed into the world, these critics claimed, were subject to interpretation. In terms of the rhetorical triangle, then, attention shifted from author to text.

But the Structuralist critics challenged the idea that meaning could reside in the text. If language itself were to carry meaning, they said, then there would be a natural and compulsory relation between words and their referents. As Ferdinand de Saussure showed, however, there is no such inherent referential quality in language. That anyone who speaks English knows what the word *cow* refers to is not a property of the word itself but an indication of a tacit, socially-agreed-upon system of language. Thus, the very notion of language is challenged and so also is the notion of text.

By throwing open the definition of language and text, the Structuralists made way for reader-response criticism. Indeed, reader-response criticism has essentially redefined author, writer, and text and challenged the concepts of determinacy and intentionality. For example, Stanley Fish (1980, 163–73; 303–21; 338–55) claims that the text is in the reader, thereby denying the possibility of either determinate meaning or knowledge of authorial intention. The very meaning of "meaning" is thereby altered and becomes the consequence of reading as process. According to Fish, meaning is created in the experience of reading. As one reads, one builds expectations, only to have them upset by further reading. Thus reading becomes a process of constructing and overturning expectations. Against the potential problem of solipsism, he has postulated "interpretive communities," groups of readers, who by tacit consent, regulate the range of possible meaning. Together, the concept of reader as creator of the text and the concept of interpretive communities help to explain why two or more people can create a text in the same way while others find the reading of the same text a different experience.

Wolfgang Iser (1978, 23–27; 42–43) believes that what allows readers to create the text differently are gaps, those areas from which information is missing. Because it is impossible for any author to render an experience completely, the reader has some freedom to fill in these information gaps. Like Fish, Iser claims that readers build up expectations in the process of reading, but they continue to read only because they expect the unfamiliar. In other words, if a text only told readers what they already knew, they would have no motivation for reading. Like Fish, Iser believes that several readers may produce similar texts, by drawing on their repertoire of conventions (acquired from society) for making meaning of what they are reading. This "intersubjective verifiability" is similar to Fish's notion of interpretive communities.

French Deconstructionist critics, however, like Roland Barthes and Jacques Derrida, radically oppose any concept of verifiable meaning. Therefore, there can be neither intentionality nor determinacy. For them, text forever delays closure because the possibilities for meaning are endless. Once the author has produced a work, he or she disappears from the scene and has no control at all over what readers do with the text. The author was never more than an instance writing. But this is a happy situation, for it calls on readers to take what Barthes calls a "writerly" approach to reading: that is, instead of consuming texts, readers produce them as they read; the richness of their reading experience is limited only by their ability to encode the text. As Derrida explains, there is no unassailable foundation to our thought-system, no foundation upon which we can construct a hierarchy of meaning. For Derrida, writing continually evades *all* systems or logic. As he explains in *Writing and Difference* (1978): "Meaning must await being said or written in order to inhabit itself, and in order to become, by differing from itself, what it is: meaning" (11).

Present controversy in criticism centers on definitions of knowledge. In the past two years, spurred by the work of philosophers Richard Rorty and Thomas Kuhn, a theory of Social Constructionism has begun to influence composition studies. Generally, social constructionists have claimed that knowledge is created by social communities that are linked by common language and is controlled by those communities that dominate the discourse conventions. To have knowledge, then, is to belong to a discourse community. Every discipline in the academy and every profession, for example, has its own language and discourse conventions. Interpretation is impossible for one who does not grasp these conventions. Social constructionism, then, is as radical as deconstruction. Not only does it undo traditional conceptions of a transcendent reality and stability of truth, but it also alters the way we perceive self: an individual can only "know" what is within the knowledge pool; even the conventions a person has for interpreting the world and the self are limited by the community. Interpretation is impossible for one who does not grasp these conventions.

Since a real motivation for reading student writing, no matter how humanitarian our concerns, is to interpret and evaluate it, we must decide, in light of current debate over the location of the text, exactly what we are interpreting and evaluating. If we believe that the locus of interpretation is in the student paper, then we must also believe that there is determinate meaning, something the student intended from the outset to say. This notion assumes that teachers can recognize (perhaps with the help of dialogue with students) the thoughts their students are trying to express and assist them in improving ideas or communication. This suggests that teachers will similarly evaluate the same paper. However, that has been shown not to be the case. In *Measuring Growth in English* (1974), Paul Diederich reports the subjectivity of essay grading. Diederich and his associates at the Educational Testing Service (ETS) gave a random sample of essays to qualified readers to grade A through F. There were two striking results. First, the ETS group found that when they stamped "honors" at the top of random essays, those essays received higher grades than others in the sample. Second, Diederich found that an average of twenty percent of the papers received every grade from "A" through "F." When such variant responses exist, how can one assume that meaning is embodied in the student paper itself and is equally available to all readers? Clearly, there are problems with locating the object of interpretation in the text itself.

If one looks to the reader as the locus of interpretation,then the teacher becomes the significant creator of student texts, a "writerly" reader who makes meaning of texts in light of personal experience. Preference for the familiar or unfamiliar will influence the way a teacher evaluates the student text, as will his or her mood, current interests, life situation (to name a few) and other contextual factors of the reading situation (time and place, for instance). Even the assignment the teacher has developed will influence the way he or she reads a paper, for one purpose in reading might be to determine whether students are meeting the teacher's expectations or requirements for the assignment. The problem with reading to discover whether students have met the requirements for the assignment, however, is that teacher expectations and students' understanding of the assignment are sometimes at odds. Students simply do not always have the genre knowledge that teachers expect of them. George Dillon (1981) explains that the mind analyzes and interprets experience in terms of models or patterns, what he calls "schemata." Schemata, he says, perform three functions in the process of a reader's text-construction: they enable the reader to organize, integrate, and predict material. Schemata become, then, ideas or models of order, "patterns of order that we expect to find, and seek to find, in discourse" (53). He goes on to explain that: "Labored reading, miscomprehension, and sheer incomprehension occur when the reader cannot find the schema or must wrestle with interfering incorrect schemata that he does find. These difficulties are not always the writer's fault, however, since ignorance, inattention, and wayward associations on the part of the reader will also produce them" (53).

Dillon's statement seems to have important applications as we consider the teacher as the locus of interpretation in student texts. Does a teacher fail to find meaning simply because she cannot find an operating schema or because she has made "wayward associations"?

This leads us to another difficulty. Barthes implies that the best reading is the richest reading, the one that brings together the most codes. But just how rich should the teacher's interpretation be? In the case of basic writing students, Mina Shaughnessy (1977) perceives that the only way for a teacher to help his or her students is to give texts the fullest reading possible. She says that "a teacher who would work with BW [basic writing] students might well begin by trying to understand the logic of their mistakes in order to determine at what point or points along the developmental path error should or can become a subject for instruction" (13). She encourages teachers to have "a readiness to look at these problems [of basic writers] in a way that does not ignore the linguistic sophistication of the students nor yet underestimate the complexity of the task they face as they set about learning to write for college" (13). So the teacher seems to be engaged in two activities: first, reading to find absences in the text, or pushing against the grain, and second, reading to fill in those gaps, imagining details the student writer hints at or might have included.

A third approach to interpreting student texts is to look at the author-student as the locus of interpretation. Of course, the question here is, if student writers are the locus of interpretation, what degree of control do they have over the texts they produce? The fact that we overturn Grice's principles as we read student papers indicates our lack of faith in their control. This lack of faith is not unwarranted. As Mina Shaughnessy has shown, sometimes students are confused about what they are doing in a paper. Because they do not know particular conventions, they will affect a style. Janet Emig (1971) and Sondra Perl (1979) found the same affectation of style in the texts of inexperienced writers. How do teachers help students feel that the texts they produce are truly theirs, not the ghost of some preconceived high style they are trying to emulate?

More often than not, we teachers give our students the impression that their papers are our property, not theirs. Often we "collect" papers from students (as if collecting a debt), silently read them, and return them to students with disfiguring, often cryptic, markings; in fact, almost all teachers assume the right to do this. Thus, even if we believe that the locus of interpretation is in the student-author, we certainly are not, at least in practice, admitting it. Don't we, in fact, deconstruct our students' texts, looking for places where meaning breaks down, for holes in logic that cause theses and arguments to fall apart?

But to consider that the locus of any given teacher's interpretation of student texts resides with only one aspect of the rhetorical triangle—reader, writer, or text—is certainly not realistic. Undoubtedly, the vast majority of teachers—regardless of both their stated and tacit theoretical views—do indeed take into account all areas of the triangle in making evaluations. That is, we teachers look at a paper in light of the writer's apparent intention and in terms of our expectations for the assignment, recognizing that our own biases influence evaluation. As teachers we do, in fact, take for granted the notion that thoughts and ideas can be bracketed, analyzed, discussed, and finally written down intelligibly. We also assume that this written language can be stabilized (shared and analyzed) in conferences and in tutorials. Furthermore, we take for granted that, as teachers, we are able to discuss, analyze and make value judgments of student ideas, that we can recognize how effectively our students' ideas are expressed in writing. Finally, we accept that we can make quality judgments which conform to some sort of objective scale, and we can rank "relative" success of a sample of student texts. If all of these assumptions are indeed made, then the act of reading, interpreting, and evaluating essays—as the overwhelming majority of teachers actually do read student essays—requires a very traditional, conservative view of thought and language.

The question for us educators is whether, in light of current hermeneutic theory, we really wish to continue to assume all that we have traditionally assumed when we read student texts. In the classroom, there has clearly been a shift from the teaching of writing as an act to the teaching of writing as a process. Theory has thus radically changed our pedagogical approaches. However, it does not yet seem to be the case that the developing awareness of the nature of text and reader-text relations has had significant impact on the way most teachers read and evaluate student texts. We feel the group of essays collected here raises a full range of hermeneutic concerns regarding student writing. Now it is time to focus more specifically on the implications of these concerns. For example, how is the way we read

texts affected by the specific nature of the class, whether it is multicultural, remedial, advanced, and/or interdisciplinary? We hope that
this collection will encourage a reconsideration of the interpretation
and evaluation practices of writing teachers and spur further research
and discussion. We also believe that the richness of these essays justifies
our conviction that student texts do indeed represent a significant
juncture in the crosscurrents of reading and composition theory and
practice.

Notes

1. Particularly interesting is Charles Cooper and Lee Odell's collection of essays, *Evaluating Writing: Describing, Measuring, Judging* (Urbana: NCTE, 1977). But as its title suggests, the volume concentrates
primarily on ways to evaluate writing, on the reliability of such methods
as holistic and primary trait scoring. While primary trait scoring is a
primitive form of reader-response criticism (it requires that the reader
establish whether certain predetermined characteristics are present in
the writing), still it does not focus on interpretation.

Works Cited

Anson, Chris M., ed. *Writing and Response: Theory, Practice, and Research.*
    Urbana: NCTE, 1989.
Barthes, Roland. *S/Z.* Translated by Richard Miller. New York: Hill and Wang,
    1974.
———. "The Death of the Author." In *Images—Music—Text*, translated by
    Stephen Heath, 142–48. Ithaca: Cornell Univ. Press, 1979.
Cooper, Charles R. and Lee Odell. *Evaluating Writing.* Urbana: NCTE, 1977.
Derrida, Jacques. "Freud and the Scene of Writing." In *Writing and Difference*,
    translated by Alan Bass, 196–231. Chicago: University of Chicago Press,
    1978.
Diederich, Paul. *Measuring Growth in English.* Urbana: NCTE, 1974.
Dillon, George. *Constructing Texts: Elements of a Theory of Composition and
    Style.* Bloomington: Indiana University Press, 1981.
Emig, Janet. *The Composing Process of Twelfth Graders.* Urbana: NCTE, 1971.
Fish, Stanley. *Is There a Text in This Class?* Cambridge: Harvard University
    Press, 1980.
Geertz, Clifford. "Thick Description: Toward an Interpretive Theory of Cul-
    ture." In *The Interpretation of Cultures: Selected Essays*, 3–30. New York:
    Basic Books, 1973.
Grice, H.P. From the William James Lectures delivered at Harvard University,
    1967.

Hilger, Thomas L. "Toward a Taxonomy of Beginning Writers' Evaluative Statements on Written Compositions." *Written Communication 1* (1984): 365–84.

Iser, Wolfgang. *The Act of Reading: A Theory of Aesthetic Response.* Baltimore: Johns Hopkins University Press, 1978.

Lindemann, Erika. *Longman Bibliography of Composition and Literature, 1986.* New York: Longman, 1987.

Newkirk, Thomas. "How Students Read Student Essays: An Exploratory Study." *Written Communication 1* (1984): 283–305.

Perl, Sondra. "Composing Processes of Unskilled College Writers." In *Research in the Teaching of English* 13 (1979): 5–22.

Porter, Jeffrey. "The Reasonable Reader: Knowledge and Inquiry in Freshman English." *College English* 49 (1987): 332–44.

Shaughnessy, Mina. *Errors and Expectations: A Guide for the Teacher of Basic Writing.* New York: Oxford University Press, 1977.

Wimsatt, W. K., Jr., and Monroe C. Beardsley. *The Verbal Icon: Studies in the Meaning of Poetry.* Lexington: University of Kentucky Press, 1954.

I Encountering Ways of Reading

Student writing has, oddly, been handled as though it were far more stable than a literary text, offering itself without ambiguity, awaiting unanimous response. But as the writers in this section show, reading student texts is at least as highly complex and problematic an endeavor as reading literary texts.

The first essay, Margaret Himley's narrative of a group evaluation experience, illuminates the complex activities that are part of reading and responding to a student paper. She and her colleagues found themselves involved in a complicated interplay of interpretative acts: at times they attempted to "unpack" the meaning; other times they tried through rich readings to assist the student's creative effort; often their own values shaped and recreated the writer's meanings. Reflecting on that experience three years later, Himley notes the degree to which the perceived meanings of that student paper were shaped by the temporal and social context of the group session.

This awareness of the contextual nature of meaning is further explored by W. Ross Winterowd and James Thomas Zebroski. Their essays make it clear that student texts are as vulnerable to trends in critical theory as are literary works. Winterowd shows how the meaning of a student essay transforms over time according to the changing interpretative values of the readers, values usually derived from literature study. Similarly, Zebroski provides responses to a sample student essay to demonstrate how the meaning we find in our students' essays is shaped to a great extent by the voices of those important critics/theorists who influence us. Both writers believe that interpreting student papers is too complex to be understood within the confines of the classroom alone. Drawing on Kenneth Burke and Paulo Freire, Winterowd contends that to understand the "hermeneutic tapestry" required to interpret a student paper, we must attend to the social significance of our behavior and to the cultural agenda we are promoting in our responses to student essays. Zebroski urges a Bakhtinian interpretative strategy involving a search for and dialogue with the multiple voices— individual and social—that constitute the student text.

Elizabeth Flynn, too, analyzes recent changes in interpretative stances, but she explains these changes not in terms of evolving literary assumptions but in terms of gender difference. Thus, while Winterowd characterizes the evaluative, authoritative stance as a New Critical one, Flynn sees it as a distinctly masculine orientation. She believes that the movement over the past twenty-five years from that stance to a "student-centered process pedagogy" reflects, therefore, not so much an evolving literary theory as a growing acceptance of specifically feminine approaches to composition instruction.

Further underscoring the complicated nature of the interpretative process, Tilly Warnock's intense and poetic essay brings insights of Kenneth Burke's enigmatic dramatistic theory of meaning to student texts, setting forth both a theory of textuality and a method of interpretation. She justifies bringing Burke into the discussion because his theory is, above all, a theory of language, and for him language is always rhetorical. Warnock foregrounds this rhetorical, performative quality of language and argues a relationship to student and text that ultimately shares Zebroski's and Winterowd's emphasis on dialogue and sense of context and cultural significance.

Finally, Patricia Murray challenges us to reconsider some of our traditional interpretative priorities. Utilizing the reader-response literary theory of Wolfgang Iser to clarify the ways in which reading student writing differs from reading literary works and analyzing responses to a student essay by several teachers, she argues that in limiting ourselves to such traditional English Department values as control, concreteness, and diction, we may devalue a piece of writing that would be better understood and appreciated if interpreted through the frame of Iserian theory. Only when we examine the discourse community in which we operate and the expectations we place upon our students are we able to lead them to explore their full potential as writers.

All of these writers share the view that it is naive to talk about a "correct way" to read a student essay. Student texts, like literary works, are complex and slippery things, and we must be intensely self-conscious as interpreters. Just as our literature classes are enlivened by multiple approaches to the texts, so our encounters with student writing may become more productive as we consider alternative ways of interpreting and responding to those dauntingly alive, complex and troubling creations our students hand us at the end of class sessions.

1 A Reflective Conversation: "Tempos of Meaning"

Margaret Himley
Syracuse University

It was time again for the six of us to gather in the seminar room of the English Department. Jacki, a graduate student in English Education, set up the tape recorder in the middle of the table, while Don, Delia, Marty, and Lib, all experienced writing instructors, settled into their seats, chatting casually about classes and glancing through the packet of twelve student texts we had been working with.

"Who wants to read the next essay aloud?"

"I will," Delia said—and so we began.

Over the next three hours, we read and talked together about three of these student texts, as part of a communal reading process that we had been engaged in over several weeks.[1]

It was an *odd* reading process for us, dramatically communal in ways that both discomforted and exhilarated us as teachers accustomed to reading student texts alone in our offices. We had embarked on it together as a specific response to a particular problem at Syracuse University.

In the fall of 1983, the College of Arts and Sciences established an ad hoc committee charged with reviewing instruction throughout the college. At that time, students in this very traditional, form-oriented Freshman English program wrote in-class, five-paragraph argumentative essays on (typically) unannounced topics, and had to achieve minimum competency (at least two passes) in order to move on to the next three modules: Fiction, Poetry or Drama, and a mini-course. The kinds and amounts of writing in each module were prescribed, and grading sessions and file reviews were designed to standardize the rather formalistic ways teachers were asked to assign, respond to, and evaluate student writing.

As part of their work, the review committee members wanted a more specific *sense* of what students at Syracuse are like *as writers* when they enter the university and in what ways, if any, they change as a result of our instructional program.

The theoretical and methodological difficulties inherent in attempting to design "a research project" (in any experimental or quantitative sense) that would answer that question completely or definitively awed us, appropriately enough, yet questions kept nagging at us: What are our student writers like? How do they change? What is the effect of our writing instruction? As the compositionist on the committee, I was asked to figure out some way for us to get a more concrete picture of our university's student writers.

So I put together a procedure for reading student texts that would at least give us some actual experience with student writing. I proposed working with a group of Syracuse University writing teachers and using the phenomenologically-based review procedures developed by P. Carini (1975, 1979) to do a reflective reading, in order then to compose a descriptive typology, according to M.Q. Patton's *Qualitative Evaluation Methods* (1980), cast in the form of a metaphor.

In this essay I would like to present a kind of "thick description" of the reflective reading that we did of just *one* of those texts; "thick description" is Clifford Geertz's (1973) term for turning a passing event into "an account" for describing, interpreting, and evoking the complex meanings of that event which you enter into imaginatively.

A Reflective Reading

Background

Our general reading procedure, based on those developed by Carini, provided a specific structure for each meeting:

1. We read a text aloud.
2. Next, we went around the group, with each of us paraphrasing a section of the text.
3. We continued around the group, making observations or publicly verifiable statements about the text, such as noting the sentence patterns or repetitions of certain words.
4. Gradually we moved into more inferential statements, such as noting an apparent sense of confusion in the writer's use of a literary term or incoherence in the development of the claim.
5. Once this reflection was "completed," usually in about an hour, we summarized features of the text and categorized it based on our working metaphor of "driving a car."

In our first meetings, we agreed that a metaphor would provide an interpretive framework for describing and charting texts. Patton makes the point that metaphors serve as "a way of communicating the connotative meanings of the various categories" (1980, 316–17) when qualitative researchers report results, as long as reification is avoided. We experimented with several metaphors, such as downhill skiing, looking for an activity comparable in some ways to writing, and ended up with "driving a car." The driver, with a certain destination or purpose in mind, selects a route along which she travels, negotiating the twists and turns and demands of the road. Drivers vary in their understanding of the car itself, of the route, and of the strategies for handling curves or rounding corners. In a similar way, a writer has a certain purpose which she strives to fulfill within the constraints and potentials of the route laid out by a particular genre. Writers also vary in their understanding of the language, of the genre, and of the strategies for negotiating textual choice points. We ended up with categories like "car careening out of control," "commuter," and "rally driver."

Fundamentally, the structuring procedure serves to bring a group of readers from a common community together for a concentrated "conversation" about some particular focus of interest (Carini 1979), in this case, student texts looked at from a developmental perspective. As the following narrative illustrates, our conversation slips in and out of the "rules," takes place in far less linear fashion, and works in interpenetrating ways both to reveal and "unpack" meaning as well as to constitute it. This kind of reading process proved complex and generative.

And *odd*. At Syracuse, teachers had tended in the past to work alone, in a kind of isolation, and to respond to texts primarily as products for diagnostic or evaluative—that is, *grading*—purposes. But for this reading we didn't have to grade these essays or place the students in appropriate courses or design instructional plans. Our traditional institutional constraints were loosened, the traditional reading framework was loosened, and we had time and space and a communal setting to enter into the various textual possibilities of these student texts, to play with those possibilities, to respond *differently* and, as it turned out, expansively to student writing.

In this particular session, halfway through the project, the text we worked on, which follows, had been written as a diagnostic on the first day of Freshman English, prompted by a topic such as, "Compare

two movies you have seen recently and evaluate which was better."
This essay is based on an analysis of a transcript from the taped
session. Following is the student text:

> As I was waiting in one of the many lengthy lines I have
> encountered at Syracuse University, a group of students began
> discussing the various movies they had seen recently. Some movies
> were thought of very highly by some people, while others detested
> them. I, of course, refused to listen to this conversation without
> voicing my own opinion. When I got a chance to speak, I
> immediately told them that I had seen two excellent movies this
> summer, but one was slightly better than the other. Everyone
> stared at me in silence, wondering what which movies I had
> chosen to discuss.
>
> When I told them I was referring to *Airplane* and *Caddyshack*,
> a roar of voices arose. Many people agreed that both movies were
> very funny and that they would even see them again. Others
> only liked one of the two, and few hated them both. As the noise
> began to die down I then decided to tell them which I preferred.
>
> *Caddyshack* was a very amusing movie. Many different things
> were going on at the same time, but it was not confusing at all.
> The actors were fantastic and they contributed greatly to its success.
> The was also a little gopher in the movie, which I fell fell in love
> with instantly. As you can see I rated this movie highly, but I fell
> that *Airplane* is slightly better.
>
> This movie was so hilarious that I came out of the theater with
> a side sticker from laughing. Every scene contains something
> worth laughing at. *Airplane* is a mockery of the many other
> airplane disaster movies. Other movies may leave you in tears
> because of sorrow, but this one will have you laughing so hard
> you'll cry. This is my opinion and I would definitely advise
> everyone to see both movies if your in the mood for a great
> comedy.

The Conversation

This session begins, as do all our sessions, with reading the text aloud.
This one occasions a bit of eye-rolling, snickering, and then outright
laughter at the "side sticker" line. After having read a number of
these diagnostic essays, the dramatic tone and attempted flair of this
text strikes us as funny, almost as comic relief. Reading as a group
seems to call forth a fuller and more open response. In thinking about
it now, I doubt, for example, that alone I would have laughed aloud
as I read the essay.

Marty begins the paraphrase, "A narrative, an anecdotal beginning.
I think that's refreshing, don't you?" The essay's narrative beginning
startles us, jars our expectations as teachers in this particular program.

The student writer either does not know about standard academic essay introductions or is willing to risk, to experiment, to entertain.

"Now this student was waiting in line and tells a story about, you know, first occasions at Syracuse and the lengthy lines, people discussing things, and movies came up in the topic of conversation, and she or he *had* to interject his own opinion because they were discussing which were the better movies of the summer probably, that's my guess, or at least which were highly entertaining movies. When the writer had a chance to put forth her opinion, she discussed two excellent movies, and doesn't name them here, but goes on with this interesting narrative. I like the word 'wondering,' as though Judith Crist were ready to speak about the two movies of the summer—and that's the introduction."

In the course of this paraphrase, Marty concludes that the writer is female, and so "she" remained throughout the discussion. She also constructs a new context/voice for this text—Judith Crist providing a clever and dramatic critique of a movie. In a sense, that intertextual connection begins to accord a certain kind of respect to this writer, to provide a context in which the writer succeeds. Marty raises no objections to a possible "decision" by the writer to move outside the expected genre and to suggest inventively a new one. In fact, she finds it "refreshing" that the writer shifts the diagnostic prompt and the task in this direction.

The paraphrase, which is actually longer than the first paragraph, reconstructs the (imagined) setting and adds the theme of "first occasions" as a focus.

On the tape, Lib's tone of voice in the next part of the paraphrase is ironic, a bit dramatic, as if she is having fun with this essay and its parody of Judith Crist. "The narrative is continued in paragraph two. The suspense is built in paragraph one, and we finally found out that the two movies are *Airplane* and *Caddyshack*, much to the amazement of the audience. Discussion of the two movies in this group of people centered on the fact that both were funny and both were popular, but also some liked only one of them, and some hated them both. Then we have a transitional sentence here, moving from the narrative introduction into the body of the paper."

Along with the other readers, Lib enters into the possibilities of playfulness provided by the text, taking pleasure in the effort at suspense and willing to go along with it, despite its artifice and awkwardness—or perhaps because of it.

Lib's paraphrase adds "writing teacher terminology" to our talk about the text, with words such as "narrative," "transitional sentence," and "body of the paper." She also uses the passive voice at one point. I suspect that, indirectly, this use of technical language serves to attribute implicitly a kind of competence to the writer, a sense of intentionality, and a knowledge of the possible choices and decisions, *as if* this too is how the writer thought of it.

Delia continues the paraphrase: "Well, she goes on to 'transit' to the discussion of *Caddyshack,* which the writer found very amusing, no, confusing, even though there were lots of things going on at the same time. The actors were fantastic. And there was a gopher in the movie with whom the writer fell in love. And she rates this movie very highly but feels conclusively that *Airplane* is somewhat better."

The reader's addition of the word "conclusively" indicates how the readers are responding to a voice, a strong voice, in the text, cued perhaps by the hyperbolic adjectives, the straightforward sentence structure in the claims, and the many uses of "I." The text creates a strong or loud sense of "author" and "authority."

"Well," Don picks up the paraphrase, "then she goes on to the discussion of *Airplane,* and it definitely affects this writer with a knife slashing . . . ?"

"I think she means 'side-splitting,' " Lib adds.

"I wondered if that was a colloquial expression. I never heard of it," Delia replies "or she might mean 'a stitch.' "

Don finishes the essay, summing up the last line by saying, "This is definitely opinionated, of course, and we get the advice again to see both movies if you're in the mood for a great comedy." At this point in the project, we have seen the opinion disclaimer/advice often, almost as a standard ending, reminiscent to us of the nearly mandatory ending of the elementary school book report that invites readers to read the book themselves and form their own opinions. We have come to see this as a "tag ending," a formula tacked on as an automatic conclusion for each and every essay.

Moving into the next phase of the reading, Delia begins to draw inferences. "I like the way it begins. . . . I'm sure the assignment was, 'Pick two movies you've seen recently and pick one that is better.' There's a real imaginative attempt to make it with a narrative. I don't think that I was laughing at this student, but with her. I'd like to meet this kid." The focus of our conversation shifts from features of the text's content and tone to the (imagined) features of the context in which it was written. We are now "reading" that first day of the fall semester when a student writer, new to the university and having been hit with a diagnostic writing task, had opted to try an imaginative or creative introduction. Aware as writing teachers of the kinds of constraints that operate in those situations, we acknowledge here a respect for a writer who rebelled or at least took a chance, even one that failed in some ways. The response also reveals a kind of defensiveness about having laughed, about having perhaps made fun of a student who was new to the university and its ways of talking, who was in transition.

Three years later, I wonder now if that defensiveness also marked a point of identification—that we, too, as teachers in a rapidly changing program, were in transition, moving between "paradigms," straddling two worlds, and sensing our vulnerability to the same charge of naivete as this new freshman writer was.

The body or "second half of the essay," as we came to call it, reveals to us that the writer was aware, at least in a general way, of the conventions called forth by this task—claims, evidence of some sort, argument or opinion. Even in the anecdotal beginning, as Delia comments, "There's a real tension between the diction and the intent in the opening paragraph because I think she wants to be humorous and yet is writing 'an English paper,' so there's a little bit of an attempt at high-sounding diction, for example, 'I refused to listen to the conversation without voicing my opinion.' And yet that works in service of the humor at the same time. And this writer never loses the thread of the narrative. I wonder about the overstatement of her judgment of the movies, giving rise to our somewhat funny perception of a nascent Judith Crist. It's nice. There is a whole little setting for the essay."

We respond here to the multiple voices in the text—the conversational and comic voice of the storyteller, the more formal or high-sounding voice of the academic critic, the dramatic voice of the movie reviewer, and the strained voice of the new student trying to fulfill an assignment and (presumably) impress the teacher. The essay, basically, pulls in several directions, yet rather than evaluate that as a failure, we are at this point in the reading more than willing to credit the writer with a range or repertoire of voices and a spirit of risk taking and playfulness.

It seems to me now, three years later, as I read the transcript and listen to the tape that we were reading this essay in relationship not only to the more traditional and "duller" responses other students had more typically provided in these pre-Freshman English essays, but also in relationship to the testing context that none of us approved of or valued. The choices this writer made were read as imaginative, perhaps even rebellious, and they were not considered to be a means of avoiding the assignment or to be a misreading of what the task called for. Again, I sense in retrospect a strong identification with the imagined writer. As we constructed her, so we also constructed ourselves.

The readers' conversation now moves into summative and positive talk about the writer's "engaging style," her sense "that an introduction is supposed to introduce the topic and catch the reader's attention," the coherence and logical sequencing of the claims.

"Technically, it's competent," we conclude. "It shows a student with potential. There's a facility here."

"If this writer learns to provide some real concrete evidence, I think she will be well on her way. A pretty good writer."

From initial and somewhat embarrassed laughter, into a playful paraphrase or "enactment" of the text, we have hit a moment of closure and move into a summative evaluation of the writer based primarily on her textual choices as read against the backdrop of the writing-as-testing context. We have invented a writer who in many ways reflects our values—and have given her our communal stamp of approval.

But we still have more time, and as our talk continues, we start to raise questions and problems. "But any good review (the genre we had now located this text in) would bring out some details, or discuss why it is a satire at a higher level than *Caddyshack*," Marty points out. "When you make an assertion, then some concrete exemplification makes it stronger. And wouldn't these kids, if they were standing in line, say, 'Do you remember when . . . ?' They wouldn't say generalities all night. Students would get to specifics."

Having agreed in some sense to judge this writer as "pretty good," the readers move into a more critical assessment of the writer's choices here. Even in the terms of her own narrative, there are problems, we decide, with credibility and development.

Another reader then describes the mixing of voices or personae as a problem with control. Another wonders if this strategy wasn't a "cop-out," a clever way to use a fictional audience to get out of the demands being made on her by a real audience. Specifics are missing, and that, Don points out, "gives us a sense of where this writer is at and how she defines audience."

The writer has been re-constructed now almost as a "basic writer" in David Bartholomae's (1986) definition of the term, as a writer pulling on fragments of different voices and interpretive schemes from different discourse communities, producing a kind of patchwork quilt text. She has presented herself as a storyteller and movie critic (and hence as a capable student writer able to work effectively with this task)—but only to an extent. Rather than "imaginative," her choices now seem to us desperate and defensive.

But, we go on—she was willing to give this task an energetic try. In that way, too, she exhibits another quality of the writers Bartholomae describes—patience and good will. Further, we conclude, the task was harder than it looks. In fifty minutes, with no instruction, a student had to identify two movies, preferably ones that were appropriate to talk about in a university setting (that is, ones that deserve "serious" consideration), draw on a discourse that she may have had limited experience with, and then rely on her memory for details and evidence.

We had been struck earlier in our reading by the ideological pressures in the diagnostic task. When a student elected to compare "M.A.S.H." with "Perry Mason," for example, she was told by the instructor at the close of the final summative comment "to consider the assignment—that is, 'of two *good* shows choose the one that is best' [emphasis added by instructor]."

As our conversation continues, we circle back to talk about how and why the text *did* work, but now in more text-specific ways. We agreed that the text got our attention and respect, that it engaged us, even though it was flawed in many ways. "She does communicate something," Don noted. "A lot of things that have to do with sound— 'listen,' 'speak,' 'conversation,' 'voices,' 'voicing,' 'silence.' Then we move into the interior, into feeling—'amusing,' 'confusing,' 'fantastic,' 'love,' and 'feel,' and 'hilarious.' So, on the one hand, it's very fundamental, very basic, using sense perceptions to develop some kind of descriptive essay. But, on the other hand, it leads to some sophistication because it drives into the interior of this person for a few, bright moments. It drives into the personality of the individual, somehow."

"Yeah," Lib adds, "and you even hear some excitement—here's a possibility, I'll start this way. Enthusiasm."

"With a subtle logical structure to it, too," Don points out.

"And the sentence structure seems quite varied, although there are lapses and strange repetitions ('fell fell') in the hurry of writing. But some dependent clauses, like the beginning of the first paragraph, and the verbal at the end of it. I also like the use of 'I' in 'I, of course,'" Marty concludes.

At this moment in the reading, we move back into an appreciation of an imagined writer, making effective choices about how to work this assignment. Writer and "intentionality" begin to dominate our discussion about the text. The writer has a "voice" that registers excitement, that sounds personable, that makes the writer increasingly "real" to the group of readers. The sixteen uses of "I" in the text forcefully locate the author's presence in the text. Against the context of the writing situation, and cued and orchestrated by certain textual features, we have constructed a writer that we like a lot. I suspect now that we would have constructed a very different writer had the context been different—had, for example, this text been a take-home essay in the middle of the semester. The "she" might have "sounded" sloppy, lazy, careless, indeed taking a cute cop-out.

Again, the readers move into a conclusion and decide that the writer has made some "smart choices." She has picked movies that she has actually seen, that are similar in certain ways, and that she has (apparently) strong and genuine opinions about.

"But this question of choices becomes curious then," Don argues, "because if we have these students with this option of choices here, what motivates that choice? 'I have read *Anthem* and *1984* last year, and I only saw one movie this summer...' so even though the mode of popular discourse is what the student is really in tune with, all of a sudden, 'I'm in college now, higher education, and this *is* English class....' "

The tensions return. We are not fully comfortable with this communal decision. One reader commented later that, in engaging in dialogue like this, he often felt a tension among what he saw/read/felt in the text, what his colleagues saw/read/felt, and what was actually being voiced in the group. In this case the group's overtly positive reaction to this text/writer shut down certain critical responses, yet the text was flawed in ways that kept announcing themselves and demanding our attention.

But, again, we want to give this writer a break. After all, we agree, it was the first day of "college," the students had been asked to write what was clearly a diagnostic essay for an as yet unknown teacher, and the assignment set up mixed messages. On the one hand, it called forth the popular discourse of movie reviews (and hence the voice of Judith Crist), yet it was also assigned in the context of an English class and thus also—and conflictually—called forth academic discourse.

And in a sense, this writer provides a bit of both. As Marty says, "She could have done a 'The two movies *Airplane* and *Caddyshack* have similarities and differences,' but instead she goes with this 'wonderful narrative opening.' " We conclude yet again that she writes forcefully, with humor and playfulness, and perhaps with a sense of confidence and trust—she trusts that her audience will respond positively to her choices and efforts here.

We speculated that this writer had had experience writing to an audience that had encouraged her. We are dismayed as we further imagine what this writer's response might have been to the "No Pass" stamped loudly across the top of the paper, with the following summative comment:

> The thesis should come in the first paragraph—structurally—though you don't follow Baker[2]—you are organized—However, there is no conclusion, the introduction is too long and involved. The development is weak—and you offer little concrete support—be sure to give specific evidence for any generalizations.

It is easy for us at this point, given our frustration with a program that demanded "Baker" before it had even been taught and that rubber-stamped comments and evaluative judgments in this formal and formulaic way, to feel even more identification with and supportive toward this "refreshing" writer.

With a bit more discussion, we assign this writer to the "rally driver" category of our typology, despite the evident problems with development and organization in the essay. This writer, as we have come to see her, convinces us that she is a risk taker, a writer with potential, with a sense, if nascent, of the imaginative possibilities of written language. In terms of the metaphor we are working with, she seems to know how to rev up the car and tackle a complex course; she seems willing to negotiate the twists and turns of unfamiliar terrain, with a certain kind of bravado and flair, ability and confidence.

"This is a definite writer," Marty sums up. "She knows what she wants to say and isn't afraid to say it. She plays. She trusts her skills, and she trusts an audience that responds positively. And she makes effective choices, given the constraints of the task."

"Tempos of Meaning"

In "Writing Time," James T. Zebroski (1987, in manuscript) discusses the role of *time* in reading and writing, the effect of temporality on the way a text is defined and hence on the way a text "means." He calls it "the tempos of meaning." He argues, for example, that "the close reader reads an entirely different text in a completely different time warp from the holistic scorer" (19).

And it is *time* that Carini's reflective procedures provide—time for readers to come at a text from multiple perspectives, to engage with and dwell in the materiality of that text, to construct a writer cued by textual choices, to remember one's own writing experiences and to imagine the writer's current one, to read and re-read the possibilities presented by the text against the imagined context of the writing situation and against the comments of other readers.

The reflective procedures also create a *communal* reading. At the end of the project, in fact, readers reported pleasure in this kind of shared time with a text and in the experience of breaking out of the lonely, labor-intensive grading cycle teachers often find themselves locked into. One reader concluded that "the opportunity to discuss writing and teaching philosophies with a peer group was a real treat— it was fun, intellectually stimulating, and educational." Another noted that "for me personally, the reading experience itself was unique and pedagogically rewarding. Although I regularly read papers for the Educational Testing Service (for the College Board and CLEP exams), I have never before analyzed writing so intensively."

Three years later, one reader suggested further that the process of reading *as a group* provided a more expansive and, hence, more complex reading. "What was prevalent and popular in the group, among the cacophony of voices, does not gain narrative courage in quiet, secular reading. Do we lose a sense of play? We relocate, in our individual reading, an identity of conventional rhetoric bounded and shackled by audience of self." He speculated that private readings tend to close off an awareness of codes or competing codes and tend to push toward those that match our own.

Reading together also allowed us to invent and reinvent ourselves as a group and as individuals, to make visible the beliefs and attitudes we held, to define our roles in the academic place. "Now," one writer noted, "the writer and the text are less important. I want to know more about those readers"—and what has happened to them during the changes in the new program.

In this particular conversation, as in all of the others, there occurred various "moments" in the reading, shifts in attention and feeling and focus. The process was complex and multilayered. The definition and meanings of the "text" changed across and through time, often in conflicting ways. And through our communal enterprise, in response to different texts, and against the context of the changes going on at Syracuse, we constructed and reconstructed ourselves as a group of readers.

Initially, the point in the text that opened up space for dialogue was the phrase "side sticker." Unsure of its actual meaning and amused by its location in a first-day college diagnostic essay, we were intrigued and "refreshed" by its use. Its colloquial quality startled us and invited us into the semantic space shared by readers and writers via text (Nystrand 1982). In our paraphrase, we responded to the text with playfulness and dramatic irony. We shared the words and phrases with each other as if they were lines from a play that we were performing. In a sense, we *enacted* the essay, and the text became a *script* for us to say aloud, to activate with our emphases, to entertain each other with. We took pleasure in our voices reading the text, enlarging the scene of the text and writer at Syracuse.

The text also opened up a space for *us* to be "rally drivers" of sorts, to be different teachers than we were accustomed to being and to take some risks with our reading.

Yet, at other points, the text held us out. The last two paragraphs, for example, even over time, did not invite our participation as the narrative beginning had. The more "academic" she tried to be, the less we "liked" her. We commented on our problems, envisioned student-teacher conferences in which we would talk about evidence and illustration to back up rather hollow claims. No longer playful, our responses to the text became serious, and we became teacherly. Now the text became a *draft*, a record of an incomplete process in which we wanted, as teachers, to intervene. Possibilities for revision and instruction occupied us, as we entered the text as teachers fretting about the problems a writer presented to us.

This position alternated with one in which the text was defined as a *product*, an example of what a writer could do, and we became judges, evaluating this product as flawed in certain ways, successful in others. We read the text then as revealing a writer's competence or knowledge of written language discourse conventions and genre. It was then that we saw this writer as falling possibly in the basic writer category.

But perhaps most frequently, we read the text as a *sign*, to which we reacted ideologically, taking a socio-political/historical stance in our reading. We were reading all these essays from within a specific institutional setting at a particular time in its history and from a particular point of view. Our reading project was embedded within a larger project that was aimed at reviewing and, we assumed, criticizing the pedagogical and theoretical model of writing instruction that had dominated the writing instruction at Syracuse University for over ten years. We were opposed to the basic theory of development in that program, were opposed to the writing-as-testing pedagogy, and we were opposed to the stultifying over-emphasis on form that had resulted in this program. So, "naturally," we read this writer's choices from a point of identification and saw her text as an act of rebellion and as a sign of the failure of the program to "make space" for divergent writers and for imaginative, risk-taking teaching. One reader wondered later "how much resonance of anarchy towards the then present paradigm flavored [this particular] reading? Were we truly trying to set up relations of power rather than meaning?" Those points of identification, of course, shifted with each reflection and each text/writer, allowing us to read from multiple points of view over the course of the project.

However, overall, in the process of reading together, we did construct ourselves into a rather *particular* group of readers, a group that came to value expressiveness and voice. Having worked in and against a writing program that pushed product, we were "refreshed" by (or we "re-freshed") this text, I suspect now, because we were open to a personalized text, to the individual stance this writer adopted in her response to this writing task. We were enlarging the possibilities of text and writer (and teacher) at Syracuse University. In this case, we constructed a writer, a presence or "felt sense" in the text, and then rewarded "her," albeit a bit ambiguously, with our communal stamp of approval, while at the same time we condemned a writing task (and hence writing program) that demanded a certain kind of conformity and conventionality from its students. This writer became, for us, "imaginative" and "natural"—values that were not legitimate in the old program at that time, values resonant with the very impulses and beliefs about language that had originally drawn us into working as writing teachers in the first place. In this sense, the project enabled us, forced us, to recognize more explicitly the position from which we were reading not only the student text, but the overall writing program, too. And it enabled us to acknowledge, in ways, the romantic and empowering mirage of self that was part of the change going on—our self, the writer's self, political self.

Three years later, with that romantic impulse played out somewhat and from a greater intellectual understanding of the social aspects of composing, I read this writer now as being unaware of the discourse community she has joined, as being naive, with only a fragmentary sense of the intellectual and discursive demands of the writing task. For better or worse, I am less willing to "enjoy" this essay or to categorize this writer as a "rally driver." For me, the text has become a different *sign*, a sign of the problematic tension between "self-expression" and "conventionality" that informs freshman writing courses. I hear the polyphony in the text—the voice of the storyteller, the nascent Judith Crist, the fourth-grade book report writer, the academic arguer, and the nervous entering freshman. While I recognize and celebrate that coherence has not been achieved through the suppressing or silencing of these multiple voices, as in so many other freshman essays written in "the English paper" voice, I recognize at the same time that the voices may be garbled and cacophonous, the tensions not worked through or perhaps even acknowledged.

I wish I had a chance to talk this new observation through with the group of readers, to open up dialogue again, to play out the further possibilities such a reading would enable for understanding this writer, the writing task, our position now as readers, the changing context at Syracuse. I wish there were more time.

Notes

1. I would like here to acknowledge and thank the readers who worked on this project: Elizabeth "Lib" Hayes, Marty Hiestand, Jacki Lauby, Delia Temes, and Don Wagner.

2. This is a reference to Sheridan Baker's *The Practical Stylist* (Harper and Row), the required textbook for the course at that time.

Works Cited

Bartholomae, David. "Inventing the University." *Journal of Basic Writing* 5 (1986): 4–23.

Carini, P. *The Art of Seeing and the Visibility of the Person.* Grand Forks, N.D.: North Dakota Study Group on Evaluation, 1979.

———. *Observation and Description: An Alternative Methodology for the Investigation of Human Phenomena.* Grand Forks, N.D.: North Dakota Study Group on Evaluation, 1975.

Geertz, Clifford. *The Interpretation of Cultures: Selected Essays.* New York: Basic Books, 1973.

Nystrand, Martin. "The Structure of Textual Space." In *What Writers Know: The Language Process and Structure of Written Discourse*, 75–86. New York: Academic Press, 1982.

Patton, M. Q. *Qualitative Evaluation Methods.* Beverly Hills: Sage Publications, 1980.

Zebroski, James T. "Writing Time." Unpublished manuscript at the time of this writing.

2 The Drama of the Text

W. Ross Winterowd
University of Southern California–Los Angeles

The Mysterious, Magical, Changing Text

Twenty-five years ago, I received the following archetypical theme from one of my freshmen, and rediscovered it just hours ago. Between 1965 and the present, the paper changed radically, and I would like to discuss the nature of that change (the sentences have been numbered for easy reference).

[Untitled]

(1) Before a person can say whether the best things in life are free, he must first deturmine what in his opinion best things are. (2) Naturally every person has his own ideas concerning the objects or things that are important.

(3) I believe that friendship, health, and beauty are three of the most important things a person can enjoy. (4) When I say "beauty" I mean having things around you that you like or being places that make you feel good.

(5) When I say that friendship is not fun [sic; "free"?] I don't mean that you can go out and buy five dollars worth of it when you need a friend. (6) Instead of using money you use yourself. (7) Your ideals and attitudes to buy friends. (8) To fit into a group you must drop some and maybe most of your attitudes before you will be considered normal by the group. (9) If you don't, you will be considered rebellious or off-beat and become an outcast from that group. (10) Therefore, to have friends is to pay by changing yourself for their benefit.

(11) Good health is very important to me because without it I can not enjoy myself. (12) To maintain a healthy physical condition one must get the proper amounts of exercise, food, and sleep. (13) Exercise and sleep are free but food is by no means free. (14) Every time one turns around he is paying for food by working at some type of job to get money for food.

(15) Beauty is the only thing that comes close to being free. (16) Aside from having to buy most of the articles that a person likes to have—such as a car, skiis [sic] or any other material

21

object—beauty is mostly free. (17) I love to go into the forest and enjoy nature's beauty. (18) The trees, forest creatures, brooks, and streams all mean a lot to me. (19) I enjoy hunting and camping in the forest and just walking there alone, thinking to myself. (20) But to keep these forests we must pay to see that some careless hunter or camper doesn't burn them down. (21) We have to set aside parks and wilderness areas so they aren't cut into lumber by the mills. (22) These parks all cost money. (23) Everywhere you go, you have to pay some way or another.

In two obvious ways, the text remains unaltered from 1965 to the present. First, certain of the mechanical errors have not changed their nature or their value. "Deturmine" (S.l) is still annoyingly misspelled, and "Your ideals and attitudes to buy friends" (S.7) remains a fragment. Second, the paper was, and today still is, ghostly in its abstractness and generality—or, to shift the metaphor, a skeleton, lacking the flesh of specificity and concreteness. It desperately needs one living, breathing friend, warts and all, for whom the author changed; a day on the ski slopes, with the powder snow flying, the brilliant, sunny coldness stabbing through the ski mask and mittens; a forest campground, with the aromas of pine trees, frying bacon, and percolating coffee.

In another way, the text has changed radically: since the time it was composed (and mimeographed), it has become sexist, as the pronouns in the first paragraph announce.

More interesting is the way in which the untitled theme changed its status and value as a text, going through three relatively distinct phases. It has been, successively, (1) an inadequate structure, (2) an inadequate statement of selfhood, and (3) a perfectly normal exemplar of a pseudo-genre.

In the second part of this discussion, I will explain why, in composition, it is better to ask "What are you doing?" than "What are you writing?"

Why the Text Resisted Stability

Among the happy aperçus of Stanley Fish (1980) is that of the "interpretive community," which "is the source of texts, facts, authors, and intentions. Or to put it another way, the entities that were once seen as competing for the right to constrain interpretation (text, reader, author) are now all seen to be the *products* of interpretation" (16–17). Thus, I have tipped my hand: I am going to show how the untitled essay on the best things in life changes according to the interpretive strategies employed by its readers. Well, yes, that's pretty obvious, but my argument is somewhat more complex than this. *I want to show how the theories and practices of the study of literature influence, even control, the teaching of composition.*

So that I can get on with the mercurial freshman theme, let me stipulate that, by and large, the English department establishment, the traditional custodian of composition, unconsciously translates literary theory into composition theory. Thus, New Critics in the literature class were pretty much tacit New Critics in the composition class, and deconstructionist literary professors will be deconstructionist composition instructors. As Colleen Aycock (1984) puts it in the abstract of her dissertation,

> In the representative text of New Critical composition, Cleanth Brooks and Robert Penn Warren's *Modern Rhetoric* (1949), we find the New Critical hermeneutic applied to composition/rhetoric: one learns to write against a background of [literary] principles and linguistic analysis, establishing a pedagogy which emphasizes texts as organic constructs of dense, rich texture, metaphor as the constitutive principle of language, and meaning as derived from language contexts.

And in a recent essay, J. Hillis Miller (1983, 38–56) has assumed that deconstruction will supply the theory that composition, according to him, lacks.

Or let me state my thesis another, less contentious, way: if literary theory does not become composition theory, at least literary theory heavily influences composition, and the reverse is not usually the case.

Three Manifestations of the Text

The Text as an Inadequate Structure

C-

> Mechanical errors weaken this paper. Check the spelling of the words I've circled. And see pages [000–000] of your handbook for an explanation of sentence fragments.
>
> You don't have to convince me of the truism that the best things in life are not free, but you do need to show me. Remember the lesson we have learned from our readings: "Show; don't tell." You need to be concrete, specific; give me images, not generalities.
>
> Your organization is "logical," but rigid. Couldn't you think of a way to make your theme flow?
>
> In "The Flea," Donne chose an astounding symbol to carry his meaning, and in "The Secret Sharer," Conrad wove together the ancient theme of the *Doppelganger* and the myth of the night

> journey. Of course, you are not writing fiction or poetry, but you
> can use the methods of literature to structure your own papers.
>   Your conclusion, the last sentence in your paper, is too abrupt
> and doesn't really summarize adequately.[1]

A number of factors make it unprofitable, if not impossible, to discuss either the ethical or the truth value of the text. In the first place, I am an English teacher, not a sociologist or psychologist. Second, positivism has made all intellectuals skeptical of statements concerning values, the only meaningful statements being those that are either tautological or empirically verifiable.

Finally, as Wellek and Warren tell us, "Language is the material of literature as stone or bronze is of sculpture, paints of pictures, or sounds of music" (1956, 22), and though certainly "Untitled" is not literature, my commitment is to language as a medium, and my training prepares me to do a special kind of "linguistic" interpretation. In particular, I want my students, in their writing, to aspire to the condition of literature, which is why I have chosen as readings for the course a collection of short fiction ("The Open Boat," "The Bride Comes to Yellow Sky," "Uncle Wiggily in Connecticut," "Bartleby the Scrivener," among others) and a collection of poetry (with an ample representation of the metaphysicals).

Wellek and Warren have shown us that "everything which persuades us to a definite outward action" is mere rhetoric. "Genuine poetry affects us more subtly" (24). And Northrop Frye (1971) widens the chasm between rhetoric and literature:

> In literature, questions of fact or truth are subordinated to the
> primary literary aim of producing a structure of words for its own
> sake, and the sign-values of symbols are subordinated to their
> importance as a structure of interconnected motifs. Wherever we
> have an autonomous verbal structure of this kind, we have
> literature. Wherever this structure is lacking, we have language,
> words used instrumentally to help human consciousness do or
> understand something else. (74)

I am not insensible of my dilemma as a composition teacher. I cannot instill creativity or genius into my students, and in that sense I cannot teach composition. However, I can give them models of excellence, analyze those models so that the class will understand their structure, correct the errors that I find in themes—and hope that in some cases at least my efforts will spark improvement.

The Text as an Inadequate Statement of Selfhood

C-

Mechanical errors weaken this paper. Check the spelling of the words I've circled. And see pages [000–000] of your handbook for an explanation of sentence fragments.

I know you well. We have drunk coffee together in my office as we talked about your problems with your parents. You are a bright, lively, sensitive person. But in this paper you hide behind bland language. Why? Why not use your true voice?

You don't have to convince me of the truism that the best things in life are not free, but you do need to show me. Remember the lesson we have learned from our readings: "Show; don't tell." You need to be concrete, specific; give me images, not generalities.

Did you have any surprises while you wrote this paper? Did you make any discoveries about yourself or about your world? If not, you weren't really writing.

Think of *Soul on Ice*, which we discussed last week.

We get to know Cleaver because he's honest; he uses language to reveal himself, to discover himself, not to hide behind. In your next paper, I want to hear you talking, in your own voice.

Students have been conditioned to write "the phony, pretentious language of the schools—Engfish" (Macrorie 1976, 1); they don't know that we write "to be surprised by what appears on the page" (Murray 1985, 3). Above all, students have never seen themselves as language users whose "lives, no less than their papers, are composed by language" (Coles 1974, 1). "All good writers speak in honest voices and tell the truth" (Macrorie, 5).

Underlying my attitude toward teaching composition is the profound belief that rather than expressing meaning, language creates meaning, to the eternal surprise of the language user. As Susanne Langer says, "What is true of language, is essential in music: music that is invented while the composer's mind is fixed on what is to be expressed is apt not to be music. It is a limited idiom, like an artificial language" ([1942] 1951, 204).

Of course, my viewpoint is extremely traditional, going back most directly to Coleridgean Romanticism, alembicated so well in "The Eolian Harp":

And what if all of animated nature
Be but organic Harps diversely fram'd,
That tremble into thought, as o'er them sweeps
Plastic and vast, one intellectual breeze,

At once the Soul of each, and God of all?

Interestingly enough, deconstruction—lately so fashionable—says many of the same things that my colleagues and I have argued since the mid-1960s. As evidence, I juxtapose Jacques Derrida:

> It is because writing is *inaugural,* in the fresh sense of the word, that it is dangerous and anguishing. It does not know where it is going, no knowledge can keep it from the essential precipitation toward meaning that it constitutes and that is, primarily, its future. (1978, 18)

and Peter Elbow:

> . . . think of writing as an organic, developmental process in which you start writing at the very beginning—before you know your meaning at all—and encourage your words gradually to change and evolve. (1973, 15)

The Text as a Perfectly Normal Exemplar of a Pseudo-Genre

C-

> Mechanical errors weaken this paper. Check the spelling of the words I've circled. And see pages [000–000] of your handbook for an explanation of sentence fragments.
>
> You don't have to convince me of the truism that the best things in life are not free, but you do need to show me. Remember the lesson we have learned from our readings: "Show; don't tell." You need to be concrete, specific; give me images, not generalities.

The expository essay—though devalued in the English department establishment since it verges on "mere rhetoric"—represents the liberal arts tradition at its best. As George Dillon has said, this genre is not intended to convey information, but to cause the reader to think about a problem; its open-minded author uses evidence and logical proof to win her point. The whole stance is that of a "liberally educated person, who is meditative, reflective, clear-headed, unbiased, always seeking to understand experience freshly and to find things of interest in the world" (1981, 23).

The erosion of the expository essay is, then, nothing less than the erosion of the liberal arts tradition.

To be within the tradition, one must have both (1) cultural information and (2) a sense of genre.

> E. D. Hirsch, Jr., defines "cultural literacy" as that knowledge that enables a writer or reader to know what other writers and readers know within the literate culture. Thus it is not only a knowledge of convention and vocabularies but is also a knowledge that this

information is widely shared by others. Moreover, since this shared culture is changing at its edges, the content of cultural literacy is also changing. New things become part of it and old things drop away—even while the more permanent central core remains. (Horner 1983, 146)

And in his recent book, *Cultural Literacy,* Hirsch, with hard data and telling anecdotes, limns the deplorable lack of cultural information among today's students—for instance, the high school girl who challenged her teacher's statement that Latin is a dead language: "What do they speak in Latin America?" (1987, 5–6).

Even if the student could score 100 percent on the quizzes in the *Mensa Genius Quiz Book,* win every game of "Trivial Pursuit," and enter the "Jeopardy" Tournament of Champions, he (or, somewhat less frequently, she) would fail, or at least fall short of excellence (receive the hopeless C-), in an expository writing class *if that student lacked genre knowledge,* which could be acquired only through reading expository essays, which are seldom part of the educational and cultural equipment that students bring with them to college writing classes. Since literary theory has devalued "non-imaginative" writing, the essay has not been represented in curricula, and the magazines that publish expository essays are hardly part of the cultural diet in most elements of society.

In short, the essay is an anachronism. Perhaps the liberal arts as they were traditionally conceived are anachronisms.

Thus, we can say that "Untitled" is a perfectly normal exemplar of a genre: the pseudo-expository essay, written by a student who has neither the cultural information nor the sense of genre necessary to carry out the assignment. We can hope for little more.

Doing Rather than Writing

C-

Mechanical errors weaken this paper. Check the spelling of the words I've circled. And see pages [000–000] of your handbook for an explanation of sentence fragments.

You don't have to convince me of the truism that the best things in life are not free, but you do need to show me. Remember the lesson we have learned from our readings: "Show; don't tell." You need to be concrete, specific; give me images, not generalities.

I can't figure out what you want this paper to do.

A Word to the Wise from KB

We take it as a given that language is symbolic action and that "Untitled" is language. That being the case, we must ask the dramatistic questions regarding Agent, Scene, Purpose, Agency, and Attitude. Full answers to these questions—even in a narrowed circumference—would extend this essay beyond the bounds at which it is already beginning to strain; however, a few remarks will suggest the hermeneutic tapestry that we must weave before we can begin to claim that we have interpreted "Untitled."

I see the student-writer as clearly as if he were before me in a class. Because the cover sheet of his theme is missing, I don't have his name, but we can call him Agent. His black hair is worn pompadour, his plaid flannel shirt and faded denims are immaculate, and his cowboy boots are scuffed and unshined. His family's ranch is thirty miles (that figure sticks in my mind) from somewhere (but I've lost the name of the Montana town). He has told me, in a conference, that he's uncomfortable in a big city: Missoula, Montana.

A survey of his interests and talents reveals him to be a genuine *bricoleur*: cowboy-veterinarian-mechanic-naturalist-entrepeneur-pilot (of the family's Cessna).

The Scene of the English class is nearly as foreign to Agent as a camp of the hunter-gatherers of the Kalahari would be to his instructor. (Remember: the expository essay defines the English class Scene.)

The Purposes of the assignment behind "Untitled" are no doubt diverse, but all of them, one way or another, relate to a central goal for the course: to initiate Agent into the society represented by the expository essay. The problem, of course, is that Agent quite possibly neither understands nor wants to join that society. Furthermore, he doesn't really understand the Purpose of the assignment, befuddlement that translates itself, I think, into the generalities and truisms of "Untitled." Agent doesn't really know what his theme is supposed to do.

If we take Agency to be both Edited Standard English and the expository essay genre, we can say that Agent does pretty well with the former and hasn't the foggiest concerning the latter. And there is no quick fix for lack of genre knowledge; you acquire such competence by immersion—reading expository essays to find out what they have to say, but in the process gaining a sense of genre.

As for Agent's and Instructor's Attitudes—well, let's give them both credit for good will. Teacher and student don't dislike one another—in fact, they develop a warm relationship during the semester. Yet at the end of the four months in English 101, Agent is no more at home in the expository essay culture than he was on the first day of class. He has no desire to integrate and, indeed, no reason to integrate. The problem, as I diagnose it, is the opposition of *Kultur* and *culture*.

Kultur and Culture[2]

Education for Critical Consciousness, by Paulo Freire (1981), is one of the central statements regarding education in general and literacy in particular. Even the term "critical consciousness" is resonant, suggesting as it does that education should give people the ability to analyze and evaluate their society and their role in that society and thus take charge of their own destinies.

Freire, with good teachers at all levels from kindergarten through graduate school, deplores the "banking concept" of education, in which a teacher pours knowledge into the passive receptacles before him. As Freire says, "Communication gives way to communiques by the teacher, who makes deposits which the students meekly receive, memorize, and repeat" (1981, 75). It is not revolutionary to posit that learning must be active, not passive, and that teacher and student must interact, carrying on a dialogue that replaces the lecture-mono-logue of the banking model of education. However, in the context of Freire's work, this good-natured, sensible position on learning becomes something less familiar and more revolutionary.

Specifically, Freire first leads us to a critical understanding of the difference between what I will call *Kultur* and a redefined *culture.* Next, he plunges us into the abyss of indeterminacy, the belief that texts have no single, stable meaning. Both of these moves have profound implications for composition.

Kultur and culture, then.

Kultur is a given, stable, immutable, and of unquestioned value. It is what institutions "pass on" from generation to generation, in the form of canons, collections, and societal norms. Manifestations of Kultur are *Julius Caesar* in the eleventh-grade literature anthology, and the literature anthology itself; the Getty Museum in Malibu; the Lincoln Center for the Performing Arts; the expository essay that Agent is asked to write for English 101. These are "given," donated, conveyed. They are pre-existent and for all practical purposes eternal. They also, of course, belong to certain classes in society.

Culture, on the other hand, is always becoming, being made. In Freire's view, the cultured person is one who sees him- or herself as creative agent, not merely a partaker, a donee. The illiterate, who stood in awe of Kultur, was puzzled by it, afraid of it,

> would begin to . . . change . . . his former attitudes, by discovering himself to be a maker of the world of culture, by discovering that he, as well as the literate person, has a creative and re-creative impulse. He would discover that culture is just as much a clay

doll made by artists who are his peers as it is the work of a great
sculptor, a great painter, a great mystic, or a great philosopher;
that culture is the poetry of lettered poets and also the poetry of
his own popular songs—that culture is all human creation. (1981,
47)

Freire, of course, is talking about Brazilian peasants, but substitute
"fifth-grader," "high school senior," or "college freshman, our Agent,"
for "illiterate," and the principle is extended—the principle that everyone can be a culture-maker and that culture is not confined to tomes,
monuments, concert halls, museums, or accepted genres.

The point, however, is to preserve Kultur (including the expository
essay and what it represents) by gaining for it the allegiance of critically
conscious beings who envision themselves as participants in the same
spheres *of action* as the "masters." Perhaps the most maligned work
of Kultur is that wonderful tale *Silas Marner,* long the staple of high
school English courses. Culture, in Freire's sense, is not a revolution
that would abolish this monument, but a creative, dialectical movement
that would incorporate it, with other diverse works both old and new,
in a dynamic process of becoming.

Freire would argue that we can achieve cultural literacy only through
what he calls "problem-posing education," which consists in acts of
cognition, not transferrals of information. It is a learning situation in
which the cognizable object (far from being the end of the cognitive
act) intermediates the cognitive actors—teacher on the one hand and
students on the other. Accordingly, the practice of problem-posing
education entails at the outset that the teacher-student contradiction
be resolved. Dialogical relations—indispensable to the capacity of
cognitive actors to cooperate in perceiving the same cognizable object—
are otherwise impossible (Freire 1982, 67).

Which is not to say that the teacher does not "know" more—about
Silas Marner and George Eliot—than the students, but that the students,
in dialogue with the teacher, must create their own knowledge, a goal
that they cannot reach if they deal only with Kultur, which is given
to them, and not with culture, which they are creating and which
includes their own works.

Culture, then, has no hard-and-fast parameters, but is continually
created by creators who reinterpret what is and was and who contribute
their own works to the immediate future. Thus, the problem of cultural
literacy is not so much one of compiling lists of works, as demonstrating
through a dialogic and loving pedagogy that every human is part of
the culture-making process. "Problem-posing education affirms men
as beings in the process *of becoming*—as unfinished, uncompleted
beings in and with a likewise unfinished reality" (1982, 72).

The danger in problem-posing education is obvious: all absolute certainty vanishes, except the faith that new insight, greater understanding, lies just beyond the next question. As Freire says,

> To exist, humanly, is to name the world, to change it. Once named, the world in its turn reappears to the namers as a problem and requires of them a new naming. Men are not built in silence, but in word, in work, in action-reflection. (1982, 76)

The world we live in gains meaning only when we interpret it, and our interpretations can be widely various. Freire gives this wonderful example:

> In Santiago . . . a group of tenement residents discussed a scene showing a drunken man walking on the street and three young men conversing on the corner. The group participants commented that "the only one there who is productive and useful to his country is the souse who is returning home after working all day for low wages and who is worried about his family because he can't take care of their needs. He is the only worker. He is a decent worker and souse like us." (1982, 111)

Education must begin with society and the environment as they exist because meaning comes from the situation and is inseparable from it.

> . . . neither language nor thought can exist without a structure to which they refer. In order to communicate effectively, educator and politician must understand the structural conditions in which the thought and language of the people are dialectically framed. (1982, 85–86)

One lives in a "thematic universe," a web of interlocking concerns, and it is these "generative themes" that form the basis for Freire's pedagogical method, which relies not so much on *technic* (for example, phonics, drills, reading "attack skills") as what might be called *rhetoric* (that is, the relationship of words to the thematic universe in which the subjects live), and of the two, rhetoric is by far the more important. Technic makes words, but rhetoric makes meanings.

As opposed to the banking concept of education, underlying which are the consoling certainties of accepted knowledge and tradition and the belief that behind every situation there is a meaning, problem-posing education sucks us into the vortex of indeterminacy, where knowledge is always constructed and "truth" ever evolves through the "eternal dialogue between man and man, between man and his Creator. It is this dialogue which makes of man an historical being" (1981, 17–18).

In problem-posing education, the students—no longer docile listeners—are now critical co-investigators in dialogue with the teacher. The teacher presents the material to the students for their consideration, and he re-considers his earlier considerations as the students express their own. The role of the problem-posing educator is to create, together with the students, the conditions under which knowledge at the level of *doxa* is superseded by true knowledge at the level of the *logos*. (1982, 68)

A humane and loving revolutionary, Freire gives us reason to support *cultural* literacy without succumbing to Kultur. It is particularly satisfying to discover such a powerful ally and equally satisfying to realize that he and we are completely within a great tradition that began with the Greeks and Romans and gained one of its most lucid and succinct expressions in Montaigne's "Of the Education of Children":

Our tutors never stop bawling into our ears, as though they were pouring water into a funnel; and our task is only to repeat what has been told us. I should like the tutor to correct this practice, and right from the start, according to the capacity of the mind he has in hand, to begin putting it through its paces, making it taste things, choose them, and discern them by itself; sometimes clearing the way for him, sometimes letting him clear his own way. I don't want him to think and talk alone. I want him to listen to his pupil speaking in his turn. Socrates, and later Arcesilaus, first had their disciples speak, and then they spoke to them. *The authority of those who teach is often an obstacle to those who want to learn.* [Cicero]

Notes

1. The commentator has missed a point that you, the reader, undoubtedly caught: namely, "Untitled" is a five-paragraph essay. If the student writer had developed a conclusion, he would have violated the norms of a rigid and widely practiced genre, for five-paragraph essays cannot contain six paragraphs.

2. Adapted in part from "Literacy: *Kultur* and Culture." *Language Arts* 64 (1987): 869–74.

Works Cited

Aycock, Colleen. *New Critical Rhetoric and Composition.* Dissertation. Los Angeles: University of Southern California, 1984.

Coles, William E., Jr. *Teaching Composing.* Rochelle Park, N.J.: Hayden, 1974.

Derrida, Jacques. "Force and Signification." In *Writing and Difference*, translated by Alan Bass, 3–30. Chicago: University of Chicago Press, 1978.

Dillon, George L. *Constructing Texts*. Bloomington: Indiana University Press, 1981.

Elbow, Peter. *Writing without Teachers*. New York: Oxford University Press, 1973.

Fish, Stanley. *Is There a Text in This Class?* Cambridge, Mass.: Harvard University Press, 1980.

Freire, Paulo. *Education for Critical Consciousness*. Trans. various. New York: Continuum, 1981.

———. *Pedagogy of the Oppressed*. Trans. Myra Bergman Ramos. New York: Continuum, 1982.

Frye, Northrop. *Anatomy of Criticism*. Princeton: Princeton University Press, 1971.

Hirsch, E. D., Jr. *Cultural Literacy*. Boston: Houghton, 1987.

———. "Reading, Writing, and Cultural Literacy." In *Composition and Literature: Bridging the Gap*, edited by Winifred Bryan Horner, 141–47. Chicago: University of Chicago Press, 1983.

Langer, Susanne K. *Philosophy in a New Key*. [1942.] New York: New American Library, 1951.

Macrorie, Ken. *Telling Writing*. Rev. 2nd ed. Rochelle Park, N.J.: Hayden, 1976.

Miller, J. Hillis. "Composition and Decomposition: Deconstruction and the Teaching of Writing." In *Composition and Literature: Bridging the Gap*, edited by Winifred Bryan Horner, 38–56. Chicago: University of Chicago Press, 1983.

Montaigne, Michel Eyquem de. "Of the Education of Children." In *Selections from the Essays*, edited and translated by Donald M. Frame, 6–33. Arlington Heights, Ill.: AHM Publishing Corp., 1971.

Murray, Donald M. *A Writer Teaches Writing*. 2nd ed. Boston: Houghton, 1985.

Wellek, René, and Austin Warren. *Theory of Literature*. 3rd ed. New York: Harcourt, 1956.

Winterowd, W. Ross. "Black Holes, Indeterminacy, and Paulo Freire." In *Composition/Rhetoric: A Synthesis*. Carbondale: Southern Illinois University Press, 1985. The essay appeared originally in *Rhetoric Review* 2 (1983): 307–13.

3 A Hero in the Classroom

James Thomas Zebroski
Syracuse University

My First Self

What do I do when I read a student text?

I listen for the voices. I join the dialogue. I search out the hero.

I turn to the work of Mikhail M. Bakhtin, the Soviet literary theorist and self-appointed "philosophical anthropologist"—Bakhtin always did feel uncomfortable locating his interests within the bounds of a single discipline—for a view of discourse that accentuates the plurality of text and the push-pull, center-seeking, center-fleeing forces of the word.

Word is a funny word in Russian. *Slovo* has the wonderful characteristic of referring, among other things, to both discourse generally and to the single word. Bakhtin's constant invocation of *slovo*, when the more fashionable *text* or even *work* would do, seems in keeping with his constant blurring of what, for us, are the clear-cut and necessary boundaries between plurality and singularity, between other and self. Bakhtin flees from pure, independent, clearly demarcated essences; he searches out the mixed, the interrelated, the borders, the boundaries. Bakhtin, then, is an ontological pluralist. *Slovo*, by being shot through with the plurality of conflicting, even opposed, meanings, is especially useful because its ambiguity reflects the deeper ambiguity that Bakhtin finds in the universe of discourse. What seems singular is already plural. What appears to be most self-sufficient and independent relies for its very "essence" on others. Arguably, Bakhtin's motto could be "from many, one."

Bakhtin's fervent ontological pluralism, matched, though with his steel-willed resistance to reducing one phenomenon to any other, or to any more general, all-encompassing abstraction, makes for an explosive mixture when we move to the idea of voice. Bakhtin talks a lot about voice and voices. I find his notion of voice to be helpful,

35

even central, to my experience of reading/writing. Yet Bakhtin is not simply latching on to a romantic ideal. Voice for Bakhtin involves a great deal more than the notion of an "authentic Self." Voice is neither intended *parole*, nor systemic *langue*. Neither autonomous self, nor pre-existent other. Rather than any inner or outer reality (or fiction), voice lives on the borderlines of what comes to be known as self and other. And, living on the borders, voice gives rise to that which we later name self and other which are always mutually contested and negotiated through dialogue.

Then to say that I listen for voice when I read a student text is not to say that I necessarily search out that single, truthful, honest, consistent, coherent, inspired, authentic soul of the student, somehow embodied, even degraded, in the humble materiality of writing. Rather, I listen for the twists and turns and confusions of the text that often point to "voice." Where voice is, whether in the student or in me or somewhere else entirely, doesn't much matter. I can join the dialogue of voices without having to have their permanent address. They tend, after all, to move around a lot. I try to discover when, how, why a voice is intoned. I listen for the mixtures of word and phrase, the breaks and discontinuities, the broken symmetries and the interrupted rhythms and temporalities. And I try to get the student to do likewise.

Notice: "the" student, seemingly singular. Bakhtin's work does not ask us to abolish the notion of self, only to rethink and reinvent it. I cannot, and will not, treat the student as a bundle of free-flowing textual shreds and threads, as a site of textual fragments, as a text-processing machine spewing forth voices, as merely one location of Intertext. Language may in some sense speak the self, but that writes only one side of the equation, setting up precisely the dichotomy between the individual and the social that Bakhtin, both under his own name and under that of Voloshinov, argues strenuously against, and which seems peculiarly the product of our society and time. For Bakhtin, the individual is precious for the unique vantage point, the irreducible site he or she occupies at the conjunction and disjunction of voices. This vantage point is always changing and is always "social." It is not just a nice, optional supplement to my perspective; it is constitutive of *me*. I need the other to create my self, as dynamic, developing, and plural as that self may be. Bakhtin envisions a world where self is endlessly being perfected through other: *Now we construct self and other through dialogue. I speak through others to others and to myself.*

The immense importance, even holiness, of dialogue for Bakhtin becomes more understandable when we recall that for him dialogue is no mere exchange of information or pleasantries. Dialogue is the place where self is born and consecrated. It is a wrestling of self with other, by the wresting of self from other, of voice from Voice, of present from past, of history from future.

Dialogue is the a-"cross-word" where wor(l)d unfolds into world and word, where Voice gives rise to self and other. As much as we may try to repress certain voices or certain historical events, we are bound to them. My reading, then, is my unique and unrepeatable transformation of my reading history. That history is bound up with others in a whole set of ways. For instance, my history lives in the very symbols I use to think and express myself, to develop my thoughts, and to share those thoughts with others. But history also permeates the ways I have learned to transform those symbols from shared signs to signs that pulse and congeal and flow uniquely and unrepeatably through my mind. My history is even present in my estimation of what counts as dialogue. Other cultures and social classes, for example, make a far more important place for silence or stillness in their dialogue than our society does.

So dialogue in Bakhtin's anti-system of thought draws in not only the apparent and present speakers who send and receive utterance, who engage in rejoinder, but also necessarily includes all of those voices through history, both from the past and from the future, who populate the word. Dialogue evokes and enacts this history, intones these voices, serving as a sort of great assembly where voice gathers.

Enter the hero.

The hero is Bakhtin's attempt in his later work to explore the very edges of the universe of discourse. The hero is that super-addressee who is infinitely distant from immediate participation in a dialogue, but whose responsive understanding of it is assumed, somehow animating and vitalizing the word. Why do people speak when no one is present? Why do people bother to talk when they know for certain that misunderstanding is guaranteed? Why is it that people in the most extreme and hopeless circumstances—in torture chambers or in concentration camps or in the prison house of their own isolation and loneliness—continue to speak? What can account for this persistent urge to raise their voices in the face of what amounts to staggering, even overwhelming odds of ever being heard? If, as Bakhtin contends, the life of a text always develops on the borders between two consciousnesses, two subjects, what happens when there seems to be no Other present? If Other is absent, then self and word would seem to disappear.

Bakhtin deals with this philosophical problem by arguing that because the word cannot be understood from the outside, a "thing," the *hero* of the discourse, must always be presupposed by anyone who even attempts to speak the word. The hero takes different forms in different periods of history, but is a constitutive aspect of the word. The hero, it turns out, also faces the word unfinalizable and open. Understanding is not immediate and once for all; rather, it presses on further and further to the very limits of the universe of discourse.

Bakhtin helps me to read any text. Bakhtin's voice with its history of our dialogue is there as I read a student text. It is now impossible for me to read if I don't read through Bakhtin.

And others.

So, I listen for the voices. I join the dialogue. I search for the hero. . . .

My Second Self

In 1979 I gave up trying to teach the so-called modes of discourse. Instead, I began sending my freshman composition students out of the classroom to observe social scenes and to talk with people at those scenes about how they view their little piece of the world. I asked students to do some ethnographic field research, observing and interviewing people about their work and how they felt about working. When you move out of the textbooks and into the messiness and the richness of the world, you run the risk of receiving a paper like this (the sentences have been numbered for easy reference):

Disabled Unemployment

(1) Disabled people United Cerebral Palsy in Smithtown are said to be discriminated against in employment. (2) For instance, Fred Lawrence of the United Cerebral Palsy said that he was up for a promotion in April of 1981; but, another client named Harry George was up for the same promotion in April of 1981. (3) Although, Harry George was a two year college graduate from (STI), Smithtown Institution of Technology, and could walk with the assistance of a brace. (4) But, was in another training program name United Way training program for the disabled disavantage. (5) Which has been established for over thirty-two years. (6) On the other hand, Fred Lawrence had only a eleventh grade education with 6 months of training, and was in a program named United Cerebral Palsy which has only been established for 2 1/2 years.

(7) Fred said he had been discriminated against just because he couldn't walk and manoeuvre like Harry George.

(8) Also, another incident took place on May 7, 1981. (9) With a client name Dan Roberts. (10) Dan Roberts is also a United Cerebral Palsy trainee for the program. (11) He said that he put in for a supervisor position two years in a row; but another trainee for Blue Cross and Blue Shield had the same interview on May 7, 1981. (12) Likewise, Dan Roberts knew that another person from Blue Cross and Blue Shield training program would be present, but he didn't know his name. (13) So they both were called into the office by the second supervisor, which called both of them into the office. (14) He then introduced his self, my name is Herb Johnson I'm looking for a man which can fill my supervisor position. (15) I'm the president of Sears distribution center. (16) Okay, Dan Roberts how many years of Training have you ad at the Blue Cross and Blue Shield program. (17) Dan said I have had 3 months of training at Blue Cross and Blue Shield. (18) What about you; Mike Bonner. (19) I have 3 years of training in blue Cross and Blue Shield, and also 4 years of college; with a Bachelor of science from Princeton University. (20) He then told Dan Roberts to step out in the hall and wait until I call upon you. (21) He then told Mike Bonner to go out in the hall. (22) Fifteen minutes later he told both of them to come in; he said both of them are good men, but I only need one. (23) So I came to the conclusion that Mike is most qualified for the job. (24) I'm sorry come back next year. (25) Now, Dan Roberts said that he was being discriminated against, and that he waited in line for a job. (26) In conclusion, I think that in each case it was the level of education. (27) The year of the establishment of each program. (28) For example, blue Cross and Blue Shields training program had been established for thirty-two years. (29) Whereas, United Cerebral Palsy only 2 1/2 years. (30) I think that United Cerebral Palsy is just a program that is not very well known, but through time it will be known. (31) I also think that the disabled people in United Cerebral Palsy are jumping to conclusions.

"Disabled Unemployment" came up the row and into my hands; for over eight years I have been conducting a dialogue with the voices of this text, trying to understand it, sensing that there is more going on in it than first meets the eye.

Composition teachers have emerged from a complicated and often discordant history. Over the last eighty years we have moved through a prescriptive, handbook tradition, across the New Criticism, and into the realm of process. Currently our fascination with discourse communities points to the reemergence of a social perspective on language. Our readings of texts enact this history. Every time we sit down to interpret a student paper, we bring to that dialogue our history of such dialogues. And with this history come what Bakhtin calls ideologies, theories of language and of the world that are not simply right or wrong. Our readings cannot be tagged as either an accurate or inaccurate (re)construction of text. They are instead loud or soft voices that we find more or less persuasive, tending toward dialogue or monologue, worrying about creativity or control. We all consist of constellations of these voices and we wring our voice, our reading of text, from this collective. I create myself anew each time I read a student text.

Let me introduce you to some of the more insistent voices that populate my reading of "Disabled Unemployment."

First in my reading is Simon Newman.

> This paper is proof of the decline in public education and the decay of the English language. The writer lacks a knowledge of and respect for the English language. Where are our standards?
>
> In the very first sentence the word "of" has been carelessly omitted. In sentence 3, a comma has been incorrectly placed after "although." That line is actually a fragment. In sentence 4, another incorrectly used comma appears after "but." The -*ed* is left off of "name" in that sentence. Sentence 5 has another sentence fragment. In sentence 6, the number "six" needs to be spelled out.
>
> The second paragraph isn't really a paragraph. It's simply a blob of disconnected discourse. The errors increase; the incoherence compounds. The writer shifts from Dan Roberts in sentence 10 to a nameless other person in sentence 12 to a supervisor in sentence 13 to a president of Sears Distribution Center in sentence 15 to a confused dialogue.
>
> Need I say more? I could go on, but it is clear that the English language is being butchered. Even when the language is correct— which it hardly ever is—it is awkward, lacking any grace or redeeming qualities. Look at that title—"Disabled Unemployment"—what does that mean? Can you think of an uglier phrase?
>
> This remedial student has no control over the language and needs to go back to the basics. When you quit teaching grammar, as so many did in the permissive 1960s and 1970s, this is what you get!

Voice two is that of John Crowe Redemption.

> I think you are being a bit harsh on the student, Mr. Simon Newman. Certainly this is unacceptable as exposition. But I find it curiously similar to, of all things, poetry—bad poetry to be sure—but poetry nonetheless.
>
> A poem is a loose logical structure with a good deal of local texture. It returns to us a denser, more refractory world. The texture of the poem tends to undermine its structure; the details and examples and other foreign matter fight to displace the argument. This appears to be what is happening in this paper. We begin with a statement of hypothesis—"Disabled people are

said to be discriminated against." Notice the tentativeness, the conjectural quality of the verb phrase, its passive voice, its distance, its objectivity. The first paragraph is a brief for that case.

Now notice the second paragraph begins in a like way, but gets sidetracked. The structure of the first argument is being undermined in front of our eyes by the texture of the proof, the testimony of the witnesses and participants. The paper breaks in two.

Paragraph one is objective and structured; paragraph two is subjective and textured. The first paragraph wars against the second paragraph. In this war there are no survivors.

The paper, then, fails to achieve unity. As my good friend Cleanth Brooks would say, the structures of meaning are confused. They do not fit together. They do not balance each other; the paper does not work. What we have here is an extremely rough draft masquerading as a finished paper. Perhaps if the student were to start the next draft with sentence 26, were to go after the indeterminacies, were to do some more writing and then some restructuring. . . .

The third voice that I hear is Mina Flaherty.

Gentlemen, I don't disagree with what you say, but I do insist that some rather critical points have been omitted.

Is this paper really as chaotic as you insist? While certainly not acceptable exposition, this paper is not all that different from the work of my own basic writers. More than anything else, this writer—by the way, what is the name of this writer? Dave. Well, Dave is simply very inexperienced in writing and probably has read very little. He is not conversant with the conventions of exposition. Yet he is farther along than many. I read a logic and a consistency, and considering Dave's inexperience, dare I say it, a sophistication in this paper that should encourage Dave's composition teacher. Dave is well on his way to becoming a writer of acceptable prose.

Notice first the errors. Yes, there are many of them. Yes, they are unacceptable.

And yet there is a logic to them that reveals some deeper psychological and linguistic processes at work. For example, the incorrect comma use after words like "although," "but," and "also" is consistent, derived from a rule that is correctly applied after "for instance," "on the other hand," "in conclusion." Dave is simply overapplying the rule, using it when it isn't necessary, but not randomly. Dave is too rule-bound in this instance. Notice also that the fragments in the first paragraph reveal an attempt to control the language, to get a complex sentence that stretches from sentences 3 through 6 under control. I would guess that Dave has been told by former English teachers that he has a run-on problem, a lack of control, and this is Dave's way of making sentences do what they don't seem to do in his mind—stop.

Similarly, the incoherence of the second paragraph is largely removed if we do two simple things—put in the appropriate quotation marks, and arrange this dialogue by using the conventions of spacing. We expect to see dialogue arranged in a certain way spatially on the page. Dave does not seem to be aware of those expectations.

And look at what Dave does do right. There is a curious, even a shocking lack of misspellings even in a paper that uses words like "cerebral," "technology," "institution," "discriminated," "distribution," "bachelor," and even "manoeuvre." I think the motivation is reflected in the effort that must have gone into getting this paper ready for class presentation—at least if the spelling means anything.

The language of the paper is awkward, but much of that awkwardness comes from the use of the passive voice and avoidance of the personal pronoun "I"; perhaps Dave avoids "I" because he had been taught that in an obejective research paper you don't use it.

And on the plus side, that bane of composition teachers, generality and lack of specification, is absent. In fact, Dave is so involved with specific examples and incidents that he seems to lose track of them. For example, Dave states in sentence 10 that Dan Roberts is a United Cerebral Palsy trainee and then in sentence 16 he implies that Roberts is a Blue Cross/Blue Shield trainee. It might be the case that Dave has more details than he or his audience need, but that's still a wonderful change from the more usual writing of college freshmen.

Finally, the essay is structured.

It begins with a statement of the problem, goes through two cases, and concludes with an inductive judgment. While certainly the elaboration of these parts is uneven, inconsistent, and unbalanced, a basic inductive structure is there. Like most of us, Dave needs to learn when to say more and when to say less; he needs to learn when to elaborate and when to cut out. If we could introduce the concept of audience as one factor that may be helpful in making those kinds of decisions, and if we could get Dave to read his paper out loud and listen to what he has written down, this elaborating/condensing problem will tend to solve itself.

So, although Dave has quite a ways to go, he is off to a better start than it may first appear to a reader who focuses more on the product than on the processes behind the product.

The fourth voice is that of Mikhail Zebroski Bakhtin.

Who speaks here? Who accentuates these words? To what worlds do these words and voices belong?

All discourse is dialogic, double-voiced, teeming with the voices of others. This paper is almost a transcription of that dialogic world.

Let us look closely at paragraph two since this is where the struggle for voice comes out into the open.

The first voice begins with sentence 8: "Also another incident took place. . . ." This is the voice of the lawyer/judge of the paper. The lawyer is investigating an incident, presenting the case, examining the evidence, cross-examining the witnesses, studying their testimony. The first voice is interrupted by a second—the storyteller. The very boundary between the two voices is a disputed zone, indicated by the repetition of "both were called into the office by the second supervisor, which called both of them into the office." We now occupy the storyteller's world which is further interrupted by three additional voices.

Voice three is Herb Johnson, the boss. Voice four is Dan Roberts, the less trained job applicant. Voice five is Mike Bonner, the more trained job applicant.

There is a movement, a kind of dialogue, between these voices, a movement that returns and centers primarily on the boss and the storyteller. A few double-voiced phrases and words straddle the borderlines, the junctures of the reported speeches. In sentence 20 "wait until" shifts from the storyteller to the boss. In sentence 22 "are good men but" marks a similar boundary. Finally, toward the end a new voice, the sixth voice is raised. This is the "I" of the paper, no longer the lawyer/judge. Here perhaps is Dave's voice finally making its entrance. We can observe then a movement in this paper from "they" to "I," from others to self. One's own discourse is gradually wrought out of others' words that have been acknowledged and assimilated, and the boundaries between the two are at first scarcely perceptible.

And yet it isn't quite this simple. There is a struggle for voice at another level. The entire paper is a word-with-a-sideward-glance. The speaker obliquely addresses the disabled unemployed who think that they have been discriminated against. My friend Valentin Voloshinov calls this subject being talked about, but also in some sense being talked to, the hero of the discourse. This is the hero in the strict sense—Dan Roberts and all of the other Dan Robertses of this society.

Yet this address to the unemployed does not quite ring true. The reader—in this case the instructor and the class—is called in not so much as an ally but as a hostile witness. The author acknowledges the silent but ever-present hostile witnesses by attempting to quiet, if not silence, Dan Roberts by placing many of his claims in indirect discourse (sentences 11 and 25). By giving the boss so much to say and so much power, by in fact giving the boss the last word in the matter, the author is also bowing to the authority of the classroom reader.

Finally, the sideward-glancing word is observable when the author states the so-called objective facts typified by the proliferation of names. Yet from whose point of view are these facts objective? Not from the Roberts's point of view, nor from Herb Johnson's perspective. Not even from the author's viewpoint since the author too is involved in talking with these people. No, the objective facts are only objective in this case for the silent but

ever present and influencing class reader who does not know the
situation or the participants personally. So even the writer's proof,
the dialogue between the participants, is an example of discourse
sideward glancing, discourse that anticipates the reader and the
reader's objections. The sideward glancing word shows up in the
boss who has been made the epitome of reason and empathy.
And to further clinch this matter, the cases that the author chooses
to discuss are the clearest cut cases possible. If Herb Johnson
cannot figure out in fifteen minutes that three years of training
beats three months of training, and that a Princeton University
degree beats no degree at all, then he is in trouble.

In sum, there are three participants in this little drama: the
author, the hero, and the reader. The hero in the strict sense is
Dan Roberts and the unemployed. The readers are hostile because
they are a part of the social structure; they represent its power of
reward and punishment, acceptance or rejection, both in the
classroom and in the university and therefore in the author's
future world of work. The author tries to mediate between hero
and reader, trying to present the people involved and their
viewpoints in a reasonable way while at the same time trying to
please or at least not offend the reader.

Yet the author is concerned with Dan Roberts. This sympathy
is clearly revealed in sentence 30 where the author asserts that
the program will become better known through time. And it is
here that the hero of the paper in the broader sense is revealed.

The hero includes not only the unemployed but history's
judgment on those unemployed and on those who create their
unemployment. This higher course of understanding will make
the ultimate decision. Dan Roberts, standing out in the hallway,
will someday come in to hear the verdict of not simply his boss,
but of history. His plaintive "How long, how long must I wait?"
will one day be answered.

"The author imagines, more or less consciously, a higher super-
receiver . . . whose absolutely appropriate responsive understanding is projected either into a metaphysical distance or into a distant
historical time. . . . In different periods and in different conceptions
of the world, such super- receivers and their . . . responsive understanding receive various concrete ideological expressions (God,
the absolute truth, . . . the people, the judgment of history, science,
etc.). . . . Every dialogue takes place, then, against the backdrop
of the responsive understanding of a present but invisible third
entity, hovering above all the participants in the dialogue. . . . [This
third participant, this hero] proceeds from the nature of discourse,
that always wants to be heard. . . . For discourse (and, therefore,
for humans) nothing is more frightening than absence of answer."
(Todorov 1984, 110)

My Third Self

Let me interrupt at this point to say that recent books and articles
about Bakhtin have tended to end with a consideration of endings.

No conventional ending will quite do when speaking of Bakhtin, who believed that the living word is unfinalizable and unending. Some current essays about Bakhtin close with the case for further dialogue about (and interpretation of) Bakhtin. Others, in a (post-)modern turn, consider the discourse that has so far passed, and comment on it, word interrogating (if not parodying) word. A few have argued for the acceptance of Bakhtin's notions of discourse as the only real alternative at a moment of Western intellectual history that appears to be torn between outworn ideas of language as self-possession-expression and new views of language as intertext and difference.

I don't want to end in any of these ways. Rather, I want to try in the remainder of this essay to let the people have the "last" word. The people I'm referring to here are the composition student and teacher.

What about Dave, the freshman in my composition class, the author of "Disabled Unemployment"? What might he say to my reading of his paper? Dave and I have been out of touch for many years, almost from the moment he finished my freshman composition course. I went on to get my degree. I wonder if he got his and whether he made it and what kind of work he is doing. He should have graduated in 1982 or so.

I would imagine that Dave would in the first instance be puzzled that his writing, for whatever reasons, merited the extended attention of his teacher and other teachers across the country, over time. I also expect that if he knew, he would be more than a bit shocked that ordinary "Paper 3" in such an ordinary freshman English course would live such a long and illustrious life. All my students know that their ethnography paper is a public paper, meaning all students will read it. That also means that I collect these papers, bind them into books, and save these books so that they can be placed on reserve at the library for my future students to read. They know that. I say that. It's on the syllabus. They have read the yellowed and tattered pages, the smeared and faded purple, from the days when I used to ditto all the papers off. Everyone knows that crazy Zebroski keeps these things, and shares them, for whatever weird reason.

Still, I think Dave would be amazed that something he did is still around and still having an effect, seemingly all out of proportion to its humble origins. No doubt Dave would tell me, politely but firmly, with great enthusiasm—that's how I remember him—that "You are really reading more into that little paper than is there." And I would smile, "Am I?"

Thus writing students flow through the writing teacher's life. Their texts and our sense of discourse are always seen as temporary, as rather humble, ordinary. Great and lasting thoughts seem to be mutually exclusive of their words, of my words. Language is a throwaway commodity, an exchange value that is only useful in that it gets us something else, somewhere else. And here I am, somewhere else, writing of that language, making of it something else.

Maybe.

Response. Response-ability. Answerability. Our word taking on a life of its own, a life beyond us. The openness of word, its ultimate return, its inevitable resurrection. That is Bakhtin's view of it. He, the optimist.

And I? I keep returning to the great unsaid of this interpretation, of any response to student writing: it is less important *what* we make of student writing than *that* we make something, something principled, of it. The writing teacher must believe that student texts are intrinsically worthy of being valued. But the simple truth is that the kind and amount of attention a writing teacher can direct toward student texts is a function of training and social circumstance. Our training, our institutional location, and our social function inevitably come down to social class.

Bakhtin, despite the attempts of scores of U.S. scholars to obscure or soft-pedal the fact, is a Marxist. The class struggle lies at the heart of this view of a dynamic, dialogic language. A writing teacher may or may not agree with Bakhtin. But a writing teacher is constrained by the very forces that Bakhtin describes. When I teach four sections of freshman composition I necessarily respond differently than when I teach a class or two of writing. Not surprisingly, the teacher who gets to teach four or five composition classes tends to teach at an institution that serves working-class students. So the students who need to get the most attention, who need to be most engaged in dialogue—if they are to be initiated or invited into the academic discourse communities that David Bartholomae and Patricia Bizzell, among others, talk so much about—those students are the very ones who will get the least attention, simply because their teachers will be the most overloaded and overworked. And the very students who need the least attention because they come from the right class will be the ones who will get the most attention since their teachers will have fewer classes, fewer students, fewer diversions. And nothing changes, as the class system reproduces itself over and over.

There is a good deal of moving in and out of doors in Dave's "Disabled Unemployment." Even though the text is one long argument for meritocracy, a giant question mark hangs over it and over Dave. Maybe that's why I really like that text, because the same question mark has always hung over me. The doors in Dave's paper remind us of the gates of the university. But the door to my freshman composition class rarely opens to the working class. When it does, Dave comes through it.

Dave and I share a set of experiences, momentarily embodied in this text. Only a person with roots in the working class can hear this voice. It is the voice of a whole class of people excluded from composition textbooks, ignored in composition research, and too often silenced in writing classrooms, silenced, as Tillie Olsen shows us, in a hundred subtle ways.

So who do *you* think the hero is?

Works Cited

Todorov, Tzvetan. *Mikhail Bakhtin: The Dialogic Principle.* Translated by W. Godzich. Minneapolis: University of Minnesota Press.

4 Learning to Read Student Papers from a Feminine Perspective, I

Elizabeth A. Flynn
Michigan Technological University

I've been teaching writing for nearly twenty years. I began my career as a T.A. in the English Department at Ohio State where I graded the papers of about fifty students per ten-week quarter, each of whom wrote a paper every other week—approximately 750 papers a year. The project was enormously frustrating. My preparation for the task consisted of one year of high school teaching and a university course, which I took the first quarter that I was a T.A., that focused on classical rhetoric and contemporary rhetorical theory. Aristotle's topics seemed far removed from the papers on high school cheerleading contests and football victories that I was receiving. Every other weekend I found myself poring over student essays with utmost perplexity. Was the paper to which I assigned a C really a C? Was it all that much worse than the paper to which I had just assigned a B? I remember reading some papers again and again trying to decide how I should evaluate them, and I certainly spent more than the fifteen minutes per paper I was told was reasonable. I know my assessments were influenced by grammar and penmanship—students did not have word processors then, and many of the papers I received were handwritten. The mandatory "in-class" essay assignments, designed to defend against plagiarism, always were. Frequently I assigned the grade B-/C+—an indication of my indecision.

In those days, the late 1960s, the teacher of composition was an evaluator of freshman English themes. Assignments were made, students tried to fulfill them as best they could, teachers graded submitted papers, returned them, and went on to the next writing assignment. Enrollments were burgeoning, and freshman English was a "flunk out" course. Instructors routinely assigned D's and F's on papers and in the course, and revision of submitted work was unheard of. Students expected low grades and harsh judgments and received them. I remember being disturbed by the approach we were taking—we did not seem to be doing much for our students' writing abilities.

I was ready, therefore, for the revolution when it came. I liked the idea of peer group critiques and an institutionalized revision policy, and I liked the idea that developing writers had to be treated gently, had to be nurtured. I was relieved, too, that I was no longer simply an evaluator of student papers. I had to read them as work in progress, to comment on them as potential products rather than actual products. I now saw my job as helping students transform their initial attempts into essays that had meaning for others. I discovered that my task of reading papers was made easier if I made careful writing assignments, if I asked my students to write papers that interested me, that taught me something. I remember one assignment that produced essays that were especially enjoyable to read. Students had to employ a "foreign" language of sorts, a vocabulary they were comfortable with but that might be foreign to someone not familiar with particular technical jargon. I read about photography, about football, about sausage-making. Students became the authority, and I became the learner.

It was not until the late 1970s, when I held a position as a teacher in Ohio State's Writing Workshop, a program for underprepared writers, that I had an opportunity to compare the strategies I had developed with the strategies of my peers. Reading student papers is usually a solitary task occasionally interrupted by sharing the best or the worst with friends and colleagues. The staff of the Workshop, however, frequently engaged in holistic scoring of student papers, so our assessments were often discussed and negotiated. I realized that my colleagues were often much more concerned with how a paper conformed to a given assignment than I was. For me, an assignment is a stimulus, a way of getting students started, rather than a straitjacket. If students reinterpret the assignment in creative ways, fine. If they misinterpret an assignment, I'm quite willing to try to work with what they give me. I also learned that I had developed a facility for reading a paper for what it could become; I could see the potential in the actual.

I might describe my story as a conversion from a masculine approach to reading student papers to a feminine approach. I was initially acculturated into a system that valued objectification and one in which the teacher of writing had one function only—that of evaluator. I was always a judge of my students' writing, never a sympathetic reader. I saw my task, in writing comments on papers, as justifying a grade, never offering advice. This definition of my role defined my relationship to my students. I was separate from them, above them, arbiter of what constituted good writing and bad writing. My position of judge and ultimate authority was a precarious one, though. I was twenty-three years old, only a few years older than my students, and inexperienced, hence my frustration and anxiety.

My conversion to a feminine stance was gradual. First I altered my usual routine by allowing students to critique each other's papers. The procedure did not change the situation drastically, though, because students critiqued papers on the day the final (and only) version was due and had no opportunity to make use of the feedback they received. Other colleagues were doing much the same, and we did not question the approach. One day, though, and this was not until the mid-1970s, Lisa Ede told me that she had decided to have her students critique each other's *drafts*, not their final papers, so that they could incorporate their comments into their revisions. I distinctly remember being shocked by the idea. Wasn't this cheating? Plagiarism? How could I evaluate a final product so tainted by others' opinions? Eventually, though, I succumbed, no doubt because I had begun to read composition theory in earnest and was beginning to understand what this talk of "the composing process" was all about. The approach, of course, increased my work load. I started taking home sets of drafts as well as sets of final essays. But the reading itself was much more rewarding. My comments on the drafts were meant to be helpful rather than judgmental, and I read the final products as documents in which I had an investment. I read to see if students had understood my comments and taken them into account. Sometimes they did, sometimes they did not. The important thing was that my relationship with my students changed. I was no longer merely an adversary. I was also on their side, a friendly advisor (I hesitate to use the usual "coach" metaphor since it introduces a world of combat and aggression that I am trying to avoid). I could relax.

In what sense is this new approach a "feminine" one? Numerous feminist researchers and theorists in a variety of different fields have argued recently that males and females process language and perceive the world in distinctly different ways. As we will see, they suggest that males tend to objectify, to detach themselves from the experiences they are observing or the individuals with whom they are communicating. Females, in contrast, tend to empathize with others and to interact with them more readily than do males. The developmental problems that the different genders have to overcome, therefore, tend to be different. Males often are able to detach themselves from parental ties but have difficulty committing themselves to others. Females, in contrast, are often able to commit themselves to others but sometimes have difficulty recognizing and insisting on their individual rights. The powerful feminist argument that the male perception of reality is chronicled and becomes the standard while the female version is suppressed, silenced, depends on a recognition of difference. Feminist literary scholars, for instance, point out that the literary texts that tend to become canonized by literary scholars and publishers are largely written by males and, for the most part, describe male experience; women's texts are often marginalized or ignored entirely. The work of such scholars makes evident the androcentrism of the institution of literary studies, gives voice to the work of lost or forgotten women writers, and provides reinterpretations of work by recognized women writers. In urging that we recognize difference, feminist researchers and theorists are urging us to make visible a previously invisible feminine perspective. Work in a number of different areas would be relevant here. I'll limit the discussion to a brief overview of work in reading, psychology, sociology, and education.

Mary Crawford and Roger Chaffin (1986), in their essay, "The Reader's Construction of Meaning: Cognitive Research on Gender and Comprehension," review research that shows that males and females differ in their interpretation of texts because they have been socialized in different ways and hence have different schemata or mental representations to draw on. Crawford and Chaffin explain that schemata are abstract representations of the original events or statements, generalized knowledge structures that provide a framework for and determine the nature of understanding. Schemata allow the understander to go beyond the information usually given in a situation. In discussing gender-related schemata, they point out that women and men are "sex-typed," that is, they differ in their degree of gender-typing. People who are more highly sex-typed are those who not only conform to their culture's definition of masculinity or femininity, but also process information in terms of the gender schema (17). They also point out that the potentially, significantly different perspectives of males and females are often lessened because women's perceptions are often affected by man's dominant viewpoint, hence their voices are "muted."

My own research suggests that males and females often interact with the texts they read in different ways. In "Gender and Reading" (1983) I show that females often oscillate in a productive way between the opposite poles of empathy and judgment, identification and detachment, whereas males tend to become fixated at either extreme—to dominate texts by judging them overharshly or rejecting them, or to subordinate themselves to texts by becoming entangled in textual detail or identifying too strongly with characters or situations described in them. The work of David Bleich in some ways complements my findings. In "Gender Interests in Reading and Language" (1986), Bleich describes studies in which he found that males tend to focus on literary narratives as objects constructed by an author whereas females tend to participate in the experience evoked by the text.

Work in sociology and psychology supports the idea that males and females interact with others and with the environment in different ways. Nancy Chodorow, for instance, in *The Reproduction of Mothering: Psychoanalysis and the Sociology of Gender* (1978), and Carol Gilligan, in *In a Different Voice: Psychological Theory and Women's Development* (1982), argue that women and men have different conceptions of self and different modes of interaction with others as a result of their different experiences, especially their early relationship with their primary parent, their mother. Chodorow finds that girls and boys develop different relational capacities and senses of self as a result of growing up in a family in which women do most of the parenting. A girl's gender and gender role identification processes are continuous with her earliest identifications, whereas a boy's are not. The boy shifts his identification from the mother to the father and gives up his attachment to and primary identification with his mother. The more general identification processes of both males and females follow a similar pattern. A boy, in order to feel himself adequately masculine, must distinguish and differentiate himself from others in a way that a girl need not. Girls, in contrast, grow up in a family where mothers are the primary parent and caretaker and hence begin to identify more directly and immediately with their mothers and their mothers' familial roles. Chodorow concludes, "Masculine identification processes stress differentiation from others, the denial of affective relation, and categorical universalistic components of the masculine role. Feminine identification processes are relational, whereas masculine identification processes tend to deny relationship" (176).

Carol Gilligan's *In a Different Voice* builds on Chodorow's findings, focusing especially, though, on differences in the ways in which males and females speak about moral problems. According to Gilligan, women tend to define moral problems in terms of conflicting responsibilities rather than competing rights and to describe the resolution of moral problems in terms of a mode of thinking that is contextual and narrative rather than formal and abstract (19). Men, in contrast, equate morality and fairness and tie moral development to the understanding of rights and rules (19). Her study aims to correct the inadequacies of Lawrence Kohlberg's delineation of the stages of moral development. Kohlberg's (1976) study included only male subjects, and Kohlberg's categories reflect his decidedly male orientation. For him, the highest stages of moral development derive from a reflective understanding of human rights (Gilligan 1982, 19).

Nel Noddings, in *Caring: A Feminine Approach to Ethics and Moral Education* (1984), argues that ethical matters have traditionally been discussed from a masculine perspective and treat the subject from a "rational-cognitive" point of view. She says that ethics has been discussed largely in the language of the father, in principles and propositions, in terms such as justification, fairness, justice (1). The mother's voice has been silent. Noddings's alternative view begins with the moral attitude of a longing for goodness, not with moral reasoning. It locates morality in receptivity, relatedness, and responsiveness rather than logic. For Noddings, human caring and the memory of caring and being cared for form the foundation of ethical response.

The "one-caring," that is, the person who cares, tries to apprehend the reality of the other and displaces her own interests with the interests of the reality of the other. Noddings says, "When the other's reality becomes a real possibility for me, I care" (14). The attention of the one-caring is on the cared-for, not on the self. To care is to act not by fixed rules but by affection and regard (24). Objective thinking may play a part in the activity of caring, but it is of limited and particular use. The rational-objective mode must continually be re-established and re-directed from a fresh base of commitment (26). In the rational-objective mode, the self moves toward the object. In the caring mode, the self receives the object, puts itself quietly in its presence. The one-caring assumes a dual perspective and can see things from both her own pole and that of the cared-for. She accepts the attitude of the one cared-for, adjusts her requirements in light of the other's interests and abilities, and supports those efforts nonjudgmentally (174). Noddings emphasizes that the relationship between the one-caring and the cared-for is asymmetrical but that both must contribute appropriately. Something from "A" must be completed in "B" (19).

We might say that Noddings describes the ideal that a process approach to the reading of student papers attempts to achieve. The teacher becomes a reader of student writing, not merely an evaluator. She attempts to receive the language of the student, to understand it and to respond to it with warmth and concern. She permits, even encourages, false starts, incomplete thoughts, incoherence. She responds to what she receives, attempts to tease out the student's intended meaning, and allows multiple revision. The teacher does not demand that the student come to her, accept her standards and values. Rather, she receives the language of the student and attempts to work with it. The approach is quite similar to the one advocated by Lil Brannon and Cy Knoblauch in their essay, "Students' Rights to Their Own Texts" (1982). They argue that teachers of writing should pursue writers' real intentions until those intentions are satisfactorily conveyed. According to Brannon and Knoblauch, "The teacher's role is to attract a writer's attention to the relationship between intention and effect, enabling a recognition of discrepancies, but finally leaving decisions about alternative choices to the writer, not the teacher" (162). They point out the dangers of attempting to measure students' texts against some Platonic Ideal Text (159). Nancy Sommers conveys a similar idea in her essay, "Responding to Student Writing" (1982). She identifies common problems in responding to student writing: (1) appropriating students' texts by confusing the student's purpose in writing the text with her own purpose in commenting on the text or (2) making comments that are not text-specific, that could be interchanged, rubber-stamped, from text to text (149, 152). She suggests that teachers should read student texts for meaning and offer commentary to motivate revision. She says,

> The challenge we face as teachers is to develop comments which will provide an inherent reason for students to revise; it is a sense of revision as discovery, as a repeated process of beginning again, as starting out new, that our students have not learned. We need to show our students how to seek, in the possibility of revision, the dissonances of discovery—to show them through our comments why new choices would positively change their texts, and thus to show them the potential for development implicit in their own writing. (156)

The caring teacher of writing starts with the student's text and works from there, praising that which is well done, and pointing out specific ways in which the writing could be improved.

This is the ideal, but is it realized? Do I realize it? How complete has my conversion to a student-centered process pedagogy been? Are there still remnants of my previous training in the way I now read student papers? Do I read in a caring, supportive way or in an overly judgmental way? To find out, I decided to examine comments I made on a set of student papers. I looked at marginal and terminal comments on "final" essays submitted in a first-year English course in which students read and wrote about literature. Students wrote journal entries about short stories, selected paper topics by attempting to answer questions raised in their journal entries and in class discussions, wrote drafts of their papers and received feedback on them from classmates and from me, and revised their essays into finished essays that I commented cn and graded. I had an open revision policy in the course, however, so that students were always free to revise their work. My comments, then, were both evaluative and suggestive. They justified the grade I assigned but also made suggestions for revision.

Many of the comments I made were clearly meant to encourage the students. Typical marginal comments, for instance, were as follows: "Interesting," "nicely put," "good quote," "good," "Good intro.," "good transition." I also always began a terminal comment with a direct address to the student and a positive comment about the paper. Here, for instance, are some examples: "Mark, I think this is quite good— an interesting approach"; "Julie, Good. This is a thoughtful, well-organized analysis"; "Sue, I think this is very good. Your essay is well-organized and insightful."

Not all of my comments, of course, aimed to encourage students; many aimed to give them constructive criticism. Some of my marginal comments, for instance, raised questions that the student might take into consideration in revising the essay: "Is this the central theme do you think?" "Some priests are gregarious, aren't they?" "How?" Or they pointed out evidence students may have overlooked: "How about mentioning the 'bridal chamber'?" "Might help to indicate which conflicts you are going to deal with here." Other comments indicated problems with individual assertions: "not clear," "a bit awkward." Others pointed out specific problems: "You are doing too much summarizing here"; "Transition could be stronger"; "In the paragraph you don't focus upon self-centeredness"; "Somehow this sentence seems out of place here." The terminal comments, which always began on a positive note, always indicated the problems that remained in the paper: "Some of your sentences are awkward, though, and a few of your transitions could be stronger"; "That second-to-the-last paragraph could have been developed more fully"; "Some of the quotes you use need more of a context, though."

To the extent that my comments are justifications of grades as well as suggestions for revision, they fall short of Noddings's ideal. Noddings argues that teachers should not assign grades to student work. She feels that caring teachers should evaluate student work along all the dimensions proper to the field they are teaching, but they have no right to report that evaluation to the world. If grades must be assigned, external examiners should do so. Noddings feels that punitive moves work against the development of a sense of responsibility. The caring teacher, then, would never feel the need to justify a grade in commenting on student writing. All comments would serve the purpose of improving student writing.

Most of us, though, do not have the luxury of working within a system where grades are optional. Is it possible to take a caring stance toward the student papers we read despite the limitations of the system within which we are working? Did I take such a stance? The open revision policy that I instituted was an attempt to mitigate the deleterious effects of the externally imposed grading system. Paper grades were not final. My comments were caring to the extent that they were supportive and helpful. For the most part, they indicated that I received the students' texts and dealt with them on their own terms. Both marginal and terminal comments always pointed out strengths and always made helpful suggestions. Often, those comments made specific references to the arguments students were constructing: "I agree that Woolf paints a unified picture in 'Kew Gardens'"; "Some priests are gregarious, aren't they?"; "How about mentioning the 'bridal chamber'?" And frequently they made explicit or implicit suggestions for revision: "I think the material in this paragraph could have been arranged more effectively"; "That second-to-the-last paragraph could have been arranged more effectively"; "I think your thesis could have been supported more effectively." My intent was clearly to interact with my students' texts, to help them improve their writing. Of course, my comments also reflected the constraints within which I was working. They could have been longer, more specific, and I did sometimes yield to the temptation of using formulaic responses—"good transition," "transition could be stronger," "not clear."

Student writers need more help than over-committed teachers can possibly give them. We always fall short of our ideal. But I have come a long way from the days when I conceived of my job as that of a judge, an upholder of standards. I now read student papers with empathy for the student writer and with an eye for what a flawed paper might possibly become with some work and some guidance. I would like to think that I have learned to resist a male mode of behavior that our institutions so frequently introduce us to and have begun to develop a feminine way of encountering student texts.

Works Cited

Bleich, David. "Gender Interests in Reading and Language." In *Gender and Reading: Essays on Readers, Texts, and Contexts*, edited by Elizabeth A. Flynn and Patrocinio P. Schweickart, 234–66. Baltimore: Johns Hopkins University Press, 1986.

Brannon, Lil, and C. H. Knoblauch. "On Students' Rights to Their Own Texts: A Model of Teacher Response." *College Composition and Communication* 33 (1982): 157–66.

Chodorow, Nancy. *The Reproduction of Mothering: Psychoanalysis and the Sociology of Gender.* Berkeley: University of California Press, 1978.

Crawford, Mary, and Roger Chaffin. "The Reader's Construction of Meaning: Cognitive Research on Gender and Comprehension." In *Gender and Reading: Essays on Readers, Texts, and Contexts,* edited by Elizabeth A. Flynn and Patrocinio P. Schweickart, 3–30. Baltimore: Johns Hopkins University Press, 1986.

Flynn, Elizabeth A. "Gender and Reading." *College English* 45 (1983): 236–51. Reprinted in *Gender and Reading,* edited by Elizabeth A. Flynn and Patrocinio P. Schweickart, 267–88. Baltimore: Johns Hopkins University Press, 1986.

Gilligan, Carol. *In a Different Voice: Psychological Theory and Women's Development.* Cambridge: Harvard University Press, 1982.

Kohlberg, Lawrence. "Moral Stages and Moralization: The Cognitive-Developmental Approach." In *Moral Development and Behavior,* edited by T. Lickona, et al., 31–53. New York: Holt, Rinehart and Winston, 1976.

Noddings, Nel. *Caring: A Feminine Approach to Ethics and Moral Education.* Berkeley: University of California Press, 1984.

Sommers, Nancy. "Responding to Student Writing." *College Composition and Communication* 33 (1982): 148–56.

5 An Analysis of Response: Dream, Prayer, and Chart

Tilly Warnock
University of Wyoming

I want to complicate matters and respond to the question at hand, about encountering student texts, with a touch of magic, Kenneth Burke's magic. He opens *The Philosophy of Literary Form* (1967) with an invitation for his readers to imagine:

> Let us suppose that I ask you: "What did the man say?" And that you answer: "He said 'yes.'" You still do not know what the man said. You would not know unless you knew more about the situation, and about the remarks that preceded his answer.(1)

In Burke's attempt to explain his anecdote about response, he raises further problems: "Critical and imaginative works are answers to questions posed by the situation in which they arose. They are not merely answers, they are *strategic* answers, *stylized* answers" (1967, 1).

In Burke's popular parlor-room anecdote, he develops this view that meaning is context-dependent, but he also implies that meaning is biologically determined, in that anyone's use of language is limited by time, space, and perspective:

> Imagine that you enter a parlor. You come late. When you arrive, others have long preceded you, and they are engaged in a heated discussion, a discussion too heated for them to pause and tell you exactly what it is about. In fact, the discussion had already begun long before any of them got there, so that no one present is qualified to retrace for you all the steps that had gone before. You listen for a while, until you decide that you have caught the tenor of the argument; then you put in your oar. Someone answers; you answer him; another comes to your defense; another aligns himself against you, to either the embarrassment or gratification of your opponent, depending upon the quality of your ally's assistance. However, the discussion is interminable. The hour grows late, you must depart. And you do depart, with the discussion still vigorously in progress. (1967, 110–11)

The dialectical give and take of conversation is Burke's model for oral and written language use and language learning—for life. Our responses to the conversation at hand are broadly context-dependent while bodily or biologically determined. Later, he explores further the notion that our answers are not simply passive responses or truth statements: they are strategic in being purposeful, directed toward a particular end; and they are stylized in being formally charged or eloquent.

These two anecdotes represent Burke's rhetorical theory of language as symbolic action, a theory of language as social act. As early as *Counter-Statement*, published in 1931 (1968a), he argues against the then current view, advocated by the French symbolist poets and adopted by Eliot and his American cousins, the New Critics, that the symbol is autonomous, separate from both the author and the audience, certainly from the circumstances. Burke shows how the symbolist poets, who advocated pure self-expression and swore against the communicative function of language, were taking up symbols from the barnyard and adapting them for their own purposes, which often were to hook their readers by their abilities to renew the common language. Their motives were communicative from the selection of symbols, to their modification, to their reception by others. For Burke, the symbol is a strategy used by writers and readers to encompass situations.

Burke is clearly a contextual, historical, and psychoanalytical critic, but he is primarily a rhetorician who knows that whatever anyone says, himself included, is grounded in motives as well as in the contexts of situations and cultures. What this means in practical terms is that Burke recognizes his own definitions and assertions as strategic and stylized; therefore, he undermines the truth of his own responses by his theory and by his exploratory rather than explanatory way of presenting them.

But why would he risk not being more persuasive by adopting conventional argumentative approaches or traditional responses in academic situations, and why would he argue for the contextualist and historicist views of language at the same time he champions biology, psychology, and motives? He does so, I believe, because as a rhetorician he deals in doubt and uncertainty, not in truth. He continually reminds us that we are no longer living in the Garden of Eden but in a motivational jungle: "In view of such a motivational jungle, a good basic proposition to have in mind when contemplating the study of motives would be: Anybody can do anything for any reason" (1961, 353). Given the circumstances, he advocates that critics use whatever means are available to interpret texts. Most of all, he wants us to use language to stay alive, in communication with ourselves and with others: he wants us to cope. Burke shows how we can do things with words, not be buried by them. To define language as symbolic action—to recognize our responses as rhetorical—is most practical.

Magic enters Burke's theory here through a paradoxical claim that language—which arises from situations and biology—nevertheless carries some of the neither here nor there. We use language to summarize a situation, to name and thereby give presence to the thing, idea, or person entitled. By saying, we make *it* so. At the same time, Burke is careful to insist that the reality of *it* exists beyond us and our language. The name is not the thing, and the very presence achieved through naming testifies to the absence.

For Burke, the magic of language, most easily seen in poetry and religious language, exists in all language. All language is metaphorical: saying that something is something else establishes not a truth but a metaphor, for the word is not the thing, and the tenor and vehicle are not the same. Names dramatize the distance between the word and object. The appropriate response to metaphor is for the reader to make connections and see anew. As Burke explores in *The Rhetoric of Religion* (1970), the gap between terms, for example, between the word and the Word, between the God the Father and God the Son, gives people the chance for bridging, for becoming one with both in making sense of both.

But Burke more often speaks of language as dramatistic than metaphorical. All language is dramatic in the sense that the word and thing exist in a dramatic—distanced and dialectical—relationship, a relationship which the viewer, not the dramatist, spells out. The dramatist is a rhetorician in gauging the distance between the situation of the stage and that of the audience, for the distance must be neither too close nor too far if the audience is to experience the sense of wonder. Language is a performance, by people, for purposes, in scenes.

While J. L. Austin argues philosophically that all speech acts are performative—a doing things with words—Burke argues rhetorically that we do unto language and language does unto us. Saying makes *it* so, while it makes *us* so; saying also makes clear the not-so. Doing things with words is not the same as doing things with guns, fire, Star Wars, but we can do things to guns, fire, and Star Wars with words. And what we do with words returns to haunt us, for better or worse.

What does all of this have to do with encountering student texts? Why have I taken this long way around? Why didn't I just proverbalize about how to respond to student texts—"Do unto others as you would have them do unto you"? Why didn't I appeal to an authority who does not undermine the stated, for example to Michael Cole and Sylvia

Scribner and their elegant learning theory—people learn that which
is valued in their community and that which they have time to practice.
I could have explained their research and then elaborated on how to
establish a classroom community, schedule time for practice, authority,
and response.

But Cole and Scribner's theory is simply too easy. We all know that
it is true, about ourselves and others, including students. And we
know that it is slippery: communities infinitely regress, as small groups
become class groups become the school, town, state, and so on. And
values keep growing, separating, taking on unfamiliar forms. What is
valued in one classroom seeps under doorways and through transoms
down the highways and byways of life. (In Wynnton Elementary,
transoms are what we called the panels of glass over doorways which
tilted back and forth if not stuck with paint.) And whose values are
we talking about anyway?

I could have used the buzz word "Derrida," which like the corporate
Burke argues that the word is not the thing and that we are living in
an abyss of indeterminacy. We also know that what Derrida says is
true, but not the whole truth, and we all know that we act under
erasure, typically under the rubber tip of a number-two pencil. But
too often Derrida sounds convinced by his own assertions, and his
wordplays read like oil slicks, at least in translation. Burke never seems
quite certain as words stumble, halt, and turn cartwheels, forcing us
to question what he says and does.

Most important, Burke defines language as equipment for living. He
pictures the abyss, not as a pit of indeterminacy as Derrida does, but
more as a pitstop for refueling, for conversation, in order to continue
on the raceway:

> Our speculations may run the whole qualitative gamut, from play,
> through reverence, even to an occasional shiver of cold meta-
> physical dread—for always the Eternal Enigma is there, right on
> the edges of our metropolitan bickerings, stretching outward to
> interstellar infinity and inward to the depths of the mind. And in
> the staggering disproportion between man and noman, there is
> not place for purely human boasts of grandeur, or for forgetting
> that men build their cultures by huddling together, nervously
> loquacious, at the edge of an abyss. (1965, 272)

Burke's view is hopeful in that we—animal symbolicum—want to
participate in the conversation at hand.

Why have I complicated matters by bringing in Burke? Because his
theory is a theory of language first and foremost, not a theory of
interpretative communities, indeterminacy, cultural literacy, response,

or error. And language for Burke is rhetorical in Aristotle's sense of the term: Rhetoric is the faculty of discovering the possible means of persuasion in a given context. By this definition, a response is action, motivated and consequential, with explicit and implicit purposes, on both the speaker's and the listener's parts. Responses to student texts exist not simply on the page or in the air but in the context of people, purposes, and places. They are attempts to discover what will persuade, and, for Burke, what persuades are strategies for coping and equipment for living.

Let me now summarize what I have been trying to build a context for:

1. We do not encounter student texts without encountering students, ourselves, and context, our own and those of students.

2. Every language encounter is a counter and a discounter.

3. Every response is an action, motivated and consequential—and we are responsible for the "why's" and "wherefore's" of what we do with words.

4. In our written and oral responses to students and their texts, we are not telling the truth about the text or about ourselves. We are primarily responding to a situation, to questions posed not only by the individual student but also by the context—of the class, the situation, and the culture. And we are making our responses for particular reasons which often we don't know but must try to unravel.

5. Students understand our responses only if they are part of the conversation at hand, if they understand the questions we are answering, our situations, and the questions that long preceded either of us. They understand only if they hang around for a while, put in their oars, and elicit responses.

6. When we respond, we are doing things with words—we are decreeing that something is and is not something else—although we know, and want students to know, that our decrees are magical and metaphorical, which means they are both true and not true.

7. When we respond, we are being done unto by language.

"So what?" as Burke asks himself at every turn. Doesn't this awareness of language only prevent us from speaking and lock us into a prison house of words? It can, but our perspective can also help us listen and respond more carefully, with full care. Aren't matters just simpler than all this? Perhaps, but the best we can do is use language to get to matters. Don't we all know all of this at some level already, how impossible the task of responding to student texts really is but how we have to proceed, ignoring what we know in order to carry on as teachers? Aren't we, in fact, using language fairly well to circle round the abyss of contextuality, the nightmare of history, and the swamps of biology?

We avoid and yet still address these problems in several ways. In conferences, we encourage students to pose to us questions about their own writing. In this way, they narrow the context, get what they want, and we join their situations. We ask them to perform their texts by reading them aloud, so that they can hear themselves as writers and develop their writer- and their reader-selves. The strategy for coping here is to help students confront themselves in the mirrors of their own writings, even though the danger exists that their self-images will continue to reflect back and forth endlessly.

Another way we circle around contextual, historical, psychological, and biological problems is by establishing response groups among students, so that they create their own discourse communities, define the rules, and operate within them. The strategy for coping here might be that in small and large groups people can practice for life in a democracy. We encourage students to take ownership, authorship, and responsibility for their own words.

We also engage in holistic rankings, which admit and train members of an interpretative community, but we flinch when we remember that in another community the student would not be assigned to a remedial course or to an honors course. We use primary trait analysis and peer evaluation, and we focus on the developmental history of the individual, the sociology of the classroom, the intentions of the author, and the historical context. We do as Burke encourages literary critics to do; we use whatever means are available to interpret student texts in order to help our students write better.

I don't think, though, that we often admit to the magic of our responses to student papers—that naming makes it so, that responses are our ways of encompassing situations which, once encompassed, no longer exist as before. We have a tough enough time responding to one paper when all papers exist intertextually, sequentially, simultaneously, fragmentarily, and comparatively. But Burke eggs us on, through context, history, and psychology: "Magic, verbal coercion, establishment or management by decree, says, in effect: 'Let there be'—and there was. And men share in the magical resources of some power by speaking 'in the name of' that power."

He continues, spinning, chanting, and evoking:

> The magical decree is implicit in all language; for the mere act of
> naming an object or situation decrees that it is to be singled out
> as such-and-such rather than as something else. Hence, I think
> that an attempt to *eliminate* magic, in this sense, would involve
> us in the elimination of vocabulary itself as a way of sizing up
> reality. Rather, what we need is *correct* magic, magic whose decree
> about the naming of real situations is the closest approximation
> to the situation named (with the greatest accuracy of approximation
> being supplied by the "collective revelation" of testing and dis-
> cussion). (1967, 4)

Burke leaves us with an impossible task—to use language accu-
rately—knowing full well that we cannot: therefore we must. Having
brought us into this maze, he suggests a way out, at least temporarily,
before language rears its ugly head—the negative—to hiss at us that
what is, is not; that what was, will be; that what will be, is and was
and never more shall be. The "being" of language is metaphorical,
but in the enthymematic distance between assertions, in the missing
premise of the syllogism, lurks the invitation to bridge, fill in, make
meaning. In other words, language is the dancing of attitudes, and
because dancers are not one, they desire oneness. Language use is a
courtship ritual, the hierarchical pecking in the barnyard, a making
do with what might not be correct but is rhetoric.

And on Burke goes, weaving words, having moved us to supply
the missing links in his progressions, his gymnastic leaps and turns,
having, in other words, compelled us by his sheer rhetoric to accept
what he says if only for the moment. He then wonders, speculates,
or remembers that "ordinarily, we find three ingredients interwoven
in a given utterance: the dream, the prayer, and the chart" (1967, 5).

Encountering here what seems an assertion of truth by Burke, and
having been forewarned by him that what looks like a locutionary of
illocutionary act is—in fact?—a performative, we look askance, out of
the corners of our eyes, and decide to sniff around the three terms,
wary of trinities, dialectics, and truth, which easily, magically, become
thirds, turds, words, swords, and worlds. We have taken a ride with
Burke, become his partner in linguistic charades, and are therefore his
accomplices. We accept, not the logic of his arguments nor his appeals
to outside, inside, ancient, or modern authorities; we are persuaded
by our own experiences, our own sayings and doings with Burke. In
order to go along, in order to make sense, we have had to supply
connections, and by doing so, we have become part of the texture.[1]

Having moved from a triad to a pentad, from the I-thou-it to the
I-me, we-us, they-them, he-she-it (double 5's), having spun out to

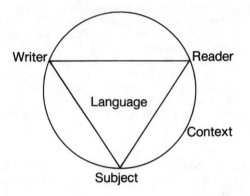

Fig. 1. The rhetorical situation.

this point, we must ask, "Now, where are we?" We must return, hang-dog but doggedly, to response, context, history, and magic, ready to chew on the not-so-solid forms Burke throws to us—dream, prayer, and chart—to get to where we might be going:

> Chart (the realistic sizing-up of situations that is sometimes explicit, sometimes implicit).

We begin in reverse to analyze responses to student texts because charting has the appearance of order, substance, and certainty. We first strengthen our position by drawing on the ancient tradition of rhetoric and the symbol of the triangle (figure 1).

Acknowledging our three-five shift in triangulating, which helps but which is not sufficient, we wish we could use 3-D or stereo, or better yet, video, television, close encounters, or even accounting ("heads I win, tails you lose"). Nevertheless, we navigate through the troubled waters of literary theory, reading theory, and response theory, steadying ourselves with Burke's view that language theory is literary theory in that all language, not just the overtly poetic or religious, is symbolic. We cross our fingers that our theories for responding to student texts and our theories for responding to literary texts can transform each other and help us cope.

Let us then chart, for fixity's sake, filling in slots and connecting dots, as is our bent as symbol-using, symbol-making, symbol-misusing animals, inventors of the negative, goaded by the spirit of hierarchy (or moved by a sense of order) and rotten with perfection (1968b, 3–24; see table 1).

Our chart is schematic, indeed incomplete and distorted—the better to involve you in, my dears.

But a little discursiveness never hurt anyone, and charting does always seem to fizzle out because things don't fit as neatly as expected. For example, do we mean the history and context of the author, the audience, or what? Is it just easier to make comments about textual features than about ideological concerns? Why can we fill in more blanks in the beginning than in the end? Do context-centered approaches defy reduction?

While we may seem to have turned our attention from product, a New Critical approach, to process, perhaps biographical, historical, developmental, intentionalist, we wonder. Our practices in responding to student texts still seem tied to New Criticism's concerns for unity and intensity of words-on-the-page. Don't we tend to mind our manners, committing neither the intentional fallacy—voyeuristically seeking for what the author meant—nor the pathetic fallacy—wallowing in our own responses? Attention to the text seems right, objective, fair, and does not implicate us. We tell ourselves that the world values order, coherence, and unity, and so should we to prepare our students for future work in the world.

But aren't we committing the intentional fallacy and liking it when we read student journals, encourage students toward expressive writing, pore through drafts, and ask students to identify their purposes? We realize often enough, though, that even process becomes a product to package and expressive writing becomes canned.

Though we might not dare to say so, maybe the norm is a reader-response approach to student texts. We talk of students' ownership and authority, but we often do as reading theorists tell us we do—we construct meaning. We take student papers and mark them, sometimes even writing in our own sentences and ideas. Recently we've hesitated to respond individually and so we reach agreement with colleagues, sometimes with students, about rubrics, scales, and traits. Like it or not, we commit the pathetic fallacy despite goals of objectivity, rationality, reliability, and verifiability.

Perhaps we also perform magic, conjure what does not exist and cannot be charted. Perhaps we engage in attitude dancing, even in our most chart-like ways. Our grids tax and taxonomize us, revealing the variety in our responses and our often contradictory purposes.

What is another ingredient in our responses?

Dream (the unconscious or subconscious factors).

Table 1
Ways to Respond to Student Texts

Schools of Criticism	Criteria	Kinds of Response to Student Papers
	————————Text-Centered————————	
New Criticism	autonomy, unity, orga- nization, coherence, intensity	Comments on papers: "Poor, difficult to follow. Lacks complexity."
Philological	origins and choice of words	Words and phrases marked. Comments: "Poor word choice. Find a better word."
Genre	conventions, kinds	Questions and discussions: models. Comments: "Is this appropriate? Out of what conditions might this have arisen?"
Historical?		
	————————Author-Centered————————	
Intentionalist	meaning (not signifi- cance), intrinsic (not extrinsic)	Listen in conferences. Work with drafts. Comments: "What do you mean? I think I get your point, but I'm not sure."
Psychoanalytic	defenses, dreams, stories, slips, displace- ment	Conferences. Work with drafts. Comments: "What patterns are repeated? What is being avoided?"
Biographical	development, truth	Conferences. Work with drafts. Comments: "Prog- ress. Lack of progress. Write in your own voice."
Historical?		
	————————Reader-Centered————————	
Response	subjectivity, honesty	Conferences. Comments: "I don't get it. Have you con- sidered this? In my view. . . ."
Deconstructive	indeterminacy	Conferences. Work with drafts. Comments: "What is

Table 1 *(continued)*
Ways to Respond to Student Texts

Schools of Criticism	Criteria	Kinds of Response to Student Papers
		vividly absent here is. . . . What is implicit? This suggests a breakthrough or breakdown."
Historical?		
	—————Subject-Centered—————	
Thematic		Comments: "Wrong. Right. Undeveloped. Unsupported."
Historical?		
	—————Context-Centered—————	
Contextual	political, economic, accuracy	Comments: "Is this appropriate? What are the assumptions?"
Ideological	political, economic power relationships	Discussion.
Feminist	gender concerns, repression, power relationships	Discussion. Work with draft. What are the assumptions? What is missing?
Historical?		

I still read student papers in order to help them revise and make their writing better, and I still read papers to evaluate and grade. I listen to help students hear themselves as writers and participate in the community of writers.

But in the past few years, as students and I are writing more, I have awakened to the fact that I am reading papers for my own sake—to improve my own writing.

For years I have surrounded myself with books that help me write—Louise Erdrich's *Love Medicine*, Sheila Bosworth's *Almost Innocent*, Doris Grumbach's *Chamber Music*, Pat Conroy's *Prince of Tides*, *The Writer on Her Work*, edited by Janet Sternburg, and others. I don't know why, but these books encourage me. I now pick up and put down books, displacing one with another. I read portions over and over. I try to copy parts and internalize forms. I know a book is good for me when I cannot read a few pages without getting up to write.

Perhaps I have gone too far. I now read student papers with an eye to finding something for myself. This means I have become the learner in my classroom, the hungry one. I comb papers for lines that move me, words which give me insights into the familiar, for forms, and for stories. I wish I had written the paper one of my students wrote about learning to weave with her mother-in-law, receiving a loom from her grandmother, and then weaving her life in with the other women around her. I long to have written Mark Jenkin's interview with Colin Fletcher and to have joined those two writers walking together. I know I'll never be able to write the dialogue Bill Strouse wrote between construction workers or capture how their conversation convinced him to return to school. And every time I read Mary Kettl's articles in the school newspaper, I regret that I didn't begin writing when I was young and keep at it as she has.

Sometimes I feel like a vulture or scavenger; at other times I feel like a bee in search of pollen, a mixer of modes, genres, and people, or a bricoleur who, like Joyce's bricklayer, Finnegan, deals in rainbows, dream symbols, and humpty dumpties, and who is always beginning again, putting in an oar, while the discussion is still vigorously in progress.

I can justify the way I now respond to student papers. I know that writing and reading are flip sides of the same action and that every writer must learn to be her own critical reader and to collaborate with others. I am modeling for students how to read in order to write. I also believe that I am modeling learning, not having learned. I have learned best from teachers who *are learning* themselves, not from people who *have learned.* I don't want to have the final word, to write the definitive text, or to be the ultimate authority, because all of these sound to me like the end of the rope or after the last midnight hour.

What this boils down to, or adds up to, is that I don't believe my cultural literacy is more necessary for students to have than their cultural literacies are for me. I often feel less literate than they, especially when I let them write, let them speak, and I listen. I am dumbfounded by their cultural literacy, functional literacy, critical literacy, and creative literacy.

I want to engage in culture-swapping, literacy-lending, with students, not just in culture-transmitting; I want to engage in the conversation at hand so that we both may learn, so that in the exchange we lose ourselves to find ourselves anew, as if in a dream, as if waking from a dream.

What other ingredients do I want in my responses?

> Prayer (the communicative functions which lead us to the many considerations of form which lead us to participate only in so far as the response has a public, or communicative, structure).

The thou shalts and the thou shalt nots. In every response, I am doing—usually trying to point out the Upward Way and the Downward Way, the Ways In and the Ways Out. I am asserting an order, a hierarchy, usually by inserting the negative, the yes-but, the on-the-other-hand, the I-wonder.

At the same time I am pointing to absolutes and almighties, I am using public transportation, the common language, but trying to take it and let it take me farther along, knowing that later both students and I will understand why.

As Burke balances expressionist doctrines with communicative programs, I want to show students in my oral and written responses that they don't have to choose between the language of the barnyard and the language of the parlor room. We have to continue learning languages from other people and places and learning when to use what kind of language. We have to keep trying to discover the possible means of persuasion in given contexts.

In every response, like it or not, my symbolic actions are motivated and consequential. I want to explore and demystify my strategies and styles and those of other writers, for myself and for students. I want to knock our socks off with our language so that we stand barefoot on the ground, pretty sure that when we understand our immediate contexts there are other lands ahead.

I am also trying to remember that telling people to do something or how to do something is not always as effective as telling stories, as representative anecdotes, which convey values, attitudes, and actions, with the understanding that listeners are qualified and eager to make connections for themselves and that they have their own tales to tell.

Notes

1. At the risk of breaking the spell, but still aiming for the gist, the gesture, let me insert Burke's telling vocabulary lesson, his Five Dogs Theory of meaning: the "primal dog" (the first dog you knew, or loved, or were frightened by); the "jingle dog" (the sheerly accidental nature of the word *dog*); the "lexical dog" (the one defined in the dictionary); the "entelechial dog" (the

perfect dog); and the "tautological dog" (the particular set of associations which in a sense reproduces his "spirit") (Burke 1986b, 73–74).

Works Cited

Burke, Kenneth. *Attitudes Toward History.* 3rd ed., Berkeley: University of California Press, 1961.

———. *Counter-Statement.* Berkeley: University of California Press, 1968a.

———. *Language as Symbolic Action: Essays on Life, Literature, and Method.* [1931.] Berkeley: University of California Press, 1968b.

———. *Permanence and Change: An Anatomy of Purpose.* 3rd ed. Berkeley: University of California Press, 1965.

———. *The Philosophy of Literary Form: Studies in Symbolic Action.* 3rd ed. Berkeley: University of California Press, 1967.

———. *The Rhetoric of Religion: Studies in Logology.* Berkeley: University of California Press, 1970.

6 Teachers as Readers, Readers as Teachers

Patricia Y. Murray
De Paul University

Studies describing the responses of readers to fiction and nonfiction, or of readers-in-the-text, focus on what happens when the "general" or "universal" or "informed" or "student" reader processes a text to derive meaning (Iser 1974; Bleich 1975; Fish 1980). Studies in reading theory and language acquisition tell us that meaning is what readers derive from reading, that meaning is a process involving the perceptions of the total human reader. What we expect from a text is largely determined by our prior conceptions ("cognitive maps") of the world which come from our experiences in and with the world. As readers mature, they acquire rules to predict and interpret events in the world, then to order that world. They do not derive meaning from the sequence of words on a page, but grasp meanings as "wholes." Further, readers analyze ideas through the symbols represented on the page; they use those symbols to organize their "mental dictionaries" to reflect past experiences and future expectations. This amounts to a process of "taking reality apart" and putting it together again (Smith 1978; Cazden 1972).

In our writing classes, we talk about the writer's intention and her audience, exploring the writer-reader transaction through the medium of a text created in a context for some purpose (Winterowd 1986). But if meaning is *constructed* by the reader, how can the reader be sure what the writer *intended* to mean? Here we point to the rule-governed nature of the language which reader and writer share, but we must also point to shared cultural and social backgrounds. Writers and readers learn a wide range of contexts in which language rules can be used. They also learn what kinds of language are appropriate, valued, and expected by different language communities. When readers read, they bring to the text not only their mental and physical characteristics, but their culture, their experiences with the world, and their experiences with the world of texts as well. One conclusion we can draw from

73

this is that the meaning of a text will be seen more directly from a reader's perspective than from a writer's.

Rhetoricians Kenneth Burke, Wayne Booth, Richard Weaver, and others remind us that language is affective. It stirs us to action, subverts or affirms, involves intention, "creates the reader," and offers the reader the freedom to make value choices. Reading, like writing, is a holistic process involving interaction among the reader's world, the writer's world, and the world of the text. David Bleich describes four phases that correspond to what readers do when they read and respond to literature: (1) they have feelings about themselves, (2) they have feelings about what they have read, (3) they judge and evaluate intellectually what they have read, and (4) they react to what other readers think (1975, 5). Readers do not simply decode meaning analytically, then. They also respond to literature at varying levels of consciousness. They respond to the formal features of language (diction, structure, use of conventions), and they respond to various contents: sociological, ideological, psychological, and ethical. Wolfgang Iser (1974) imagines an arena in which reader and writer participate in a game of imagination. The reader "imagines" the world of the text (Iser is speaking of literary texts, but I extend the idea to nonliterary texts as well), and works out the meaning for herself. The dynamic process of reading involves two poles: the artistic work of the author and the response of the reader. But there is something between: that which happens when reader engages text at the point of convergence. The reader is constantly doing two things at once while reading: remembering what has been read, and predicting or anticipating what is to come. As a story progresses, the parts (character descriptions, episodes in the plot) enter the reader's memory and add up to what the story is about. At the same time, characters change, themes take a different slant, plots twist and turn, and climaxes occur. The reader thinks ahead, wonders what will happen next, sees developments in a different light, changes her mind or attitude about a character—in short, *anticipates* what is to come, how things will turn out. The author controls the words on the page, but the reader controls the anticipation through active imagination. She is constantly "filling in" the gaps through the imagination, making connections, providing links, bringing to this process her own preconceptions, her own background, her own "world."

You can test this process by thinking about your own reading of a literary work; a second reading reveals more than the first or different things from the first. We say, "I didn't see that before" or feel differently about the outcome or characters than we did on first reading, or alter our conclusions, or respond with a deeper, richer reaction. Time is a factor: it is impossible to absorb a written text entirely on one reading or in a single moment. Thus the reading process always involves viewing the text through a perspective that is continually moving, continually being constructed. Again, think about reading a literary work more than once. When you finished the work, then read it again, your extra knowledge resulted in a different set of connections, a different awareness of what was to come; and so certain parts of the story assumed a significance you did not attach to them on first reading. But it was always the processes of anticipating and remembering that led to your formation of what the work meant and how it affected you. One more aspect of thinking about readers reading and responding: while the reader's expectations during the act of reading may continually be modified, and images continually expanded, the reader will try to see a pattern, to fit things together. She groups parts of the text together, seeing them interacting as a whole. Where do these patterns come from? Clearly from two sources: from the words, the sentences on the page put there purposefully by the author, and from within the reader herself. One problem for readers of some contemporary fiction is that they find fewer deliberate, familiar guides to help them interpret. There are more gaps to fill in, more indeterminacy, details that contradict each other, and so on. On the other hand, some texts—detective stories, for instance—provide so much detail, so much information, that nearly every detail of the fictional world is supplied, everything coming together like pieces of a puzzle at the end. The vast differences between these two kinds of imaginative worlds demand that the reader adjust and be able to read differently, with different expectations.

If readers open themselves to the writer's language, they open themselves to the writer's unfamiliar world without being "imprisoned" within it. They move into the presence of the fictional world and become "immersed" in the text. Being immersed is not the same as being interested in the work, however. Immersion involves lifting the restrictions the reader places on meaning and simultaneously co-constructing a meaning by interacting with the author's text. Think of it as a "balancing act," which Iser describes this way:

> The act of recreation is not a smooth or continuous process, but one which . . . relies on *interruptions* of the flow. . . . We look forward, we look back, we decide, we change our decisions, we form expectations, we are shocked by their nonfulfillment, we question, we muse, we accept, we reject; this is the dynamic process of recreation. (1974, 288)

So far I have discussed the reading process as it pertains primarily to the act of reading literary texts. Do these same features apply in some way to reading of nonliterary texts such as the informal essay, the process paper, the library research report, the kinds of papers our students produce? Yes, but with some differences.

First, the world created by the text of a research report does not invite the reader's recreative imagination to the extent that a novel will; still, the reader must interpret the data it offers, absorb the details, make the information part of her understanding. The paper's structure leads to anticipation: What will I learn next? Or, what is this leading up to? It requires remembering: Where did this conclusion derive from? How has the thesis developed logically?

Second, the techniques of description and narration which are commonly used to construct an essay or a report and which are methods of developing arguments and statements of opinion invite the reader to interpret, to envision, to form a picture in the mind in order to understand the world being created by the writer.

Third, the reader is trying to build consistency, to see a pattern, in the nonliterary work just as she does in a literary text. If there are not as many possibilities of interpretation in the nonliterary text, there are nevertheless interpretations and misinterpretations that are possible: the mistaken conclusion, the poorly understood argument, the confusion resulting from an overdose of unfamiliar data.

Fourth, just as something happens in us when we read fiction or drama or poetry, so does something happen in us when we read nonfiction. Readers respond emotionally, aesthetically, and intellectually to every kind of text.

I turn now to a look at our students' most frequent if not only reader, the classroom instructor—more specifically, the classroom *composition* instructor. What troubles me about the composition instructor as reader leads to these questions which I will touch on as we examine some student writing and teacher responses:

- What roles and role adjustments does a teacher of writing adopt when reading student texts? Especially, how extensively does the role of authority shape the response?

- How do teacher-readers respond to different forms of student writing? What views do they bring to a reading of an abstract, a research paper, a proposal, an expository paragraph? Do their expectations differ from those of a business supervisor, a co-worker in an office, another apprentice writer?

- When student schemas for a paper conflict with the instructor's expected schema, what happens?

Each of these and related questions deserve thorough discussion and are being explored in NCTE conference talks and journal articles. Just as we know that readers read and respond differently to literary and nonliterary texts, we know that teacher-readers respond differently to student texts. A holistic scoring session of English placement exams with one's colleagues is convincing evidence of the range of interpretation and evaluation among English teachers. The scoring rubric for a writing prompt is intended to bring readers to a consensus; even that rubric reflects a compromise among readers with varying standards. Standards imply an authority of judgment that teacher-readers establish and hold over student writers and their texts. We say a paper scores high or low, earns an A or a C-, depending upon such features as error-free surface structures, a clear and sincere "voice," familiar and expected patterns of organization, an evident sense of audience, and good development of thesis or central idea. These make up the canon of "good writing" in most of our writing programs.

In some classrooms, students contribute to the construction of evaluation rubrics and advise each other in critiquing and editing sessions. But for the most part, teachers read student papers from the perspective of their own academic training and experiences with writing papers. Much of that training has been in writing the critical essay, a form that, as Keith Fort (1971) points out, establishes the credentials and authority of the critic to "prove" a "thesis" not only through the development of an argument but through the critical essay form itself. Sharon Crowley (1986) traces the development of the freshman English course as institution, pointing to those periods when "etiquette" or conventional correctness, theme writing, and traditional grammar have defined the course and promoted mechanical literacy. I suspect that today's liberated, process-oriented, Elbow-inspired composition teachers *still* bring with them to a reading of a student paper much of the baggage of the "hyperliterate" (Crowley's term) English major or instructor.

We exhort our students to find their own, their *real* voices and to project a voice in their writing. "Find something to say," we urge them, "something you *really* want to express." But how do teacher-readers respond to student voices that do not "sound like college students" writing academic prose? How do student writers learn which voices are and are not acceptable? Is the voice most praised in the English critical essay going to get the same degree of acceptance and praise in a business document? A physics report? A research report in anthropology? A law brief? I. Hashimoto (1987) details our textbooks' promotion of voice as a feature of good student writing, citing such educators as Peter Elbow, Donald Murray, and Ken Macrorie as evangelists for the development of a personal voice. But Hashimoto also points out that good readers bring their own voices to a reading and engage in a transaction with the writer that affects the voice or "juice" of the text. What happens when the student's voice meets the teacher-reader's voice?

If the match is satisfactory, pleasing, within expected bounds, the result is good. If the student's voice does not match the expectations of the teacher-reader, we're apt to hear, "Well, I like your enthusiasm, and yes, you do project a strong voice. But you must provide more detail (or arguments or evidence), or write a stronger thesis, or improve paragraph cohesion, or cite two primary sources, or. . . ." In short, we too often exhort students to find and use a voice, but instead reward other rhetorical or formal features in their writing.

A major advantage to teaching different kinds of writing for business, technology, social services, science, law is that the instructor learns to *respond* appropriately to writing in these communities. Wearing more than one teacher-reader hat helps the freshman composition instructor see the student paper with different eyes. A personal experience can illustrate. One of my students struggled for days to find a way to organize a research paper that did not lend itself neatly to the thesis paragraph—development and transition paragraphs—conclusion form we had discussed in class. I suggested he borrow a form common in technical and business writing: problem statement—recommendation or problem solution—background—discussion—findings, conclusions or recommendation. This pattern helped the student sort out the chunks of material and arrange them logically. It also helped him get around the transition problems he had not been able to solve. A simple, yet powerful, change in thinking about the organization of a research paper in an English class enabled the writer to get on with his project.

John Ruszkiewicz (1987) urges us to think of student writers as apprentices, for treating them as apprentices anticipates that they will improve, even succeed, at becoming capable writers. This attitude further assumes that the "master" is able to train his apprentices in the writing they will need for their individual success. Since few of our students will become contributors to *PMLA* or *College English*, the burden on the instructor is to provide student-apprentices with an understanding of and practice in the kind of writing expected of a community that the writer wants to join, a professional or social community with its peculiar discourse features, not excluding the community of literature and composition scholars. This charge to the composition instructor has also been discussed at length recently in our English journals and at conferences. I am not sure to what extent composition instructors *can* assume such broad responsibility. But I am convinced that the teacher-reader who is equipped to bring only the perspectives and values of a literary or composition training to a reading of student texts may not serve those students well. Students may very well learn that what we preach is not what we practice.

I recently participated in a workshop at which teachers read and discussed student essays, exchanging ideas about how to assess student writing. I offer the following student essay and notes on our discussion of it to illustrate what features of writing teacher-readers typically notice, comment on, and use to evaluate student writing:

Anne

Many people experience turning points in their lives and these turning points can be an enhancement to their lives or a devastating experience. I would like to focus on the turning point in Anne's life.

When Anne was 20 she got married, at the age of 22 she had her first child. Once Anne was married, she said it was an adjustment because she never spent so much time with one person before. She couldn't just get up and leave when she got upset with her husband. Anne expressed that one has to make the effort to see that things work out. However, after Anne was married for a couple of years, she and her husband were finally adjusting to married life, she became pregnant with her first child. Anne now had a new group of responsibilities; husband, child, and work.

By Anne being 22, she was still young and had some growing up of her own to do. It was a new experience to realize that she had someone who depended on her for their very existence. This new little person will need guidance and understanding from now on. To say the least, Anne and her husband adjusted and the child gave them great pleasure.

At the age of 27, Anne had her second child, a girl. During this time, Anne had made a career move to another company; she was working as a secretary for a marketing firm. A few years went by and the baby wasn't quite a "baby," she was five. Anne started to feel restless, she wondered where her life was going and trying to figure out what else was she going to do with her life besides being a mother, wife, employee. Anne said she was not putting down all of these things because it is, indeed, no easy

task for everybody. However, she was aware that she wanted to
do something else, set new goals.

Anne eventually did set new goals, but she had to wait a while
because of her children, and also in the beginning she didn't quite
know what those new goals would be. Anne is 39 now, still
married, her children are 17 and 12. Her new goal is to go back
to college and receive her degree in management. At the present
time, Anne is an executive secretary at the same marketing firm,
and will be seeking advancement their once she receives her
degree. Anne made the decision to go back to college because
she was watching the company expand, the new people were
male and female, some her age and younger. Anne admitted that
she mostly noticed the women, the younger ones who were
achieving so much more than she had at their age, and the older
women her age still achieving so much more. She realized she
could receive more gratification out of her life by pursuing a new
goal.

There are many women today who feel just as Anne does,
needing something else outside of the home to give them that
feeling of accomplishment. Some of these women are pursuing
these new goals, like Anne, others are less fortunate and can't.
I'm proud that Anne is pursuing these goals, and I'm sure she
will find satisfaction in them.

Directions for the assignment included advice to tell enough of the
story so that a reader could understand the significance of the turning
point. (Writers had interviewed another person to gather material for
their essays and so were reporting, interpreting, and translating from
an oral to a written medium.) In addition, students were advised to
have a focus and to consider their readers, to anticipate their readers'
reactions. These were the teachers' comments:

Nice diction; not high falutin' or too simple.

* * * *

There's a problem with sentence structure.

* * * *

I don't see a resolution.

* * * *

Problems bothered me; there's no resolution.

* * * *

There's no controlling focus.

* * * *

I liked it; I'm a marshmallow for women's turning points. It has
sentence variety.

* * * *

Not spunky enough for a B.

* * *

I'm lenient and encouraging on the first paper.

* * *

I'd urge this writer to give more examples.

* * *

It lacks relevance to how the turning point affects the woman's life now; it lacks a sense of the turning point.

* * *

How much do usage and grammar count? I'd lower the grade for mistakes.

* * *

A difficult topic to write about; the student should have created more concrete stuff to "feel" it.

* * *

The paper looks awful; it's poorly laid out on the page.

* * *

Diction is the main problem.

* * *

Writing seems directed toward a friend or person like her; not appropriate for a college paper.

* * *

No evidence of great thought or sense of insight as to a turning point.

* * *

Writer needs to know the difference between writing down what someone says and interpreting.

* * *

I feel it's below average; but a C looks better than a C− or D+.

* * *

I tend to let them get away with murder on grammar, but jump on them on the last paper (in the course).

* * *

I'd come down hard on this first paper so I don't have to deal with all this as much by the second paper.

These evaluations, many of them valid, reflect the familiar and expected reactions of teacher-readers. As hyperliterate readers trained to value the characteristics of the "English Department Essay," we focused on *control, concreteness, sentence-level features,* and *diction. Control* elicited comments about the value of organization, the direction of movement in the essay, the lack of focus or thesis or point, and relevance. *Concreteness* brought on comments about the paper's needing "more stuff," more examples and detail, more fleshing-out of the paper's structural bones. In teacher talk, these features fall generally under "development." *Sentence-level features* focused on sentence variety, considered good, but also on sentence "problems," considered a hindrance to reader understanding. And while one reader thought the *diction unpleasing*, others found it dull or nonstandard. Perhaps that is what one reader thought not quite "spunky enough for a B" and may even account for the comments about grammar. Other comments are less easily categorized, but it is interesting that at least one reader responded to the "image" projected through format ("Paper looks awful . . .").

Had we not been reading only in our teacher-reader modes, we might have considered the features of the paper differently and commented on quite different questions:

- What happened as you read? What did you expect?
- Did you fill in the gaps? Were there too many gaps?
- In what way did your memory function to help you anticipate what would happen next?
- What writer-reader transaction was established?
- Was it successful? Why or why not?
- Did you get the "gist" of the paper easily? What was it? Did you have feelings about the paper? What were they? (Note the "I'm a marshmallow. . ." response.)
- Did you become immersed in the text?
- Is there a voice (or voices) in the text? How would you characterize it (them)?
- What persona did the writer ask you to assume as you read the paper?
- What persona-as-grader did you assume (proofreader, editor, coach, peer, expert)?
- What *succeeds* in this paper?

Had we teacher-readers shifted our focus to such questions, we might have noticed, among other things, that the Anne paper *does* project voices: first, that of the reporter narrating the substance of the interview with Anne; second, that of a responder commenting on the universality of Anne's predicament and relating personally to it; third, that of the apprentice writer trying to comply with the directions in the assignment. If the voice does not sound like that of a college writer, perhaps it is because the writer's purpose was to sound like someone else: a friend or peer or reporter.

We might have noticed that the writer *does* address the "turning point" issue, but no single, dramatic epiphany marks a turning point for Anne. Instead, the writer reports Anne's gradual awareness of the need to change, because of Anne's recognition, after some years of married life, that she needed to find out "what else she was going to do with her life besides being a mother, wife, employee," and also because of Anne's decision to seek a college degree. Perhaps the student writer did not know how, during the interview, to extract a statement from Anne that pinpointed a precise turning point. Perhaps there *wasn't* one after all, but only the growing acknowledgement that new goals were needed. But the teacher-readers condemned the essay on just this point: "It lacks relevance to how [sic] the turning point affects the woman's life now; it lacks a sense of the turning point." As teachers of literature and composition, we expected to find a clearly developed narrative line leading to a climax (the turning point) followed by a *denouement* or logical conclusion. Our expectations were thwarted. We might have noticed, too, that the student succeeds in telling enough of Anne's story to enable us to follow the sequence of events, perhaps even to concur with the writer's generalizations in the final paragraph. The directions had been to "tell enough of the *story* so that a reader could understand the significance of the turning point." *Story* suggests a narrative form to most readers. The teacher-readers, on the other hand, seem to be criticizing the paper more in terms of an expository essay than a narrative, although the two forms are certainly not mutually exclusive. Do the form expected and valued by the teacher-readers and the form produced by the student writer conflict? Is the scheme of one being superimposed on the scheme of the second without allowances for the differences? Could the directions of the assignment have been made clearer, more explicit, more formulaic if the instructor expected one form in particular? If the *form* specified in the assignment had been an interview with its dialogue format, or a feature article for a newspaper or magazine with its special format, or a clinical report with its peculiar language ("The subject reported that . . ."), perhaps the student/apprentice writer, given these specified formats, might have been able to respond more successfully.

To be fair to the group of teachers whose actual responses are presented earlier, we turned our talk toward suggestions for helping student writers revise. For example, students can benefit from writing descriptive outlines of their works, paragraph by paragraph, specifying what each *does* rhetorically and what each says in content. They can read each other's work in peer-group critiques, they can consider problems in finding forms to fit messages and audiences, and they can benefit from looking at examples of what different discourse communities expect in form, content, and style. We can talk to them about the transactional nature of discourse and provide work in designing documents for various kinds of readers. We can treat our students as apprentice writers, starting with their inexpert efforts and helping them to learn expertise.

But the need remains for teachers of writing to take what we know about the reading process and apply it to a reading of students' papers. We need to recognize that we bring with us to a reading of student texts an inevitable evaluation that stems from a discourse community that more often than not is different from that of the students. We need to look at how our responses *as teachers of composition* affect what we advise our students, and to judge whether that advice is appropriate in all rhetorical situations. We need to consider how we can use the knowledge we have about how readers read—specifically how teacher-readers read in asking questions about student texts vis-à-vis other kinds of texts. Until we do, we may be denying the very freedom to develop many of the possibilities for finding expression in writing that we exhort our students to explore.

Works Cited

Bleich, David. *Readings and Feelings.* Urbana: National Council of Teachers of English, 1975.

Cazden, Courtney. *Child Language and Acquisition.* New York: Holt, Rinehart and Winston, 1972.

Crowley, Sharon. "The Perilous Life and Times of Freshman English." *Freshman English News* 14 (1986): 11–15.

Fish, Stanley E. *Is There a Text in This Class? The Authority of Interpretive Communities.* Cambridge: Harvard University Press, 1980.

Fort, Keith. "Form, Authority, and the Critical Essay." *College English* 32 (1971): 629–39.

Hashimoto, I. "Voice As Juice: Some Reservations about Evangelic Composition." *College Composition and Communication* 38 (1987): 70–80.

Iser, Wolfgang. *The Implied Reader: Patterns of Communication in Prose Fiction from Bunyan to Beckett.* Baltimore: Johns Hopkins University Press, 1974. See especially chapter 11: "The Reading Process: A Phenomenological Approach."

Ruszkiewicz, John. "Assuming Success: The Student Writer As Apprentice." *Freshman English News* 15 (1987): 13–18.

Smith, Frank. *Understanding Reading: A Psycholinguistic Analysis of Reading and Learning to Read.* New York: Holt, Rinehart and Winston, 1978.

Winterowd, W. Ross. *Composition/Rhetoric: A Synthesis.* Carbondale: Southern Illinois University Press, 1986.

II Encountering Conflicts in Theory and Practice

"Wonderful disjunctions occur in our field. We don't always seem to notice them, or if we do, we don't blush, as we might or should," writes Jim Corder in the essay that leads off this section of the book. Recognizing that a gulf often exists between our "wonderfully sophisticated" textual theory and the reality of classroom practice, the four contributors to this section—Corder, Sharon Crowley, Norm Katz, and Janice Lauer, each an experienced writer and teacher—raise questions about the concept of intentionality in student writing. As Corder notes, for every paper a student submits to the writing instructor, there are parallel texts: what has been written, what the student thinks has been written, what the student would like to have written, and, significantly, the text the instructor creates in the reading.

Although they provide differing perspectives and sometimes even appear to contradict one another, the contributors to this section seem to move in a similar direction as they perceive their own and their students' roles in the classroom. It is a movement away from the traditional (and ego-satisfying) representation of teacher as authority and power-broker to an acceptance of the teacher as *cointerpreter* of student writing and *facilitator* of the revision process. It is not surprising, then, that these essays reveal an especially intense awareness of the compelling presence of the student writer and, more significantly, a conviction that students are capable of taking a more responsible role than they have in their own writing, even in current workshop settings.

Perhaps this is best illustrated in the essays as the authors address the issue of intentionality—in theory and in classroom practice. Building her case on her firm knowledge of the history of rhetoric, Sharon Crowley suggests that the modern obsession with intentionality—and the ubiquitous use of the term in classroom procedure—grows out of the eighteenth-century rhetorical theory of George Campbell. Crowley argues from several perspectives that intention is far too problematic and unstable a concept upon which to ground either theory or classroom instruction. Most compelling, perhaps, is her observation that such emphasis is fundamentally incompatible with our widely held assumption that intention is *discovered* in the composing and revision process, that ". . . students find out what it is that they can write while they are in the process of writing it."

Initially, it might appear that Norm Katz's essay is proposing the very thing Crowley opposes. However, it becomes clear that the statements of intention or "METAs" that Katz asks his students to write are something quite different from the pre-existing, bracketed intentions described by Campbell. The METAs function not as something prior to, but as an extension of, student texts. As he says, "Students' intentions are subject to the same sort of scrutiny as any other part of their writing performance." Thus intention, as Katz utilizes it, is actually an *interpretive* tool, a form of student self-evaluation; as such, it is a part of the revision process and has the effect of shifting valuative responsibility back to the student.

Janice Lauer's dialogues with her students serve a similar interpretive purpose, requiring students to articulate what they are attempting to do as they are in the process of doing it. Perceiving writing as inquiry, she argues that part of the writing process is "exploring broadly without coming to judgment prematurely and of focusing at appropriate moments"; writing "cannot spring from unexamined or comfortable judgments and theses." The teacher's role, then, is to lead students in a workshop setting through those critical moments of focus, helping them to articulate what they find significant and, by "echoing their texts as intended reader, assisting them in judging the sufficiency and appropriateness of clues and evidence they have given readers to guide interpretation." Both Lauer and Katz thus share Crowley's view that intention can only be discovered in the writing. And they go beyond that in suggesting that a deliberate articulating of those discovered intentions facilitates the revision process.

What the contributors to this section ask, then, is that we shift the focus in the writing workshop from teacher evaluation to student interpretation and critique. When emphasis is placed on the process of inquiry rather than on the product itself, students are empowered. All of this suggests that the writing process can more effectively be enacted if the students are encouraged to liberate themselves from dependence upon teacher as critical authority and are taught instead to be expert readers and *interpreters* of their own writing.

7 Asking for a Text and Trying to Learn It

Jim W. Corder
Texas Christian University

Wonderful disjunctions occur in our field. We don't always seem to notice them, or if we do, we don't blush, as we might or should.

Try these two.

First, in our professional research and publications, we mostly examine fiction, poetry, and drama. We mostly do not examine and write about nonfiction prose. Most of us have never been held accountable for nonfiction prose in general or for essays in particular, except as historical artifacts or as philosophical documents—*Walden*, say, and the *Tatler* and *Spectator* and *Rambler* papers, and perhaps a little of Lamb and Hazlitt and Emerson and Carlyle and Ruskin, but probably no twentieth-century works. But almost every day, when we go to freshman composition classes, we expect freshmen to analyze specimens of nonfiction prose from their readers/anthologies, usually what we call essays or articles or excerpts from longer works.

Second, over on one side of our lives, the "literary," the "real," the "scholarly research and publication" side, we enjoy and explore wonderfully sophisticated views of "the text," or "interpretation," or "hermeneutics," or whatever the hell else. We banish the author from the text and from our lives in post-structuralist theory. Then on Monday morning, the other side now dominant, we go to our freshman composition classes and say, "Show yourself to me in your nonfiction prose essay so that I may edit/correct/indoctrinate/acculturate/grade you."

Odd, our behavior, but then we're sometimes troubled. I reckon that texts do exist, though we don't always—or ever—know them. People live, events transpire, and texts take shape without my participation; they are real apart from my interpretation of them. Texts—even freshman essays—exist, but they keep sliding out from under us: the author is still inventing them, and the texts are inventing themselves, and we're still inventing them as readers. Both because I fear for my own existence and because I remember what I have asked of freshmen, I have to resist when Harold Bloom, for example, observes that "there are *no* texts, but only interpretations" (1979, 7). The version of the author's death that he and others have given eliminates both me and texts. Bloom nevertheless seems undeniable when he remarks that "I only *know* a text, any text, because I know a reading of it, someone else's reading, my own reading, a composite reading" (8), or when he says that in our reading "There is always and only bias, inclination, prejudgment, swerve . . ." (9). But texts exist, I believe, though we may always misread them, troping them, reinventing them as we work our way toward ourselves. To be sure, we make our own text of the text we read (or hear, or watch), but that other text exists. As we read (or hear, or watch), we work toward ourselves, always provisional self-makers, but what Bloom calls the "verbal agon for freedom" is not inevitably *against* the other text(s), but sometimes is *toward* it as well, as we try to catch it, miss it, and come again, and sometimes learn interesting things:

- That freshmen exist, for example.
- That freshman essays/texts exist, for example, though they are sometimes lost behind or alongside or in front of the mess that actually gets turned in to us.
- That freshman essays may even be loci where we can face, examine, and—if it is indicated—heal the disjunctions that occur in our work.

But if freshmen exist, and if their essays exist as texts, we don't always notice that they exist or take into account what it means to ask for and to judge their texts. That means, I believe, that we don't always notice that *we* exist; we don't always notice what is entailed in the text of our asking for their texts—we sometimes imagine different selves and different texts in our own assignments.

Who do we suppose that we are, as we give our assignments, check them in, grade them, and return them? Guardians of the culture? Yes, of course, sometimes, gone off to our ten o'clock class to wage war against ignorance. Protectors of the English language? Surely. Monitors of freshman misdeeds? Yes. Those who will indoctrinate and acculturate? Yes. And gladly teach the great tradition? To be sure. We *expect* to change our students, and we *expect* to be their editors, and sometimes as we edit—that is, mark and grade—their papers, we edit to achieve *our* text rather than theirs. And what do we suppose our assignments are? Requests for precision? Obviously. Opportunities *we grant* for the statement of clear propositions and the presentation of sure evidence? By all means—if we know what evidence is. Expectations for the demonstration of analytical skill and the power to synthesize? Yes, indeed, it goes without saying—this demonstration belongs, some would say, at the center of education. Mastery of processes and stratagems? Oh, Lord, yes—they have got to write good definitions and comparisons and contrasts and cause-effect studies.

All's well and good, so far, right enough, and perhaps part of our responsibility. I believe we are supposed to tell and show students how others have thought and seen and written. I believe we are supposed to show and tell the values and privileges, but not the imprisonments, of common usage. I believe we are supposed to ask and to expect that they perform as public citizens in the common language.

But what else are we asking when we ask for their texts to be turned in, and can it be asked of each of them in the same way? What do we ask for when we give an assignment, asking for a text to come toward us from our students?

We should stop, I think, to remember our expectations or what we demand of their writing. We have many high hopes and great expectations and exacting requirements. I want to recall just one, but I believe it is very nearly universal among us. I believe that almost all of us would forgive "frag," "sp," "agr," "dang," or "DM," "CS," "Trans," and a host of other transgressions, if among them we found what I believe we are mostly looking for—sharp and compelling images, sure and revealing details. We all have agendas to observe when we grade papers—it would be foolish and probably hopeless if we did not. These agendas remind us of what we do and do not want to see on freshman papers. I reckon that almost all of us, quite consciously and deliberately, put *specificity* at or near the top of our desired agenda, *vagueness* at or near the top of our most unwanted list. Even if we did not put *specificity* high on the list, we would still be sufficiently struck by sharp images and revealing details to acknowledge and applaud them when we come upon them. "Ex?" and "Illus" may be our commonest red marks; if they are not, I would judge that examples and illustrations are nevertheless what we want most to see.

What does it mean to hope for, to ask for, to expect specificity, examples, illustrations? Among other things, it means that we are asking them—and I believe I am talking only about freshman writers— to remember their lives, their histories, and to notice the particulars there. That is asking rather a lot: professional writers do not always

manage to do it well. And there are young people still *waiting* for the
world, hungry for it, still waiting for history. When they look at their
lives, they may not see clear images and sure details. Apparently, some
never do. History does not exist in the same way for all. Some notice
and remember images and details, to be sure, but some do not. Some
notice and remember general patterns of behavior, but not particulars.
You cannot notice and remember particulars if you do not see them.
But every time we make an assignment, we are asking our students
to cherish themselves and their histories (while they're still waiting
for history) enough to make themselves before us in their very
particulars. That old pattern, the *oratio*, grew out of greater wisdom
than we sometimes acknowledge. *Exordium* begins things, and *peroratio*
closes things, not in assertion that we have gone back to the beginning
and gone on to the end, but in testimony that we have artificially,
temporally, *made* texts. We ask them in every assignment to cherish
themselves and their texts, to be authors of themselves and their texts,
and simultaneously to believe that we cherish them as authors.

I am not about to plead or to recommend that we accept anything
they write as acceptable. I am trying to shape a reminder to us all
about the mutual effort that is needed to gain a text and to learn it.
And, after all, how many texts are there on the desk when our students
turn in a set of papers, and how many of us are present? I think there
is a text that each wanted to write. I think there is a text that each
thought he or she wrote. I think there is a text that each did write
and turn in. That's three, but not all. There is the text we hoped they
would write (ours). There is the text we hoped they would write
(theirs). There is the text we try to read. That's six, and no doubt there
are other permutations. Will we reconcile them all, or pick one out,
by writing notes in the margins, by talking to each other, by revision?
I don't know. Even supposing that we are at our best, that we are
waiting, hoping for them to get their own rhythms right, for them to
get their own history in, for them to treasure and to show their blessed
particulars, will we find a way to match what they wanted to write/
thought they wrote/did write with our expectations? I don't know.
Will they try to crowd their living time into our reading time so that
we can see them, know them, hunt them, look for *their* plot, the way
they are composed in language? I don't know.

The thing is, you see, that when I get a glimpse, or think I get a
glimpse, of a person speaking toward me, I lose all sense of grading.
I do not know how to grade any more, or why.

How am I to grade my students if, as I suggested above, they quite
literally cannot see, therefore write, what I think I am hoping to read?

How am I to grade them when I remember that for most of them writing is unnatural? They do not yearn to write. They do not need to write in any intense, personal way. They mostly have no occasion to write, except to satisfy assignments, and a semester or two may not be enough time for them to discover that most occasions for writing have to be of their own creation.

How am I to grade them when I remember how I feel when I am graded? I do get graded, more often and more regularly, probably, than I know. Because I think it is important that we remember how we feel when we get graded, I want to single out three kinds of grading that I have experienced recently.

I get graded every year when it's time for chairperson, then dean, to submit recommendations for salary increases. They are *always* in error in the grade they give me. They *must* always be in error, for there is no way in which they—outside interpreters—can know the splendor of myself, or the desperate need I have for recognition. They *cannot* give me a grade that makes any sense to me.

I get graded every semester when it's time for the students in each of my classes to complete the teacher evaluation questionnaire that is required where I teach. For each class, a packet of questionnaires is delivered to my mailbox. I take a packet to class, give general instructions, then must absent myself while a designated student monitors the evaluation, collects the questionnaires, seals the packet, and delivers it to the departmental office. On the questionnaire, there are thirty-two questions. Each can be answered (by blacking little squares) in one of six ways—"insufficient knowledge," "poor," "fair," "average," "above average," "excellent." Every semester I turn the process over to a student monitor and leave the room, thinking to myself, sometimes screaming to myself, "Good God. I'm not to be found in thirty-two questions," or "Dear God, I don't reside in a little blackened square." In such a setting, grades *cannot* be just or understandable: I don't come in thirty-two segments.

And I get graded—in one way or another—eight or ten times a semester in my freshman composition class. Some years ago, I started writing my own essay assignments with my freshman students (see Corder 1975). Since then, I have tried to continue the practice, more out of stubbornness than from principle, and my success in doing so—not success in writing splendid essays, but success in getting them done at all—has fluctuated considerably. My common practice has been to scrape an essay together by the date the assignment is due, to make a copy for each student, and to hand them out as they turn in their essays. Because I think it may be useful as we think about evaluation, I want to tell a little about what has happened to me as I have turned in my essays.

I have become moderately adept at lying, cheating, showing off, and other classroom practices. In the earlier paper I have cited, I told about an advantage I had over my freshmen when we wrote. Since I am more or less accustomed to writing and expect to write hereafter, I keep a little notebook where I jot down words, phrases, paragraphs that I hope to make something of later. In addition, I frequently carry around folded napkins and wadded scraps with other scribblings. When it came time to write, then, I could often cash in something I had already scribbled about. That practice has continued in the years since the first paper—but it hasn't always been enough. Sometimes I have come up short of both ideas and time for writing. When that has happened, I have, of course, lied and cheated. I have recycled earlier papers and turned them in as new. I have taken parts of earlier papers, made more of them, and turned them in as new. I have rewritten rough drafts that I had submitted as finished essays in former semesters. Sometimes I like to imagine that in doing these things I was conducting my own private little writing workshop—trying things out, revising, working through writing projects. Mostly I was just deceiving. Sometimes I had the grace to tell my students what I had done. Sometimes I did not. Despite everything, though, once in a while an essay worked out pretty well, and I knew that I was showing off when I turned such an essay in for my students to read. I have told myself that it's all right—early rhetors were expected periodically to make public speeches, testifying that they knew how to do what they taught, and we can reasonably expect that violin teachers will know how to fiddle. Still. . . .

As I have written essays through these years, spent time talking to students about theirs, revised and worked through my own essays, I have come to be less and less sure of what composition textbooks are for. When you are caught up in a semester's work, living a life, maybe doing a little research, trying to read—and I am talking about freshmen as much as about myself—and you are also trying to write eight or ten essays, then it's the *writing* that preoccupies and instructs, not the textbook, as, for example, when you write yourself into a muddle and then have to work your way out of it. In my own mind, textbooks have receded further and further into the background until they are only reference works that we have in common to which we can point once in a while for help on particular questions. Perhaps everyone else already knew that.

Sometimes, when a piece of writing seemed to be going well, I found that the attention it required would distance me from the students (see my earlier remarks on "showing off"). Quite simply, I sometimes got to paying more attention to my own writing than to theirs. I got interested in my own performance. That's probably wrong for a teacher to do, but it is not all bad: I would like my students to be intensely preoccupied with their own performance as writers. Wouldn't that be something—if they cared intensely about their essays? At any rate, if I had to choose between being preoccupied with my own writing and being preoccupied with the students, I would chose the former. The latter, it seems to me, chiefly generates earnestness in the classroom, which is nice but not necessarily productive.

For two reasons I came gradually over the years to give more and more nonspecific assignments. One is decent. The other is selfish. The more I came to understand what I took *invention* to mean, the less likely I was to give specific assignments, reasoning that students needed room to invent and had responsibility, as writers, to invent. I think a reasonable case can be made for thinking and acting so. If so, my other reason for giving more nonspecific assignments is considerably less noble: sometimes I did not want to be boxed in by my own assignments, prevented from using notes, scribbles, ideas that were already lying around.

I became a poorer, or certainly more doubtful, grader. Looking at my own essays a last time before copying them for my students, I would sometimes mutter to myself, "I hope they see what I'm getting at" or "Surely they can understand why I put it together this way" or "God, I hope they realize how clever I've been" or "Well, it's the best I can do in the time that I have." I came to imagine that these or similar questions were probably in the students' minds as they let go of their essays, and, reading them, found myself saying, "Well, given what is, it's all right, I guess" or "I see what he/she is getting at—maybe we can work it out if we talk about what to do next." With my own doubts in my mind, I became more and more reluctant to give lower grades, however just they might have been—I did not want to be graded; I wanted to be understood, appreciated, answered, cherished.

Have I learned anything about evaluating student writers' essays that might be useful to others? Probably not. Have I learned anything that might help me live through another semester of freshman composition? Perhaps. I'll try these:

1. I have learned that, despite whatever reverence we may have for whatever sacred canon, a freshman essay is worth at least as much time as a short lyric poem, at least as much time as the speeches of a single character in a novel.

2. I have learned to consider the possibility that any essay turned in to me may be as good as it can be at the moment. Once again,

I don't mean to suggest that I am pleading or recommending that all be forgiven in student writing. Hardly anyone, except my cousin Duane, gets up in the morning and decides, "I'm going to be evil today." Hardly anyone, not even some freshmen, gets up in the morning and decides, "I'm going to turn in a half-assed essay today." Most probably all believe that when they have turned in an essay, it's an okay essay. We probably ought to remember that. We probably ought to remember that any judgment we make of their writing may be rape of their judgment. All of us want justification, not denial; validation, not repudiation. If we are editors, not police officers, perhaps we can help them find their own authentication.

3. Students have asked all of us, far too many times, "What do you want?" I have learned, I hope, not to want anything except that *they* will want—will want to be real in their papers, intense, interesting, present, *there*.

4. I have learned that many of the correction marks that we put on their papers do not signify much to our students. Abbreviations and grading symbols, in particular, do not create a genuine occasion or need for revision.

5. For that reason, I have decided not to scrawl "awk" in the margin again, or "clar," or "ex?," or "illus?," or any of the other shorthand forms we have used in the past. Where I am concerned with punctuation and grammatical usage, I believe I will use a standard proofreader's system of correction, and then, periodically if not regularly, talk my way through papers with their authors and try to ensure that they understand proofreader's marks.

   Where I am concerned with matters other than punctuation and grammatical usage, I am going to try either to go over the papers with their authors or to write at least semi-intelligent editorial queries and alternatives—an alternative construction here, a transitional passage there, a question yonder about adding anecdotes and illustrations with observations about why I think them desirable. Good teachers, I suppose, have been doing this for years; however, I think even the best and most conscientious of us still frequently use a language that is valorized for us, but not for them, a language that signifies much to us, but is never present to them.

   It's relatively easy, of course, for me to talk about going over papers with students. I am old and lead a privileged life and have only one freshman class (because I choose to). I don't know what the hell to say to a youngster who has five freshman composition classes. I do know what to say to his or her chairperson or supervisor—fight; change the system; don't do that to teachers; give teaching assignments that will allow teachers to teach.

6. I have learned that I must work harder with my writing students to find or to create genuine occasions for their writing. Until they need to write, their work is not likely ever to be more than adequate.

7. I have *not* learned what to do about grades. The chairperson, the dean, and the registrar all think that there should be grades assigned at the end of the semester. So do the students. I do not. Especially in writing classes, I think that about all I should indicate at term's end is "Hey, neat work, I've enjoyed reading it," or "Thoughtful work, there, keep at it," or "You're okay, and you'll see more to do as you go along," or "Why don't you practice some particular writing chores with me for a while longer?" I suppose to some that's just a substitute for grades. To me, it is notice that writing counts, and that we ought to keep working at it for as long as we can while the student is in the university. But the chairperson, the dean, and the registrar still want grades assigned at the end of the term. Often, early in the semester, I do not put grades on students' papers, but that makes them uneasy. It makes me uneasy if I do assign grades. I don't know what I'll do. While I'm still trying to learn, I would not be surprised if the grades in my composition classes are generally pretty high. I don't think I am going to worry about that too much.

8. Finally, I think I have learned that high standards of evaluation should not be simply announced and exacted. We often tell our writing students, "*Show* me, don't *tell* me," or at least, "Tell me *and* show me." We owe as much, I think. High standards of evaluation should not be simply announced; they should be enacted in our performance.

Works Cited

Bloom, Harold. "The Breaking of Form." In *Deconstruction and Criticism*, edited by Harold Bloom et al., 1–37. New York: Continuum, 1979.

Corder, Jim W. "What I Learned at School." *College Composition and Communication* 26 (1975): 330–34.

8 On Intention in Student Texts

Sharon Crowley
Northern Arizona University

Writing teachers have disposed of a good many canards about writing instruction in recent years, among them the notion that student writers can "get it right" on a first draft written out of class and without assistance. Nevertheless, other notions associated with the traditional practice of assigning out-of-class themes have not died so willing a death. I refer specifically to the assumption that students always write with a clearly defined intention, an intention which should govern their work while composing, and which should be clearly discernible in the structure of the completed text.

Let me illustrate, first of all, what I mean by "intention," as the notion usually surfaces in writing instruction. Students buy into intentionality when they say things like, "Well I know what I mean to say—I just can't seem to get it down on paper." And when students bring drafts of their work to us, we often find ourselves saying something like, "What did you mean to say here?" Or, even more abstractly, we ask, "What was your purpose in this paper? To inform? To persuade?" No doubt some of us teach in composition programs where "aims of discourse," such as exposition and argumentation, are used to organize courses and syllabi. The notion that discourse has discriminable "aims" is of course derived from the notion of intentionality; the assumption is that a writer's aim or intention is discernible in the formal structures embedded in a finished text.

I want to question the appropriateness of the notion of intention to writing instruction on four grounds. First of all, the privilege accorded to intention in contemporary composition pedagogy is a historical remnant. The foregrounding of authors' intentions or aims occurred during a remarkably nonrhetorical epoch in the history of rhetoric, an epoch in which discourse theory aspired to achieve the status of a science. Second, the notion of intention has recently come under fire from theorists of writing because it distorts the nature of writing.

Third, the notion compromises contemporary assumptions about the composing process and its attendant pedagogy in serious ways. And—most compelling for me—the notion of intention is untrue to my experience as teacher and writer.

Campbell and the Aims of Discourse

In 1776, the Scottish philosopher and theologian George Campbell published his enormously influential *Philosophy of Rhetoric.* On the very first page of that work, Campbell defines "eloquence" as "that art or talent by which the discourse is adapted to its end" (1). Campbell discriminates four such ends: "to enlighten the understanding, to please the imagination, to move the passions, or to influence the will." That is, the art of rhetoric is aim-centered, the rhetor's aim being to affect the mental faculties of an audience in some desired fashion. Campbell apparently assumes, as givens, that a rhetor's intentions are always clear and available, and, further, that there are only four kinds of intentions which merit attention.

To define rhetoric as aim-centered is to place serious limitations on the scope of rhetoric, since the definition bypasses invention.[1] Campbell's assumption is that speakers or writers have already determined what they wish to say or write before they come to the rhetorical act. All that rhetoric can offer are means of helping a rhetor to realize some intention, such as informing her colleagues about a recent discovery or moving the citizenry to vote for her candidate. While the omission of invention is not systematically made in Campbell's *Philosophy,* later rhetoricians who adopted his aim-centered definition of the art were careful to point out that invention precedes, and is separate from, the rhetorical act.[2] For example, A. S. Hill remarks in his popular *Principles of Rhetoric* (1878) that rhetoric "does not undertake to furnish a person with something to say; but it does undertake to tell him how best to say that with which he has provided himself" (iv). The school of rhetorical theory indebted to Campbell's *Philosophy* assumes that the stuff of invention—subjects, ideas, knowledge, discoveries, and thoughts, as well as aims or intentions—precedes discourse, that it exists in some coherent way outside discourse, or at least that it exists outside of its expression by speakers and writers.

Granting for the moment that an author's formulation of her intention can be separated from the rhetorical process, the transmission of this intention in and by language remains problematical. Campbell devoted most of the *Philosophy* to determining the sorts of social and linguistic interference which might prevent rhetors from achieving their aims. For example, the adherence by members of an audience to "party spirit" or their motivation by self-interest could interfere with the easy transmission of a rhetor's intention, Campbell thought, as could a rhetor's misuse of words or indulgence in garbled syntax. Rhetorical theorists who adopted Campbell's aim-centered definition of rhetoric, however, tended rather to assume a trouble-free model of transmission between a speaker or writer and her audience. They achieved this model of communication in two ways: by ignoring altogether the potential social and political differences which exist among members of a rhetorical community; and by developing a theory of style which privileged clarity above all other virtues. That is, such theorists assumed that if rhetors are careful to make their language exactly representative of their thought processes, such language would automatically signify their intentions to any other rational person.

To give only one example of the tradition's univocal faith in the efficacy of linguistic clarity, I cite Hill's definition of rhetoric in the *Principles,* where rhetoric is "the art of the efficient communication by language." Hill posits that rhetoric "shows how to convey from one mind to another the results of observation, discovery, or classification" (1878, iv). Such conveyance is achieved when writers see to it that every word they choose expresses "the exact shade of meaning intended" and that their words are "so arranged that each clause, each word, helps to carry the sentence as a whole into the reader's mind" (1892, 201). That is, language is a medium which can be made to reflect intended meanings with a high degree of precision.

In their anxiety to reduce language to an exact representation of thought, nineteenth-century rhetorical theorists were interested in determining whether linguistic elements could be directly associated with the "parts" of thought. The handbook definition of a sentence as "a group of words that represent a complete thought" resulted from this attempt to equate the structures of language with those of thought, but theorists in the tradition also attempted to make the identification hold for larger discursive structures as well. For example, in *Paragraph-Writing* (1893), F. N. Scott and J. V. Denney introduce two entities they call "inductive and deductive paragraphs." In these constructions, the ordering of sentences within paragraphs represents the movement of "the two orders of progress in thought" (48). In deductive paragraphs, "the sentences applying the principle to the particular case in hand, usually follow the topic-sentence, which states the principle." In inductive paragraphs, on the other hand, "the sentences stating the particular facts usually precede the topic-sentence, which states the general conclusion" (48–49). That is, the arrangement of words and sentences on the page was to represent the movement of a writer's thoughts in graphic form.

It was but a short step from this assumption to a second one, that writers' intentions would manifest themselves in the structure of completed discourses. While Campbell himself did not associate each of his "ends of discourse" with distinct discursive genres, his followers certainly did so. For example, in his influential *English Composition* (1866), Alexander Bain names five categories of discourse that correspond to appeals to some of the faculties discriminated by Campbell. For Bain, exposition, description, and narration appeal to the understanding, while argument moves the will and poetry excites the passions (1). Thus any piece of exposition, for instance, will have as its aim an appeal to a reader's understanding; moreover, given the tradition's representative theories of language and discourse, any educated reader should be able to trace the movement of the author's mind as she composed by paying attention to the structure of her finished composition. Out of such soil grew the assumption, or wish, that a linguistic structure, a discourse, can exactly re-present an author's intention, without disruption, derailment, or failure. Omit any possibility that readers are apathetic, inept, perhaps even hostile—and the picture is complete: rhetoric exists in an ideal discursive world where clear transmission of a rhetor's intentions always and inevitably takes place.

The realization of this ideal discourse depended on the assertion of yet another notion which proved to be of immense importance in modern composition theory. I refer to the principle of discursive orderliness, which posited that all worthwhile discourse manifests a unity and coherence which is easily discernible by its readers. If discourse is an immediately representative medium of thought, then it ought also to represent the movement of those thoughts in the highly ordered fashion that minds, working at their best, necessarily employ. The connection between intentionality and order is nicely illustrated in the composition theory of James McCrimmon, whose *Writing with a Purpose* (1950) focuses on author's intentions as the generative center of the composing act. Positing that "all effective writing is controlled by the writer's purpose," McCrimmon argues in good Campbellian fashion that a writer always "is trying to do something to . . . readers: to inform or convince or delight them, to explain something to them, or to make them see or feel what he has experienced" (3). McCrimmon is confident that discernment of one's purpose precedes and controls the entire act of writing: "Each of these general purposes will exert its own influence on the selection and presentation of [the writer's] material." Accordingly, he characterizes the task of invention as a matter of defining what it is that a writer wants to accomplish; once this is settled on, the writer can be confident that her work will be unified, and that digressions and irrelevancies will be immediately identifiable and subject to purging (5). In Mc-Crimmon's work, the availability of a clearly defined intention secures a number of desirable qualities for discourse, among them unity, consistency, harmony, direction. As he notes in summary, if the writer "understands the implications of what he is trying to do, his choices are more likely to be harmonious. His writing will be all of a piece. It will have unity of style as well as unity of subject" (9). Thus it is that a writer's intention can dictate both the shape and substance of the completed composition.

One last point: adherents of traditional composition theory offer a monolithic account of intention which overlooks its potential complexities. McCrimmon, for instance, continually confuses intentions which might be stated in such terms as "Here is the point I want to make" with those which might answer questions like "How can I succeed on this assignment?" These two quite different sorts of intentions would seem to inaugurate two very different composing procedures. I would also suggest that the second intention is much easier to formulate before writing begins than is the first. To sum up my historical account, then, the model of intention utilized by traditional composition theory is not only too simple—it makes a number of specious assumptions. First, the model assumes that all writers should not only know their intentions before they begin to compose, but they should also be able to express these clearly and without distortion in discourse. The model assumes further that language will faithfully translate writers' intentions, and that readers will interpret these correctly and without distortion. When laid out so bluntly, the vulnerability of this cluster of assumptions begins to be apparent; and, as might be expected, they have recently come under attack by theorists of writing.

Derrida on Intention

In his essay "Signature, Event, Context" (1971) Jacques Derrida argues that the crucial feature of written discourse is not the mark of an author's intention, but rather of her absence from her text. Were writers not absent from readers for temporal or geographical reasons, after all, it would not be necessary for them to write. But given its author's necessary absence, writing has the ability to generate a plenitude of readings or interpretations, a multitude of meaning. According to Derrida, "a written sign, in the usual sense of the word, is therefore a mark which remains, which is not exhausted in the present of its inscription, and which can give rise to an iteration both in the absence of and beyond the presence of the empirically determined subject who, in a given context, has emitted or produced it" (317). That is, any piece of writing, even the smallest scrap, makes itself available to appropriation by readers and other writers, who can, and do, interpret it in multiple ways.

The author's absence also permits writing to do its work with or without a context: according to Derrida, "it belongs to the sign to be legible . . . even if I do not know what its alleged author-scriptor meant consciously and intentionally at the moment he wrote it, that is, abandoned it to its essential drifting." Often readers have no information about the specific context within which writing was composed, but this lack does not keep them from being able to read the text which results. But since any "written sign carries with it a force of breaking with its context, that is, the set of presences which organize the moment of its inscription," any "real" context we might imagine for a text is always constructed by its readers. For example, when we find a scrap of paper with grocery items listed on it lying on the floor of a deserted hallway, we have no immediate way of knowing who its author might be or under what circumstances it was composed. We know only as much about it as our own experience with grocery lists and their uses can supply us. And yet our desire to know what the writing might "mean" is so strong that we can seldom resist the temptation to supply a context for its composition—"Aha!" we say to ourselves, "Jones and her family are having artichokes for dinner tonight." That is, our desire to construct a stable and specified meaning for texts is so strong that we invent contexts when none are available. Such contexts are sought precisely so that they might ground an (absent) writer's intention.

English teachers are familiar with this process as it works in literary studies; scholars attempt to find out all that can be known about, say, George Eliot's "life and times" in order that we may have a context which will permit us to understand her intention while composing, say, *Middlemarch*. But Derrida would insist that we can never have complete access to Eliot's intentions, as long as we look for these in writing by or about her. Writing, which makes itself available to anyone who can read, never authorizes a given reading all by itself, never tells us exactly what it "means," least of all what its writer's intention might have been. If writing could do this, after all, a definitive reading of *Middlemarch*, a reading which foreclosed the possibility of all other readings, would have long since been made.

But aside from its break with "external" contexts, another rift characterizes the sign's "semiotic and internal context," according to Derrida. This internal context, any stable formal structure posited for a text, is broken by virtue of its "essential iterability; one can always lift a written syntagma from the interlocking chain in which it is caught or given without making it lose every possibility of functioning, if not every possibility of 'communicating,' precisely." This iterability, or repeatability, of the written sign is what permits it to be cited, grafted into other chains of signs, and harnessed to other uses than the original author may have intended or foreseen (as I have just illustrated by inserting "Derrida's" text into "mine"). But it is also this feature of the written sign, its characteristic "breaking" with its internal context, that compromises its status as "the vehicle, transport, or site of passage of a meaning, and of a meaning that is one" (309). In other words, since written texts can be radically dissociated from their authors' putative intentions, the ability of their internal structure to signal coherent units of "meaning" is also put into serious question.

Intention and Process Pedagogy

Since about 1970, a new pedagogy has come to the fore in the teaching of writing. This pedagogy focuses on students' acts of composing, rather than on the finished products of their work. Process pedagogy assumes, among other things, that a student's response to a writing assignment can only be realized in the course of writing that response. That is, students only find out what it is that they can write while they are in the process of writing it. This process of finding out what is there to be written may consume several drafts, most of which are submitted to readings by other students and the writing teacher. In process pedagogy, each draft of a work is supposedly regarded not so much as nearer approximation to some foreordained intention as it is valued as a partial unfolding of a previously unrealized point of view. According to this model of composing, if intentions are realizable in language at all, they may be formulated within the course of writing, or they may change from draft to draft. This pedagogy, then, explicitly contradicts the viability of the notion of intention advanced by traditional composition theory. I would like to shore up the implicit rejection of intention made by process pedagogy by arguing that, aside from its theoretical unsoundness, the intentional model poses at least three serious impediments to teachers who want to make useful readings of their students' texts.

First, the intentional model allows teachers to assume nearly full responsibility for their students' work, not only with regard to its instigation and format, but in terms of its supposed meaning or interpretation, as well. If we buy into the notion of intention, when we are confronted with an unreadable student text we are inclined to ask the writer what she "meant" while she was composing it. If she can supply us with an oral account of her putative intention, we are likely to ask her why, indeed, that account does not appear within the pages of her discourse. This posture explicitly denies the possibility that the student may only have realized her intention after the fact, that the composition of the first draft helped her to grope toward an intention for it. And, if she cannot offer an account of her intention, we are likely to construct one for her, saying, in effect, "I know what you meant while you were writing this text, and your next draft will incorporate the meaning I have just designated." But now who is writer, and who reader, of the text? In this, as in other ways, traditional composition pedagogy systematically deprives student writers of responsibility for their own compositions, an observation which might explain why students often hold their classroom writing in contempt.

Second, to assume that all well-formed discourses will manifest some unified intention is to reject as inferior those which do not. On the traditional pedagogical model, students compose successive drafts with an eye toward approximating an idealized model discourse which has been pre-scribed (that is, already written) for them; texts which do not approximate the model, regardless of their quality, must be rejected. But since no text (if Derrida is right) can unequivocally demonstrate an integrated intention, to uphold such an expectation for texts composed by novice writers is unrealistic, to say the least. At best, such an expectation elicits student texts in which statements of intention are painfully overt, and which lend a mechanical quality to the ensuing discourse: "In this paper I intend to prove that abortion is murder," and so on. And at worst, to expect an overt statement of intention in every text may cause teachers to overlook texts which are superior, or which hold promise, simply because they do not conform to an expectation which, after all, issues from teachers rather than from students.

Third, the intentional model seriously distorts the nature of the reading process. The model makes an important assumption regarding reading: that texts manifest relatively stable meanings. But a more realistic view of reading insists that, like all readers, when teachers read drafts of student writing, they actually construct "meanings" for them as they read. Too, the constructed "meaning" of a text may change from reading to reading, which accounts for the fact that student papers may seem more sound on a second or third reading than they did on a first. (The instability of reading, by the way, also accounts for the fact that successive readings of *Middlemarch* can be undertaken with pleasure and/or profit.) To assume, then, that meanings constructed during reading ought to have a necessarily univocal relationship to whatever "meaning" a student writer may have had in mind for her text while she composed it is to make a great leap of faith. The congruence of the writer's intention with a reader's interpretation can only be substantiated by subsequent conversation with the writer, who will often tell her teacher just what he wants to hear. That is, the authority relation which obtains between students and teachers is such that students will try to do whatever they are told to do by a teacher, including adopting whatever intention he may have created for their texts while reading them.[3]

I think that teachers can do greater service to student writers if they are willing to say something like "I'm a pretty skilled reader, and here's how I interpret this text of yours." This stance is, of course, rhetorical, in a way that the intentional model is not; the more rhetorical response opens students to the realization that an author's intended meaning is carried or impeded, "seen through" or not, by the levels of understanding, skill, and patience brought to it by her readers, as well as by the care she takes with the language in which she couches it. When she has begun to think of readers as persons who, like herself, are groping for understanding, she will have begun to understand the essentially rhetorical nature of any act of composing. More, she will have begun to see why it is necessary for people to try to write at all.

Teaching and Writing

Just yesterday, a graduate student stopped me after class to ask if I had yet had an opportunity to read the draft of a major paper she had recently submitted. When I replied that I had not, she said, "Good. I've changed my mind about what I was after. I see now that my characterization of its subject was incredibly naive." She then asked me to return the piece, unread. I refused; and when I read the draft I saw that her insight into her work had been good. In conference, we agreed that the blind spots she had detected in writing out this early version of her work were indeed impeding her progress, and she is now at work on yet another draft. This sort of sophistication about the vagaries of the writing process is rare enough among graduate students; it is almost nonexistent among younger students.

For freshman writers, whose naiveté about the complexity of the composing process often keeps them from writing at all, the traditional notion of intention serves as an immense roadblock—how, they ask, are they to know what they mean before they write? Or, thinking they have such a meaning in hand, as it were, they become frustrated when it does not appear, as if by magic, on the page before them. In the case of young writers, I am afraid, intentions are often operative, indeed; but they are of a very different kind than those acknowledged by traditional textbooks. We teachers tend to overlook the distressing facts that students' intentions may amount to little more than getting a passing grade on an assignment, or pleasing us by demonstrating their ability to observe the formal strictures we have laid down in class. I think that if we were to acknowledge frankly that younger writers feel the force of such pressures very strongly, we might be able to discuss them with our students in such a way as to move them toward attitudes about composing which are shared by more practiced writers.

Some time ago, the editors of this collection contacted me, asking me if I would consider contributing an essay to it. I immediately wrote back to them, assuring them that I would be delighted to be included among a group of writer-teachers who were concerned about how we read students' texts. At the time I wrote that letter, I apparently "intended" to write an essay about the negative ramifications of the notion of intention on writing instruction. (I just now looked up a copy of the abstract I prepared at the time, in order to reconstruct my then-intention.) In the meantime, however, the editors contacted a publisher, who insisted that the essays included in the collection be unified by some consistent approach to reading student papers. The editors then wrote to all us potential contributors, asking that we "deal in a concrete way with real student writing by reference, quotation, or excerpt" and that we "convey the conceptual framework" that bears on such reading.

I remember being absolutely stymied by this request. I ordinarily write on a fairly abstract level, dealing with the theory or history of rhetoric and composition. I have always been reluctant to share with readers what I take to be the relatively intimate relation that obtains between me and my students; I have never figured out how to write with candor about my own pedagogy for a faceless audience. After vacillating for several weeks, I wrote to the editors, asking if I could be excused from contributing (although I "misrepresented" my intention to chicken out by couching the letter in terms of my inability to meet a deadline). In the meantime, I read a draft of an essay composed by another of the contributors to this volume. I remember being impressed by the clarity with which she discussed both her goals as a teacher and the pedagogy by means of which she tried to realize those goals. Reading her work bolstered my confidence that people could write about their teaching without falling into either dogmatism or sentimentality. Nevertheless, I put off composing my own essay until the deadline loomed disastrously near, even though I had been thinking and worrying about it for almost two years.

I tell this story to make a point about writers' intentions: the various intentions I have entertained while completing this essay are not simple or autonomous. Obviously, my intentions changed over the time that elapsed between the essay's instigation and its composition; they ranged over a wide spectrum of emotional and intellectual desires, from a wish to be included in a useful collection of work to raising my potential readers' awareness about the history of "intention." Perhaps it is the case that writers' more immediate and pragmatic intentions, such as getting good grades or getting published, are susceptible to fairly clear formulation, and may be carried out with relative dispatch—writing the paper along the lines the teacher dictates; trying to conform to a publisher's dictates. But I am quite skeptical about any idea of intentionality that includes "knowing what I'm going to write and what it will mean" or "knowing what I intend to do to my audience." I have no assurance whatever that either of these last sorts of intention will be realized by my completed discourse, even assuming that I have finally articulated what I intended, or that I am fortunate enough to have sympathetic readers.

Notes

1. Campbell's move constitutes a decisive limitation of the scope of rhetoric. Classical rhetoricians began the study of their art with invention; for example, Aristotle defines rhetoric as "the faculty of seeing in the particular case what are the available means of persuasion" (*Rhetoric* 1355b). Aristotle's definition foregrounds invention insofar as the rhetor's first duty is to find out what arguments are available in a given case. The Greek term *theorein*, often literally translated as "to see," carries overtones of discovery, or finding.

Many commentators have noticed the limitation of eighteenth-century rhetoric to arrangement and style; see, for example, Bevilacqua's "Philosophical

Influences," which characterizes the rhetorical theory of the entire school as "managerial."

2. I have assumed—without trying to demonstrate—the indebtedness to Campbell of the rhetorical school now called "current-traditional," or, as I have done here, "traditional." The textbook tradition includes not only Bain, Hill, Scott and Denney, and McCrimmon, but H. N. Day, John Franking Genung, Barrett Wendell, and Sheridan Baker, among others. A good account of current-traditional rhetoric and its indebtedness to Campbell is readily available in James A. Berlin's *Writing Instruction in Nineteenth-Century Colleges* (1984).

3. I cannot resist pointing out that some English teachers try to do to their composition students what they can only do to the so-called "great writers" in the pages of *PMLA*: that is, they try to rewrite writers' texts so that they "make sense" to the reader-currently-in-charge. E. D. Hirsch's elaborate reading in *Validity in Interpretation* (1967) of what is obviously a slip of Poe's pen provides a fine case in point (234).

Works Cited

Aristotle. *The Rhetoric.* Translated by Lane Cooper. New York: Appleton-Century-Crofts, 1932.

Bain, Alexander. *English Composition and Rhetoric: A Manual.* Am. ed., rev. New York: D. Appleton and Company, 1866.

Berlin, James A. *Writing Instruction in Nineteenth-Century American Colleges.* Urbana: NCTE, 1984.

Bevilacqua, Vincent. "Philosophical Influences in the Development of English Rhetorical Theory: 1748 to 1783." In *Proceedings of the Leeds Philosophical and Literary Society*, vol. XII, part iv: 191–215. Leeds: W. S. Maney and Son, Ltd.

Campbell, George. *The Philosophy of Rhetoric.* [1776.] Edited by Lloyd F. Bitzer. Carbondale: Southern Illinois University Press, 1963.

Derrida, Jacques. "Signature, Event, Context." [1971.] In *Margins of Philosophy*, translated by Alan Bass, 309–30. Chicago: University of Chicago Press, 1982.

Hill, Adams Sherman. *The Foundations of Rhetoric.* New York: Harper and Brothers, 1892.

———. *The Principles of Rhetoric, and Their Application.* New York: Harper and Brothers, 1878.

Hirsch, E. D. *Validity in Interpretation.* New Haven: Yale University Press, 1967.

McCrimmon, James. *Writing with a Purpose.* New York: Houghton-Mifflin, 1950.

Scott, Fred Newton, and Joseph Villiers Denney. *Paragraph-Writing.* 3rd ed. Boston: Allyn and Bacon, 1893.

9 Reading Intention

Norm Katz
Harvard University

Like the students they teach, writing teachers spend most of their time reading. Students read (and reread) as they write; teachers read (and reread) as they grade. I find that for every hour I spend teaching in the classroom I spend five hours reading student papers in my office—five slow, difficult hours. I do not read for pleasure (even though most papers provide it) or for knowledge (most papers provide plenty of that, too). And I do not read in order to label errors or categorize students (although I do both). Rather, I read in order to help my students read (and, consequently, write) more like the mature writers that many of them will one day become. The present essay illustrates with excerpts from a recent assignment how I read student papers.

I tell my students that writing is largely a matter of fixing things. And that the better they get at fixing things the better they will get at writing. Now, fixing things requires reading. Students who do not learn to read their own papers with a discerning eye will not be able to fix things. Such reading, such self-monitoring, is an essential skill for the writer and one that every student who wants to write well must learn.

My procedure is simple. I require that *every* paper submitted to me be accompanied by a letter that explains what the student is trying to do and how he or she is trying to do it: the letter explains the student's compositional intention. I call this letter of intention a "META," a term which suggests the notion of METAcognition (self-monitoring). Since the reason for explicitly stating the purpose of their papers makes intuitive sense to students, they find writing the META a straightforward task. I encourage them to be as honest as they can by allowing them to write informally and by disregarding mechanical faults. I may, of course, challenge the content of a META—some intentions are better than others—but all such criticisms take into account the quality of the paper actually produced.

The last assignment of the semester asks students to choose two of their previously graded papers and revise them for style. My job is to read the intention that motivates each revision and to use that intention to help me read with greater understanding what the student has done. In spite of the risks—who is to say what a writer's "true" intention is?—a useful pedagogical approximation of student intention may often be achieved by reading a paper in the light of the META which accompanies it.

Where do my students' style intentions come from? They come from the entire pedagogical context that frames the assignment, including in particular: (1) the concepts of "clarity," "coherence," "emphasis," "concision," and the like that I introduce in class and that are celebrated in our textbook, *Style: Ten Lessons in Clarity and Grace* by Joseph M. Williams (2nd ed. Glenview, Ill.: Scott, Foresman, 1985); (2) the comments (echoing those concepts) I write on their papers; (3) the comments (also echoing those concepts) I make to them in conference; (4) the comments (also echoing those concepts) other students make to them about their papers during workshop. The concepts are not new—almost all students come to college knowing that their papers should be clear, concise, coherent. What is new is the seriousness with which the concepts are treated and the explicitness with which they are considered. By requiring students to spell out their intentions, the META holds them publicly responsible for standards that previously may have been only professed and verbal.

To illustrate how METAs guide my reading, I have selected excerpts from revision papers completed during the fall of 1986 by three of my students—Charlie Ball, Murry Gunty, and Khursheed Imam (used with permission). Charlie revised for clarity; Murry revised for accuracy; Khursheed revised for diction and coherence. The assignment stipulated that no revision be longer than the original paper (four or five pages) and that no META be shorter than two pages.

First Student: Charlie Ball

Charlie chose to revise "A Hairy Business," a paper in which he had profiled a local barbershop. His data came from two observational visits to the barbershop and an abortive interview with the owner. The META immediately focuses one's reading on his intention: "I approached this final revision process on this paper with two main goals in mind: fixing the minor cosmetic errors, and improving the piece's overall clarity." Since no algorithms exist for "improving overall clarity," Charlie had to determine specifically both what to do and how to do it. Such a task demands imagination as well as a critical intelligence.

In order to improve clarity, Charlie made three "large" (his word) and three "small" revisions. His META explains one of the small revisions as follows (my comments are in brackets):

> One small change I made in the paper are in my final thoughts at the barbershop. After being told by Old Oil Hair [George, the chief barber and owner] that he couldn't help me [by granting an interview], in the first paper, I simply accept it and leave. In the revision, though, I added one sentence [italicized in the excerpt below]. In this sentence, I wonder why he asked me to come in to talk to him on Thursday, his busiest day. This relates to an observation I made [during a conference with me] that, though barbers seem friendly, they are only doing their job in acting as a friend to the customer, and are sometimes actually no more generous than the typical man on the street. I thought about actually writing this observation in the revision, but decided I would leave a hint—the thought in the added sentence—instead. This, I feel, will let the reader know my thoughts without "hitting him on the head" with them. ["The reader" includes the two members of Charlie's workshop.]

Apparent at once is the fact that this letter assumes that I remember the original paper—written a month before—and that I also remember what was said in conference about the upcoming revision. Charlie assumes, in other words, that he and I share a common classroom experience as well as a fairly extensive body of information. Notice, too, that Charlie reports on what he decided *not* to add to the revision.
    Charlie first wrote:

> On Thursday, I walked over to the barber shop. "Hi," George greeted me. I noticed a change in the shop's appearance. Something was different. I panned the chairs and realized that Orange Shiry [one of the barbers] was missing. "I'm sorry, Charlie, I was surprised that George remembered my name, "but I've got one out sick and Thursday is my busiest day. I'd like to help you, but it just gets crazy sometimes."

This was revised to:

> On Thursday, I walked over to the barbershop. "Hi." George greeted me. I noticed a change in the shop's appearance. Something was different. I panned the chairs and realized there were only three barbers working. Orange Shirt was gone. "I'm sorry, Char-lie"—I was surprised that George remembered my name—"but I've got one out sick and Thursday is my busiest day." *I wondered why George had told me to come in on his busiest day if he truly*

planned to help me [italics added]. "I'd like to help you, but it just gets crazy sometimes."

I judge this passage to be an improvement over the original. The italicized sentence clarifies Charlie's reaction to George's refusal to grant him an interview, and the META makes sure that the reader does not miss its significance. On an unrelated point, note that not all changes are announced. Charlie silently fixes a "minor cosmetic error," an error picked up by one of his workshop members: he changes commas to dashes before and after the words "I was surprised that George remembered my name" in order to set off cleanly the interjected sentence. Without the META my reading of Charlie's paper would be less secure.

Second Student: Murry Gunty

Murry revised a personal narrative entitled "Living a Nightmare." It describes his behavior just after his best friend, Stevie Jacobsen, was fatally injured in an accident caused by a drunken motorist.

Murry concentrated his revision efforts on "four major parts." The META sets out his intention for the third part as follows:

> The next big section that I undertook was the transition from the accident site to the hospital. In the original draft, I went straight from the site to the hospital, and Stevie was perched in his hospital bed already through with surgery. *That is not what I tried to convey* [italics added]. What happened was that I went to the hospital, and we had to wait for him to come out of surgery before I actually knew if he was alive. I saw his mother and father, and had a few moments to be alone to reflect on what had happened. [In the revised version] this is where I really decided to let the reader get inside of me to see what I was going through and how I was feeling. I described my anticipation of walking down the hallway toward his room. I told of the smell of the hospital which most people are familiar with; it almost cleanses your nose as you walk down the halls. And then, I described what it was like seeing mom (I call Mrs. Jacobsen mother). I tried to capture the emptiness that I knew she must be feeling because I sure as hell was. And I spoke of our embrace which must have lasted for close to an hour. Then I led in to when I first saw what Stevie looked like, rolling in on a stretcher, with many tubes and monitors trailing. The only other detail I added was how "his body was held together with screws, bolts, and plaster of Paris." By *expanding on this whole sequence* [italics added], I feel that the reader is with me every step of the way, and can really feel to what extent I am hurting inside. Also, I decided to give the reader a little jolt at the end of this sections by just saying, "Two weeks later, he

died." I feel that it is time to shock the reader so that he/she understands that this is not a dream, but a very harsh reality.

In conference, Murry told me that he intended to fill in what had been left out of the original text—the waiting. In the META, he criticizes the handling of the transition because it falsifies his experience: "That is not what I tried to convey." No reader other than the author could have made that criticism.

The first version goes like this:

> When it happened, I reacted as most people would, not believing that it was true. I ran down to the accident site, only blocks from my home, and the sharp odorimmediately struck me. It did not take long, though, 30 seconds at the accident site seeing the red stains of Steven's soul smeared on G-d's [sic] earth, before I realized what occurred. I stood there, staring, yet not seeing as tears welled up in my eyes.
>
> I immediately headed for the hospital. He was still alive. But it was no longer my friend that I was seeing. He was breathing with a respirator. He was eating through a tube inserted into his throat. It was not Stevie. It was something the murderer had left behind that only looked like my friend, but could never be that person again. All we could do was wait, and watch. I spent day and night at the hospital, hoping and praying. I felt so helpless, and so useless. In two weeks, all I would have would be memories.

All eight of the written comments that I originally made on these two paragraphs concern diction and syntax. I said nothing about content. I said nothing about what was omitted. How could I have? I cannot read minds.

The revised version goes like this:

> When it happened, I reacted as most people would, not believing that it was true. I ran down to the accident site, only blocks from my home, and the sharp odorimmediately struck me. The acrid smell of ammonia pierced my nose and I felt a rush of warmth from my toes to my cheeks. It did not take long before I realized what had occurred. I stood there, staring at, yet not seeing the red stains of Steven's soul smeared on G-d's earth.
>
> I immediately headed for the hospital. His father was in the waiting room. I ran over to him and he told me that Stevie was still alive. Stevie was in the operating room; there had been no word of his conditions. I had to find out something. I walked down the empty hall toward his room. My insides churned and I felt that rush of warmth again. Everything smelled sterile—the way things smell at a dentist's office right before he drills a hole in your tooth. I turned down the hallway and say that his door was open. My pace slowed, as I peered around the corner. I saw his mother standing there, looking out the window, trying to find

strength somewhere in the darkness of the Portland skyline. She
saw me and started to cry. I went to her, and she held me; after
all, to her, and us, Stevie and I were brothers. And I was her son.
We stood there for the longest time, but then again what would
time be like without Stevie.

Many hours later, the doctors came to us without bringing
any news. Stevie was rolled in on a stretcher—still alive. But it
was no longer ny friend that I was seeing. He was breathing with
a respirator. He was eating through a tube inserted through his
throat. His body was held together with screws, bolts, and plaster
of Paris. It was not Stevie. It was something the murderer had
left behind that only looked like my friend. All we could do was
wait, and watch. I spent day and night at the hospital, hoping
and praying. I felt helpless, and useless. Two weeks later, he died.

The METAs that my students write work to prevent me from
substituting my intentions for theirs. Here, Murry's META prevented
me from reading his paper in terms of the ideal syntactic revision that
I might have at first preferred: it prevented me, in other words, from
reading Murry's changes and additions as anything less than successful.
When students' intentions are insufficiently ambitious or poorly exe-
cuted, however, my job is to hold them to higher standards than they
have set for themselves. Students' intentions are subject to the same,
sort of scrutiny as any other part of their writing performance.

Third Student: Khursheed Imam

Like Murry, Khursheed revised his personal narrative essay. The META
states his intention:

> My aim in doing this revision was to make my paper clearer by
> concentrating on diction and coherence. I have included an extra
> copy of my revision with the parts that have been changed or
> added [italicized].

We talked a good bit about coherence in class. Students who underline
make the teacher's reading task easier, as can be seen below. Some
students color code their revisions.

The following excerpts consist of selections from Khursheed's META
together with matching passages from the original essay and its revision.
Khursheed is unusually good at explaining *why* he makes changes.

META:

> First, I changed the title from "Death and Life" to "Learning
> About Death and Life" since I had not written a general discourse
> on death and life and the words "learning about" prepare the
> reader to hear about someone's experiences.

This change is a result of my having criticized the generality of the original title in my written comments on the first draft.

META:

In paragraph 2 I changed "we" to "the entire family" since it was unclear who "we" referred to. I inserted the sentence, "It had practically. . ." to give a better sense of the atmosphere. I changed "I didn't do much talking" to "I did not talk much" because this phrasing is more direct and active. I rearranged "to occasionally point" to "occasionally to point" since the split infinitive poses an obstacle to some readers [Khursheed here refers to my dislike of split infinitives]. I changed "topic . . . was" to "topic . . . turned to" since this phrasing is active like the verb in the preceding sentence [I had circled the verb "was" on the first draft].

Original:

Then it happened. One night, after dinner, we were all sitting in the living room talking. I didn't do much talking myself, except to occasionally point out something funny in what someone else had said. As usual, the conversation drifted quite aimlessly from one subject to another. Presently, the topic of discussion was car accidents. My older sister, Ishrat, was speaking: "One of my friends told me that she knew a guy who was burned alive when his car exploded on the highway." "Is the man all right now?" I asked, genuinely concerned but unaware how absurd my question was.

Revision:

Then it happened. One night, after dinner, *the entire family* was sitting in the living room talking. *It had practically become a custom for us to have discussions in the living room right after dinner. I did not talk much* myself, except *occasionally to point* out something funny in what someone else had said. As usual, the conversation drifted quite aimlessly from one subject to another. Presently, the topic of discussion *turned to* car accidents. My older sister, Ishrat, was speaking: "One of my friends told me that she knew a guy who was burned alive when his car exploded on the highway." "Is the man all right now?" I asked, genuinely concerned but unaware how absurd my question was. [All the italics are Khursheed's.]

The change from "we" to "the entire family" is the result of complaints made by members of Khursheed's workshop. The inserted third sentence ("it had practically. . .") is the product of what can only be called Khursheed's "creativity." Had I not known Khursheed's intentions—to improve diction and coherence—I might have misread the revisions: that is, I might have failed to appreciate how much Khursheed

had improved the paragraph and fastened instead on, say, the awkwardness of the newly introduced phrase "it had practically."

The next passage comes shortly after Khursheed's father says:
"Khursheed, the man in the car died in the explosion. That means he
has left our world forever. . . . When a person dies, he cannot become
'all right' again. . . . Everyone has to die sometime."

META:

In paragraph 12 I inserted "someone let out" because it made it
clear that a person had let out a cry and that I felt God was
reclaiming someone's life. I change "it will be one of us" to "we
will all be lifted up . . ." since the meaning of "it" was unclear. I
inserted "I was scared" to show how I felt (outside my dream).

I changed the 13th paragraph completely since its original
form was very confusing. I began with "This dream" to assure
the reader that he had just read the description of a dream.

Original:

He [Khursheed's father] said, "Perhaps you should try to take
your mind off the subject [death and dying] for awhile and get
some sleep."

It was dark and I was lying outside on cold soil in a ditch.
There were tall, gray slabs of stone all around me. I knew that
my brother and sister were lying in other ditches not far from
mine. Every few seconds I would hear a horrible, piercing cry
that slowly died out. Trembling with fear, I thought to myself,
"Soon it will be one of us." Then I jerked awake and found
myself in bed.

Many weeks had passed since I discovered death. The days
went by all right. It was at night when I was again haunted by
thoughts of death. When I was able to fall asleep, I often had
dreams like this one, which was my vision of the Day of Judgement.

Revision:

He said, "Perhaps you should try to take your mind off the subject
for awhile and get some sleep."

It was dark and I was lying outside on cold soil in a ditch.
There were tall, gray slabs of stone all around me. I knew that
my brother and sister were lying in other ditches not far from
mine. Every few seconds I would hear *someone let out* a horrible,
piercing cry that slowly died out. Trembling with fear, I thought
to myself , "Soon *we will all be lifted up and will never be able to
see each other again.*" Then I jerked awake and found myself in
bed. *I was scared.*

*This dream which was my earliest conception of the Day of
Judgement was only the first of many such dreams that I would have.
Every night for the next few months I found that I could think of
nothing but death until I was able to fall asleep.*

Khursheed's META helps me to focus my reading on the changes that he thinks important. I need it to limit what I am to look at: no revision can fix everything that could be fixed. The reworking of the Day of Judgement paragraph is a response to my written criticism on the first draft that the time sequence was unclear.

Writing teachers face a dilemma. Our college freshmen have good ideas, yet they are fragile, easily discouraged creatures who are not yet able to write as well as we might wish. How should we read their papers? How can we simultaneously criticize their writing and support their compositional efforts? In my classroom I have found that METAs partially resolve this dilemma. By highlighting—and affirming—student intentions, METAs help readers distinguish goals from achieved written results: they help students monitor what they have written, and they help the teacher understand what students have attempted.

Letters of intention help my students write better because those letters are embedded in a pedagogical context that supports them and gives them meaning. When I read style revisions, for example, I depend first upon their accompanying METAs for guidance. But I also depend upon what I know about our collective classroom history: the revision assignment itself; what I said in class about style; what students read about style in our textbook; what I wrote on earlier drafts; what I said in conference; what students' workshop partners said. All constrain what I see when I read. All affect how I interpret the texts before me. METAs are grounded in the way that I teach, and it is the way that I teach that determines how I read.

At the end of every semester, students tell me that the METAs were "the best part of the course." They tell me that they have learned to be better readers—to be better monitors of their own writing. I would like to believe that what is true for most is true for all, but I know that it is not. METAs do help most students become better readers. Students like Charlie, Murry, and Khursheed benefit by thinking on paper about their intentions: METAs help them internalize the standards necessary to control their own production. A few students, however, resist systematic reflection on their own work; for them, linguistic self-monitoring is too subtle an art. METAs aren't for everyone. And maybe writing isn't either.

10 Interpreting Student Writing

Janice M. Lauer
Purdue University

My responses to students' writing are multiple, adapting to the changing contexts, shifting needs, and varied tempos of the writer's progress. I am coach, setting contexts, offering strategies, and engaging students in interactive practice. I am co-creator, teasing out students' incipient meanings. I am dialoguer, echoing, questioning, challenging. I am evaluator, assessing goals reached. Let me illustrate these interpretive practices through several dialogues between a student (*S*) and instructor (*I*), which take place during the writing of the first paper. In this first writing experience of the course, students have the opportunity to investigate the ways in which one of their environments influences their development. As they write this paper, they create different "pretexts" (written pieces of planning), drafts, and revisions, engaging in either written or oral dialogue with their instructor as their paper evolves. During the class periods, they also interact with peer groups, trying out strategies to guide their work and collaborating on planning, drafts, and revisions. The dialogue presented here captures some of this interaction between a student and instructor.[1]

Dialogue 1

This dialogue occurs at the beginning of the first paper.

S: "What do *you* want in this paper?"

I: I'm not surprised you didn't believe me when I said in class that these writing experiences would offer you a chance to reach new understanding about things that are important to you. That's what I want—writing that works for you, that enables you to make sense of your experience, to work with others to create and share new meanings.

S: I never had a writing class like this before. I thought my college course would help me with types of paragraphs and punctuation.

I: It will, but these are means, not ends. The real challenge for you will be to open up to puzzlement, to be willing to struggle with uneasy questions that bother you instead of with safe thesis sentences that you can easily pad with three narrative paragraphs.

S: But how do I go about writing that brings me new understanding?

I: I wish I could give you a neat formula, but none exists. Together with your group you will be using some strategies to guide your efforts.

S: Sounds like work. I'm used to dashing off a paper the night before it's due. I didn't expect to put much time into this class because I have a heavy schedule this term.

I: You're right. This kind of writing takes time. But you might want to ask yourself some questions: Would it be worth your time to learn to use writing for thinking about what matters to you instead of just for meeting assignments?

S: But I don't see how writing can do this.

I: You can only find this out for yourself by using writing to help you raise and answer your own questions.

S: Is this what you meant in class about choosing a subject that puzzles you? In fact, I've been spending time worrying about my family farm. I used to help my dad a lot before coming to college. Now he writes me about selling a large part of our herd. Maybe even selling the farm. I'm torn between staying in college or going home. I'm even having trouble explaining to my roommate why I'm thinking of a career in farming.

I: Your worries about your farm seem to be a good subject for you to tackle because you don't have answers and you won't be satisfied with slick solutions.

S: But how can I sort all this out in a paper?

I: In our next class we'll be working with a strategy that shows you how to begin investigating these worries.

Dialogue 2

This dialogue takes place after the first planning assignment, in which the student uses a strategy to raise questions that initiate his search for meaning.

S: Well, as you know from my planning, I chose to work with my farm problems. I used the strategy you showed us to figure out what values of mine were clashing with the situation at the farm. Just pinning this down got me past worrying. My group showed me some inconsistencies between the values

I've taken for granted and what's really happened on my farm. I'm having trouble, though, deciding what question I want to answer. I have written down questions about the financial problems on the farm, about my own goals, and about different kinds of careers in agriculture. I have even questioned farming altogether and my relationship with my roommate. The group noticed that one of my questions was a dead end—I could answer it only with yes or no. One person in my group pointed out that I already had an answer to one of my questions.

I: Your group has given you some good responses, but you have to decide which question you think is most pressing to answer. I agree with the person in your group who noticed that one of your questions already implies an answer, which obviously hasn't satisfied you. Your other three questions, though, seem worth pursuing. One of them demands extensive research. Perhaps you should save that for later.

S: I'll think about the other two. But how do I go about answering them?

I: You need to do some exploring, to spin your question around, examining it from several perspectives, creating different meanings. In class you and your group will use some strategies to help you explore. We'll also look at some examples of other writers exploring their questions.

Dialogue 3

This dialogue takes place after the second planning assignment, in which the writer examines his question from several perspectives, using a strategy to help him shift points of view.

S: The question I ended up exploring was this: "What aspects of the situation on my farm are pulling me away from college while at the same time pushing me to stay in college and even to get out of farming altogether?" When I listed the way I see the farm and the way my father does, I kept finding a lot of negatives in my list. Then when I wrote down the changes in the farm since I was a kid, I began to realize that those changes have something to do with my attitude toward the farm now.

I: You're on to something through your exploration. I noticed that your planning mentioned a time when your father sold your pet heifer. What was involved there? Why don't you probe that more deeply.

S: Yes, I'll never forget that. I guess my father and I have different feelings about a lot of things. I'll think more about this.

I: You seemed to have trouble making connections between your problems and other situations.

S: Yes, when I tried to compare my farm to others, I couldn't think of any group it fit in. Sure we had neighbors and I belonged to 4-H but we didn't have a typical farm. I guess I don't know much about other types of farms and their problems. I also thought it was a waste of time to put my farm experience into unusual categories. What good is thinking of my farm as a circus or as a casino?

I: Why don't you give it another try? If you could find a good category, you might profit from the solutions that other farms in this group have used. Maybe something as simple as "small family farms" might work. I was fascinated with your analogies. They seem to reveal your deep attitudes toward your life at the farm. Maybe these feelings are part of your problem.

Dialogue 4

This dialogue takes place after the next planning assignment, in which the writer used a strategy to help him frame a tentative answer to his initial question.

I: I was very interested in the tentative answer you reached.

S: It had never dawned on me that one reason I have such mixed feelings about the farm is that my dad never considered me a partner, just someone to do the work. Even though I feel guilty about leaving home, I don't think it's my responsibility to solve the farm's problems. When I wrote more about the sale of my heifer, I realized my dad never explained to me why he did it or how it fit into the whole running of the farm. Then when I thought about my two analogies, I seemed to be standing outside the farm, looking at it like a show I was watching.

I: Does this understanding satisfy you? Does it answer the question you posed?

S: Yes, but I'm sure it's not the whole story. I'd like to share it with my father so he can see why I think it's important to stay in college to assume a different kind of responsibility for the farm. I have to be careful, though, not to blame him but to let him know I realize he was trying not to burden me.

Dialogue 5

This dialogue takes place after the student has written a first version, with his father as audience.

I: You have made a good start in sharing your insight with your dad. Your letter, however, doesn't allow him to see how you came to this understanding. He may have forgotten the heifer incident. You need to re-create it for him, sharing what you saw and felt. As you do this, you will sharpen your own meaning.

S: That's what my group said. I thought I just had to mention it. I also see now that I have to write more about how I felt about the loss of the bank loan that he didn't tell me about. When I revise I also need to tone down a few phrases. They will only turn my dad off.

I: You're developing some important principles to guide your writing. Your choice of narrative makes sense as a way of drawing your dad into your process of realization. You've invested a lot in this paper. I sense that it's been worth it.

These dialogues illustrate some of my assumptions about writing and learning to write that motivate my responses to students' writing. Let me translate what I have illustrated, capsuling some of my underlying views on composition and its facilitation.

1. I consider "writing to inquire" as a discourse function worth helping students to experience. I have found that when they develop a taste for insight, they are no longer satisfied with merely fulfilling assignments. They may have to use writing in the future to meet deadlines or to get by, but they know the difference.

2. If inquiry begins with enigma and its transformation into guiding questions, then writing as inquiry cannot spring from unexamined or comfortable judgments and theses, whether posed by students or by me. I discovered, in the early days of my teaching, that when my students began with a thesis, they often started with an answer to a question that they had neither raised nor were interested in answering.

3. When my students, as developing writers, in collaboration, raise and answer significant questions, their discourse as new understanding becomes its own end. That writing for them is no longer just an exercise in learning how to write, to master modes such as description or narration, or to improve their control over the conventions means that we as a profession have often turned into ends.

4. In this challenging process, students benefit from having powerful strategies to guide their efforts. I have found that setting stimulating assignments and giving positive feedback are important but not enough. Students deserve the benefit of all four components of the best, centuries-old rhetorical training: the exercise of individual talent, the use of powerful strategies, practice in genuine contexts, and the imitation of models.

5. It is important that students realize that good writing does not exist in the absolute. Writing succeeds when its development,

organization, and style are motivated by its insight, aim, and audience, when its syntactic choices and conventions support these important ends.

6. My writing courses work best as workshops that center on the creation and interpretation of texts. Instead of spending class time teaching principles of style, dissecting models, or engaging students in doing exercises unrelated to their ongoing writing efforts, I try to create environments in which the focus is collaborative work on their evolving texts.

7. I have come to see that my students need opportunities to inquire within a range of discourse communities: in personal environments, in academic courses, and in public communities in which they are situated. Freshman writing courses may be the last opportunity that they have to gain such rhetorical flexibility—to resolve their personal exigencies as well as to reach probable judgments in the complex affairs of their shared political, social, and academic communities. They need to experience the power of writing in all of these areas, to see for themselves both the differing challenges and the similar skills at work in a range of types of discourse.

8. Finally, I have realized that the writing process is an intricate movement of openness and closure, of exploring broadly without coming to judgment prematurely, and of focusing at appropriate moments. A writing class that respects this movement does not force students too early into the linearity and structures of discourse that radically limit and shape understanding. Students need time, space, and collaborative work to engage in playful explorations, lists, diagrams, and plans before shaping texts for readers. My assignments, pacing, and classroom activities therefore affect not only my students' work but, in turn, my interpretive practice. If I schedule too many pieces of writing, I preclude acts of inquiry. If I set writing assignments too narrowly, I prevent some students from raising questions that are meaningful to them, a circumstance with another implication for my interpretive acts. If I dominate the classroom with lectures, I exclude collaborative experience.

These eight assumptions about writing and learning to write govern my hermeneutic practice. How do they influence my reading process? When students are posing questions, exploring, and framing answers, I help them articulate what they find to be significant, praising their successes and encouraging them to stretch beyond limited efforts.

When students are shaping their texts for readers, I echo their texts as intended reader, assisting them in judging the sufficiency and appropriateness of the clues and evidence they have given to guide their readers' interpretations. I tell them how their texts deconstruct for me, showing them what formal expectations they have aroused in me as a reader and where their texts' structures violate those expectations. I point out the interference caused by vague or inappropriate language or conventional mistakes. My final stance as a reader is that of evaluator, not only of the revised text, but of the entire process of inquiry. I make assessments in light of the writer's evolving insight, purpose, and readers.

Students also offer these kinds of responses to each other, thereby developing critical and co-creative habits. Thus the course engages students in an experience of intertextuality: pretexts of a paper's evolution interweave and appear in the finished discourse, students' reading and oral discourse become a part of the fabric of that discourse, and texts from larger discourse communities influence and assert themselves in students' finished papers.

My acts of interpretation are situated in layers of context: in the entire writing course, in the discourse communities of these students, and in the social, political, and professional worlds in which I and my students live. If I confine students to writing in personal contexts, I privilege this expressive writing and fail to empower them to reach new probable judgments in arenas of public or academic discourse. Students find it helpful if their writing courses show them how to move flexibly from expressive to persuasive and expository writing, enabling them to see how their planning, drafting, and revising powers and strategies can be adapted to different discourse purposes and communities.

These differing communities place obligations on me as an instructor. For example, if students write expository (including research) papers in different academic fields for general audiences, they need to know such differences as MLA or APA conventions. I, in turn, need to adjust my responses to student work accordingly, not imposing my own set of professional conventions on all texts or restricting their writing to critical papers on literature. My adaptive reading strategies help illustrate for students the rhetorical nature of discourse.

I am aware that my interpretive practices place more emphasis on the unique value of each process of inquiry than on the cumulative value of a portfolio. I prefer to read, dialogue about, and assess texts in progress, including final drafts, than to confine myself to a holistic assessment of completed work at the end of a course. I do not thereby criticize either portfolio or holistic grading, but rather distinguish my practice from them. Nor am I uninterested in students' development. In conferences, students and I discuss their progress, examining expanding portfolios, which contain each of their "papers" (all the writing as the paper evolved), noticing continuing problems and improvements, and tracing difficulties with finished discourse back to earlier pretexts. I do not, however, delay commentary or evaluation until all work is completed. Using analytic evaluation with each writing process has allowed me to show students their achievements in different kinds of writing, each of which poses a different set of challenges which cannot be easily equated in a portfolio judgment.

These acts of interpretation—mine and the students'—form an important part of the social conditions that drive student writing, conditions which are, in turn, motivated and shaped by my theories of writing and teaching and my own experience as a writer. These are influences which I can see at the moment; I cannot now conceptualize other assumptions and social structures which compel and constrain my hermeneutic of texts.

I have yet to articulate a final assumption of mine—that teaching writing, especially responding to students' texts, is a moral act, high in my hierarchy of values. For students, reaching higher levels of literacy is a liberating achievement with important consequences for both individuals and the communities in which they are situated. Helping students to raise and answer questions, to become inquirers, able to go beyond their own knowns and share new understanding, remains for me a responsibility worth a life's dedication.

Notes

1. For a complete description of this strategy and for examples of students using it, see Lauer, Janice M., Gene Montague, Andrea Lunsford, and Janet Emig, *Four Worlds of Writing*, second edition (New York: Harper and Row).

III Encountering Ethical Responsibilities

The writers in this section—John Flynn, Charles Bazerman, Lisa Ede, and Stephen Kucer—concern themselves with the ethics of reading student papers. As they point out, when we examine our interpretation of student papers and the kinds of responses we choose (and sometimes feel constrained) to give students, we discover just how complex a task lies before the composition teacher.

John Flynn expresses frustration with the pedagogy of authoritarianism, that method of teaching which unyieldingly insists students satisfy rigorous but vague professorial expectations. A European historian and composition instructor, he advocates what his wife, Elizabeth Flynn, has called a feminine perspective to teaching writing—one that is helpful, open, and constructive in its approach to students. As he demonstrates in his narrative about working with a "near-to-finishing Ph.D. candidate," often a nurturing attitude toward students, coupled with high expectations for them, helps them to discover their own potential. Student anxiety is lowered when expectations are clear, when revision is possible, and when a teacher makes him- or herself available for conference. And only when anxiety is lowered can learning take place. Whether one is working as a teacher in a composition class or a philosophy class, Flynn contends that to be an effective writing teacher one must be a facilitator and model; most of all, one must care passionately about students and the pursuit of ideas.

Like Flynn, Charles Bazerman sees the tremendous responsibility the teacher has in the writing classroom. No matter what methods one uses to try to displace the reading of student papers onto others, the teacher remains in the power position and, inevitably, students write to communicate to that teacher/evaluator. Therefore, "[h]ow the student perceives the teacher as an audience will influence what the student will write, with what attitude and with what level of intensity." It becomes the teacher's responsibility, then, to constantly adjust the teacher-student relationship "so as to draw the student into ever more ambitious problems and successful solutions." The classroom thus becomes a complex, dynamic social setting within a larger social context, wherein "[w]e invent what we do and thereby construct an order in this protean world."

Lisa Ede and Stephen Kucer also discuss the competing obligations and moral concerns of responding to student papers. Both raise a significant issue: that we read student papers to discover how successful we have been as teachers. Like Flynn, Ede feels great empathy for her writing students, and yet, as she says, she cannot help but feel that reading freshman composition essays is work. The reason for her feelings is her recognition of the complexity of the task before her. Not only must she question her own predisposition to the text she is about to read (such as knowing that a student has worked hard), but when she reads, it is with an eye toward the kinds of comments she will make. When a student fails to achieve her expectations, then she, too, feels responsible. Finally, with the sheer paper load a composition teacher faces, even a dedicated teacher—maybe especially the dedicated teacher—can feel overwhelmed. No wonder writing teachers, as they read their students' work, begin to feel they are "walking a tightrope of conflicting demands."

As a way to balance these conflicting responsibilities, Stephen Kucer has developed a framework for reading student papers. He reads student papers based on the same criteria he would use to read nonstudent texts: informativity and logic, global and local coherence, intentionality, situationality, and intertextuality. An instructor of literacy theory, he argues that when he finds disruptions in the continuity of a text, he, as the reader, assumes the initial responsibility for repair; the author is to blame only as a last resort. But as he pointedly contends, "to critically evaluate student papers is to evaluate ourselves." Thus we have a love-hate relationship with student texts: whatever evaluation we make of authors as students becomes an evaluation of ourselves as teachers.

11 Learning to Read Student Papers from a Feminine Perspective, II

John F. Flynn
Michigan Technological University

On one level, I want to argue the proposition that gender is a necessary determining condition of my interpretation of reality, a Cartesian existential predicate, so to speak. However, I would also want to argue that the politics of being are always complex, frequently contradictory, and that, more often than not, the condition of gender is complemented and completed by wider circumstances of existence. I would claim that even if we admit gender as a first principle, an essential attribute of being, my view of reality, and my perspective as a reader of student texts, needs to be elaborated by counting other qualifiers. So I would describe myself as a male, working-class, Brooklyn Irish Catholic, social-democrat, feminist, environmentalist, conservative, antifascist, disabled Vietnam veteran, peace activist, and recovered cancer patient. It is because of circumstances such as these that I read headlines such as "Vietnam Vets Found to Have Higher Cancer Rates" with an intensity, more than likely, not shared by the majority of my male and female colleagues in academe. It is because of circumstances such as these that I react strongly to comments made by contemporaries about Vietnam. A male member of my department, for instance, at a cocktail party, once said to me that, although he had not gone to Vietnam, because he was in graduate school at the time, he regretted having missed "his war." His uncles and father had had "their wars" and he had missed his. "And probably missed your cancer, too," I thought to myself, and said that, for my part, "I regretted not having been in graduate school at the time." On another evening, I had to listen to another male faculty member tell how he had "gotten out of the war by staying in school," although he was a strong supporter of Nixon at the time. "And still are, no doubt," I thought to myself. I listen silently, in some potential preholocaust twilight, to such fragments of language while sipping white wine in comfortable and tastefully decorated homes and remember friends who died innocent of adult-

131

hood and the sinful pleasures of middle-class academic life in a time of suburban abundance and indolent comfort. I wonder in what sense language is real and whether or not, our only hope, it can save us. I teach language as a salvation, I read student papers as a faith.

If we accept gender as experienced by an upwardly mobile, working-class male during the 1960s as a condition of my reading of student texts, then I wish to claim my pedagogy as feminine and women as my teachers. I came to teach writing, and then learned to use writing as a teaching means, after having completed my graduate work in modern German history. As with most things in my life, my becoming a teacher of language was unplanned. However, according to my mother, who at eighty-two is one of the last remaining medieval, immigrant Catholics in the Brooklyn neighborhood I grew up in, and who to this day is a Friday eater of fresh fish, a midnight faster for Holy Communion, and an aggressive sidewalk sweeper, I pick my way through the world only by means of divine intercession. Once, at a family holiday dinner when I asked if God had sent me to Vietnam and given me cancer (New Yorkers will no doubt recognize the tone of the genre), my mother answered, "He brought you back and cured you." You will also note, no doubt, that God's gender is not an issue with my mother, nor have I ever raised the question with her.

To continue . . . as an unemployed Ph.D. who refused to contemplate either Law School or Business School, or to follow up the only solid lead I had for gainful employment—a feeler from the CIA—I gladly took a job as a typist-clerk in the then starting-up Ohio State Writing Workshop where Beth had an instructorship. Desperate for clerical help only days before hundreds of students were to arrive, the civil service labor pool at the university being empty, I was hired on the spot for my very shaky typing skills by Sara Garnes, the director.

Built, in part, upon the theoretical foundations of a dissertation by Andrea Lunsford and the social necessity to meet the needs of entering students who lacked the language skills to do university work, the Workshop opened in an underground bunker on Ohio State's new West Campus which was nestled near a bedspring manufacturer and a lifetime-guaranteed muffler works. Sara Garnes was a newly appointed, untenured assistant professor, a mother of two teenage children, and a scholar struggling to publish. She would arrive before eight each day, wrestle with the incredible knots of administrative detail in the midst of hundreds of students, mimeo machines, phones, requests for reports, staff meetings, and leave each evening with a briefcase stuffed full of homework. Her staff were new Ph.D.s, ABDs, part-time people, or local high school teachers between jobs. With the exception of two staff members, all were women. Of the year I spent at the Workshop, what I remember witnessing most, for the first time since leaving my Catholic high school, was an atmosphere, not merely the eccentricity of one individual teacher, in which teachers were actively and heroically committed to the interests of their students.

Days, weeks, disappeared once one entered the bunker at 8:00 a.m. Some time in mid-October, during an afternoon lull in the chaos, Sara came out of her office and introduced me to the young woman with whom she had been conferencing since after lunch. She suggested we go into the instructor's room, a space which had all the fluorescent friendliness of a sales office in a near bankrupt restaurant supply house in the Bronx, and talk. The young woman and I sat at a table piled high with mimeoed handouts and began to talk. She was in the middle of a history dissertation, her time was about to run out, and she was already on an extension. Her dissertation advisor had sent her over to the Writing Workshop for help. He believed she could not write and that she needed remedial help. Her humiliation was obvious, and yet, without recourse, she had come. As we talked, I recalled that we had once both been TAs in a gigantic Western Civilization section years earlier. We had not done any seminar work together, and we had gone to opposite ends of Europe for our dissertation work. I said I would be glad to look at what she had written and see what I could see.

Beth and I both read the chapters she gave to us. Whereas I was speechless in the presence of the confusion, Beth had a language of description whereby one could begin to categorize the problems of organization, argument, claims, evidence. Beth talked to me, I began to acquire the language of the editor, and I talked to the despairing, struggling writer. The task was of personal significance as well, for I had covered much of the same frustrating ground with my own dissertation advisor. Writing had always been my academic strength and yet I could not satisfy my advisor. I met with judgmental rejection, and I would come away from a withering conference over a chapter without the slightest idea of how to revise it to make it satisfactory. I now know, through discussions with my colleague Carol Berkenkotter, that my work was being read by a reader with the conventions of a discipline in mind. I, however, had not yet mastered those conventions and so I could not satisfy the reader. Unfortunately, the reader was, of course, unaware of this problem, nor did he have the language of an editor, nor the skills of a teacher to help me to revise. I wrote, he read and rejected, I rewrote, he rejected and so on until I had something he would accept without my ever fully understanding how I had gotten there—an extremely painful and counterproductive way to produce a piece of writing. This same method was being exercised against our struggling writer, and the effect was devastating. She was trying to learn to write as a historian without anyone willing or knowing how to help her become a historical writer.

This reading experience, for me, concentrated a general dissatisfaction with the pedagogy I had been socialized into from the days of my undergraduate years. It was authoritarian and judgmental, and in large part dishonest. What had become clear to me after I was given full responsibility for teaching undergraduate history courses as a graduate student was that it was simply impossible for anyone to speak in detailed argument about the vast economic, social, intellectual, scientific, and aesthetic developments of an entire culture or any particular national segment of that culture without relying on references. And so a lecture was written from the open books of scholars who had labored long and hard with other books open before them. I began to consider lecturing a form of cribbing and a fraud. Its purpose was apparently to test the students at the end of a period of time on the material you had given them in class, and then to take off points for some obscure omission. It was a defensive pedagogy. Its purpose was to conceal. The audience knew it to be transparently stupid.

The following incident, more than any other that I can remember, illustrates one of the final stages in my frustration with the pedagogy of authoritarianism. I was the graduate reader for a senior professor in the department in an undergraduate course in one of my specialties. The format was lecture. There were to be two exams, in the typical exasperating format for a history class—five identifications, several short answers, and two essays to be written all in an hour from memory based on weeks of lectures and the textbook reading; there was also to be a writing assignment, a book report on a book assigned by the professor from a preselected group of approved scholarly books. I sat in the back of the lecture hall and took notes along with the students. I was expected to grade all the exams. The professor would read the book reports. There was a date set for the book reports and five points were to be taken off the grade for each day the report was late. No instructions were given as to expectations of how a book report was to be done, what it entailed, what an excellent book report looked like. The professor was fearsomely unapproachable by undergraduates. As the deadline neared, a student who sat in the back of the room near me asked if he could talk to me about the book and the book report. I agreed. By some coincidence—he was not a devious man, and in his own way an attractive and admirable person for all of his limitations—the professor had *found out* about our discussion. I put "found out" in italics because I had not been under the impression that I had done anything wrong. I had. In a stormy conference in his office I was told that to discuss the book report with any student was to give that student an "unfair advantage," and that employers and graduate schools relied on grades to judge students, and if they were given an "unfair advantage," how could the judgments be correct! Clearly, all of western civilization hung in the balance. (This is the honest truth, dear reader, whatever your skepticism.) I answered that I thought universities were places where people were supposed to talk about books. Well, yes, but not to anyone's "unfair advantage," evidently. I promised not to talk about books or writing assignments again with his students.

Both Beth and I recognized some similar predicament operating with our now frustrated, near-to-finishing Ph.D. candidate, with one difference. Her advisor, unable to advise, had clearly washed his hands of the whole affair, had sent his student to the Writing Workshop, and was no doubt waiting for the clock to run out for the final and last time, whereupon he could simply say, "Well, she just couldn't get the dissertation written." Our writer friend wrote, we read. Beth read, I read. We would get copy, read it together, then our writer would come over to the house after dinner, we would clear away the dining-room table, and I would begin discussing the text with her in my newly acquired editorial language learned from Beth. We, of course, talked about much, much more. We talked about the nature of historical argument. I argued for the necessity of a theoretical premise for her work, an interpretive structure, that it could simply not be one damn fact after another, that it needed to be integrated from a point of view. What was her historical point of view? She did not know. It was the first time anyone had asked her. How could she write without it? She did not know. We argued theory. How could she write if she did not know Marx, Weber, Horkeimer, Adorno, Marcuse, Mannheim, Christopher Hill. No one ever told her she had to know them to be a historian. What had she been taught? What had I been taught? She wrote, we read, I argued. She was an incredibly hard worker. She rewrote while we read what was new, and wrote what was new while we reread the rewrites. By the spring of the year she had a document that looked like a dissertation, and read like one as well. Her advisor, much relieved evidently, signed another petition for an extension and agreed to pass it on to another member of the committee. The member of the committee he passed it to was a new hire in the department, a mid-career, distinguished scholar in the field of the dissertation.

One sticky summer night the phone rang. The dissertation had been read and rejected by the second reader. She was devastated, despairing. "What had he said?" "He wrote a ten-page critique." "Bring it over and we'll talk about it." What we had spread out on the dining room table sticking to our forearms was a reasoned, detailed critique on both major and minor problems, problems of argument and theory, problems of interpretation, problems of esoteric detail, problems of dates and references, by an experienced scholar, writer, and editor. I was absolutely delighted. I recognized immediately what we had in front of us and what she had to do with it. I told her that for the first time she had gotten a close reading of her work by an expert in the field who was willing to commit his deep reservations about the writing to paper. What she had to do was merely to go to the reader, negotiate all his reservations with him, and she would have a finished dissertation. Immediately, she saw that too. Indeed! She did. After several more desperate extensions she finished an approved dissertation, and received the degree. Shortly after the happy conclusion of this experience, Beth and I moved to Michigan Tech where Art Young and Toby Fulwiler were developing the strategies of writing-across-the-curriculum with a bunch of new assistant professors, Beth among them. Art and Toby had no reservations about hiring a European historian to teach freshman composition. I identified the pedagogy as feminine. I worked with other instructors, mostly women, in the freshman writing program. The approach to students was helpful, open, constructive. We were more experienced writers working with less experienced writers. I described myself to my students as their editor. My purpose was to read their work, give them comments, and allow them to revise. Grades would improve as the writing improved during the course of the quarter. It was not a do-or-die situation with each finished piece. Deadlines were flexible as long as we negotiated them. If they had a pressing midterm in flunk-out freshman chemistry, they should let me know. We could move deadlines. Anxiety decreased. I talked with my students about writing experiences. I wrote with them in class and then shared my comments with them. We shared our journals. We spent the class hours, after we had read our in-class writes to one another, talking about the essays we had read. Under Toby Fulwiler and Randy Freisinger's direction, the composition instructors met weekly and shared their best classroom practices with one another. I made my first professional presentation on writing to my colleagues. They liked it. I began to like teaching in a new way. I was not standing in front of a group of people boring them to tears with material I had cribbed the night before from a text. The classes were planned but spontaneous, there was much free play of language, there was humor. I could relax. I began to use popular film in my classes. I knew a lot of stuff; I had been reading for years and years; it came out in the most relaxed and unpedantic way, naturally, just in the course of talking with the people in the class. They seemed to like it; I liked it. It seemed to be the way to teach that I had been looking for.

All that was in 1979–80. Over the years, as the Humanities Department's needs have changed, I have been asked to assume responsibilities in addition to freshman composition. I have joined the Philosophy Committee and teach courses in Ethics and Technology and the Philosophy of Religion. (I accepted that last responsibility by noting the irony—my mother's fondest hope, never realized, was that one of her two sons would become a priest—of discussing religion, after having been raised a medieval Roman Catholic, from the tradition of western European rationalism.) In the philosophy courses I teach, my method remains the same. It is writing-based. I read books with my students, we keep journals, we do in-class writing, we spend our hours together talking about our reading. The students get to conduct the discussions. They write their examination essays at home or in the library with the aid of references that they cite in the text of their arguments. Revision is possible. The work gets done, the books get read, the discussions are lively; no one sleeps. The students are a pleasure. I like my job.

I read their work critically. I read their work passionately. I argue with them on their papers. I do it as their editor and their teacher. I do it as a conservative male, working-class, Brooklyn Irish Catholic, social-democrat, feminist, environmentalist, antifascist, disabled Vietnam veteran, peace activist, and recovered cancer patient. I do it because I know our lives depend on it.

12 Reading Student Texts: Proteus Grabbing Proteus

Charles Bazerman
Baruch College, CUNY

This has been a hard essay to write. It has unnerved me. My pedagogical schemas and schemes have run up against the ghosts of former students, with resolution on neither side. Writing this essay has been like trying to climb out of a revery with only a theory of communication as a ladder. Lots of luck.

The truths of how we read student papers have remained secret and obscure, hidden in unexamined private experience. How we comment on student essays is an easier subject, visible and open to inspection—and already discussed in numerous studies. But how we read student papers is a deep uncharted ocean, containing creatures we barely imagine until they come into our view. Yet the forces that swirl there are the forces out of which the writing classroom is born and out of which we construct our self-esteem as writing teachers.

Our writing courses are our reactions to our student writing—the "Oh my god, they better take care of this." When we measure the student papers against whatever we believe writing is, we recognize our pedagogical priorities. The course we set for them is the projection of what we think writing ought to be. For these students are the one group of writers we have some putative influence over, the ones who we can make into the people who might write the things we would like to read.

Through the term, our readings of our student papers also provide our psychic rewards and punishments, as we measure the distance the students remain from our ideal writers. But also we are rewarded by watching the emergence of unanticipated people. Through our projections of the way the world is and should be, we catch glimmers of students' projections of what the world is and can be. We become our students' readers. In reading student papers we watch people coming and going, hiding and faking, being and becoming, and sometimes those people are ourselves.

How protean are we as readers? How protean should we be? Where should we stand fast? And what control do we have over our responses? A hard look at classroom realities is called for, but it all seems to be swimming before me. In earlier drafts of this essay I offered a confident vision of the teacher in control of a complex set of relationships, finely tuning mental set and reactive repertoire based on an assessment of the pedagogical process. I will get back to this—I have not totally abandoned my professional arrogance or responsibility—but the more I think and remember and look into myself, the more I see how ramshackle and ad hoc the process is. But honesty is the best policy, so onwards.

For sound institutional reasons and less certain reasons of educational psychology, composition specialists have devoted great energy to the issue of evaluation. But evaluation is a weak and faulted surrogate for reading, for it is the reading of a bureaucrat. We are all bureaucrats of course, functionaries in large educational/political/economic institutions known as universities and administrators of cultural institutions, such as standardized spelling, the direct American Hemingway sentence, and the autobiographical anecdote in support of a thesis statement. But bureaucratic readings call forth only the bureaucrat in the student, as students respond to the kind of audience we offer them. Our institutional address in a liberal arts college guarantees that we will feel tensions with our perpetuation of the constrained life form of bureaucracy, even the bureaucracy of an arts council.

But other things happen in the reading. Other forms of life leak through. Sometimes we as liberal-minded teachers insist on it, saying the students must bring their experience and thought and concerns into the classroom, into the text. We do this because we think students need personally urgent material to propel them to good writing and to reveal its power to master their worlds. But they write this material for us, even as they discover it for themselves. Our demand to the student has created a demand on ourselves to respond to this material. It is not the occasional dramatic revelation of family struggle, criminal activity, or mental anguish that makes the most demand on us, for we all can play the measured adult when the student asks for it. The description of their room, the letter complaining of a minor injustice, the confession of their career goals, or the obviously constructed fiction meant to mask the student's life and to feed what the student perceives of our need for vicarious engagement—these are the texts that most strain our human imagination, that tempt us to the condescension of thoughtless approval, or press us to rejection. How do we place ourselves when we read about their lives? What kind of reader is the student asking for? What kind of reader do we want to be? What kind of reader is best?

A similar issue of placement enters when we as teachers bring into the classroom the future worlds we wish to move the students toward, whether of humanistic literary culture or of the technological corporation. Do we stand with students in naive puzzlement before these arcane communities, or do we embody these communities, rendering judgments on outsiders and setting initiation exercises for neophytes? Or do we stand on the sidelines as coaches and advisers to the students we throw into the fray? What kind of intermediate ground do we create on which we can accept and respond to the students' writing?

The dilemma of placement is, however, not just of our making. Even if we could create a class sealed from the outside world, working with genres unknown and without parallel in the world outside the English class, writing about personally unmoving and unmotivating material, we would still meet the challenge of unexpected constructions of our readership, for each person in that hermetic classroom will make of it what he or she will. Individuals will enter that classroom with a unique history which will shape their perception of and participation in the events that there transpire, and thus they will each want to make of us a creature to fit their own perception and skills.

In conferences and journals of our discipline, writing teachers have told many stories of the dilemmas posed by personal encounters with their students, so I doubt that the issues I raise here will come as news. There seems to be no other form of teaching at the university that creates such a personal bond between student and teacher, that grants the teacher such personal knowledge of a student as a sufferer and maker of his or her own life. Our subject creates the frequent occasions for students to tell us about themselves and to relate to us in a variety of relationships and situations. Both in the content of their writing and in their manner, students present themselves to us with a variety, fullness, and intimacy of revelations. Yet although we have regularly considered our relationship to our students, we have not (until this volume) confronted this relationship in its most central form in the writing classroom—what transpires between teacher and student across the written page.

In order to gain some grasp of our reading processes we must gain some grasp of those relationships. Reading (from all current research) seems to be a highly contextual activity, related to the readers' goals and the readers' schematic representation both of the material of the text and the situation in which the text is presented. What we as teachers think is going on in the classroom, the text, the student, and the worlds that surround will affect how we read the paper, what signals we send to the students about what kind of audience we are, and ultimately how students will write to us. Where we stand and where we wish to move the students will affect our reading and their writing. Yet, as I have already suggested, this classroom world is not only of the teacher's making. If the presence, expectation, and perception of students reorganizes the world on which we are to set our feet, the fixed point from which to read becomes unfixed.

Perhaps one reason we have separated the question of reading from the question of the appropriate relationship with the student is that we have tried to displace the readership of the papers onto others, whether class peers or fictional outsiders, or even very real test-giving outsiders. The teacher then is free to become the editor, facilitator, confidant, to aid the process rather than receive the product. I find these wonderful classroom strategies and would be the last to deny them a major place in our pedagogic repertoire. However, the basic fact of classroom life, which I have seen very few classroom configurations overcome, is that the teacher is the most powerful person in the room, with the authority of the institution and the even more important authority of greater mastery of the skills to be learned.

The value of a piece of writing for the student is deeply shaped by what that student can glean of the teacher's response, directly through comments on the paper, and indirectly through the evolving relationship with the teacher. The student writes to the teacher, and we as teachers have a responsibility to accept that piece of writing according to our best lights. Even when students reject the judgments of their teachers (as I often did as an obstreperous lad), it is against those teachers that the student defines the self. My earliest and most formative impressions of the academic audience that resides in English departments and for whom I now write regularly came from my teachers. The professional voices and self-perception as a writer I developed then (and carry with me still) were in relation to those readers.

Given the importance of the teacher's role in the classroom, students inevitably write to communicate to that teacher. The student's perception of the teacher's level and focus of interest in the student's writing will influence the student's desire and goals in communicating with that teacher. How the student perceives the teacher as an audience will influence what the student will write, with what attitude and with what level of intensity.

Many of these perceptions will depend on the student's past history, but some, we hope, can be influenced by what the teacher communicates in the classroom. The teacher can, of course, communicate salutary lies about the teacher's reading. But I am a terrible liar, and I suspect that teachers' responses are likely to be richer, more useful, more believable, and more consistent with all the relationships and dynamics of the classroom if they are based on real reactions to reading. Thus it is important to consider how we construct ourselves as readers, what influences that construction, and how that construction acts as a variable in student writing. Our reading of student writing forms the basis not just of after-the-fact evaluation of a text, but of the entire dynamic of language production through the term and after. The student carries the class as a consciousness- and skill-shaping experience when he or she steps into new writing situations.

All the complications I have been worrying about for the past few pages are the complications that arise from recognizing the student's contribution in defining the situation in which I read the papers. When I first viewed the subject from my perspective alone, as though I were fully in control of how I read, the problem seemed simpler. And I still think that is the situation that frames the other interactions, for the class is an institutional creation for which I have immediate responsibility. Both the university administration and students hold me to that responsibility.

The interaction that occurs between student and teacher across the student's papers is framed and driven by the reason we have come together in such a contrived dyad: for the students to learn to write better. I do not delude myself that if such a mutually agreed upon (and usually institutionally mandated) purpose did not exist for coming together, the student would have other spontaneous reasons for communicating with me. That does not mean that other relationships that might occur once we are locked into this primary relationship might not develop and possibly be mobilized for pedagogical purposes, but these other relationships must be kept in the perspective of pedagogical responsibilities.

With skill subjects such as writing, mastery comes with solving of increasingly difficult problems. The teacher-student relationship, I believe, should be constantly adjusted so as to draw the student into ever more ambitious problems and successful solutions. Sometimes this is encouraged through various rewards, such as the simple and powerful one of successful communication with another human being. Sometimes this is accomplished by the help of a writing collaborator. Sometimes this is called forth by well-stated expectations, upheld in after-the-fact inspection. Sometimes this is challenged by a curmudgeon. In order to know how to position myself in reading a paper, I must first read the situation—the kinds of lessons we have been working with, the kinds of tasks set in the assignment, the kind of student, the processes and problems likely to be on the student's mind, and my ongoing pedagogical relationship with the student. Sometimes this positioning of myself is an obvious and unreflective outcome of events leading up to the reading of the paper, but sometimes it is a matter of conscious adjustment. Only when these fundamental issues of relationship have been settled, do I know what my goals in reading are. Most generally my goals are usually to respond in some way to the student writing, but what kind of response is appropriate in each case? Would it be most useful to this student at this moment and in this situation to give advice concerning surface editing? Or do I want the student to reconceive the problem of the paper in some deeper way? Do I simply want to raise the student's consciousness about what he or she has achieved? Or do I wish to communicate my pleasure as a reader of a finished product? Must I remind the student that something more is expected, whether grammatical propriety, density of detail, or intensity of concentration?

When I know what I want to do, I know how to read, whether with a proofreader's eye, a textual analyst's structural vision, an editor's helpful hand, a professorial challenge, a marker's red bludgeon, or a companionly ease. Each of these stances invokes separate reading processes. In each way of reading I look for and respond to different things. I generate different thoughts that are reflected in different comments on the paper or in different responses to the student sometime later in the term.

The situation of reading is also remolded by the paper itself. As the paper offers various things for my consideration and demands certain kinds of responses from me, I come to reconsider the right level at which to respond to it. Sometimes I must read certain papers or whole sets of papers through before I know how to position myself, how to read them. And some papers manage to break through my crusted middle age to my own passions, anxieties, concerns, and sense of surprise.

Reading student papers thus shares several features with all forms of reading. It is a situated, goal-directed, schema-laden interaction, negotiated between the reader's entering conceptions and the writer's invitations and imperatives embodied in the text. It is special insofar as the teacher's pedagogical vision, goals, and role define the reader's opening stance; the student's needs and attitudes generate special kinds of texts; and the educational enterprise creates and defines the interaction.

Trying to make sense of the ghosts of students who haunt me as I write this, I see some who within our interactions lived entirely within the anticipatable life of the classroom: students who wanted to avoid the sin of grammatical error and happily displayed their competence for my correction; other students who without enthusiasm would produce pro forma work and would have been pleased with my indifference and a passing grade. The former I could easily cooperate with, then introduce into the more powerful mysteries of writing; the latter challenged me to find sparks of fire as I read. Sometimes I failed, leaving sleeping souls asleep. There were the students who entered the classroom with the fire to learn and would gallop down any path I pointed to; as I read I could watch how far their discoveries and inventions exceeded the poverty of the assignment.

Other students in their writing challenged the classroom life: students whose papers in their shoddiness showed contempt for the enterprise of classroom composition or in their otherness refused to be harnessed to the classroom. The writing of both such students often evokes a dual kind of reading within me, which I must then convey to the student: the pedagogue's response that this is not what I asked for or will accept and the confidante/adviser's response of attempting to understand why this student seems unwilling or unable to engage in the enterprise. I look for what students may not understand about the classroom enterprise or how their compelling passions may be harnessed into the classroom forms of life.

And then there are the students who bring into the student-teacher classroom life the overflow of their already powerful lives: students who look for confirmation of their worldviews, students who are struggling with problems and ideas, students coming to recognize the quiet outrages that have constrained their lives, students who have a depth of wisdom or feeling that illuminates my own soul, students who embody in their behavior and expectations cultures strange and enlightening to me. Each of these students calls forth a complex response in the reading, a response that tries to rise to their human needs and express my own human discovery while still maintaining the editor-collaborator's eye for possible revision and the teacher's sense of the lesson plan.

Looking back over the text I have written and comparing it to the editor's call for papers, I sense I have sidestepped the requested account of the particulars of what happens when I sit down with a stack of papers. I have not presented a protocol of my reading process nor an interpretation of the papers nor even a description of my state of mind. I have externalized the problem from seeing reading as a matter of my psychology and cognition or as a hermeneutic endeavor. Rather I have seen it as a matter of interaction in a complex social setting. My thoughts have been of how I conceive the situation, the dynamics that seem to shape and reshape the situation, and the concerns I have as I participate in the situation.

Perhaps the abstraction might have been reduced by turning it into a single case study, but since I have been on leave for an extended period and will not return to the classroom for another eight months, that option would be only a fiction. Moreover, any particular account I gave would move in and out of the same ground I covered here of the classroom project, the history and personality of the student, my history and personality, our joint history in the classroom, and our evolving interaction on all these grounds. Texts are not simply words, but forms of interaction, having meaning to participants. The best I could do would be to share that interaction. I would find it difficult simply to tell the story of myself with a disembodied set of papers. Evaluating examination papers, as I suggested earlier, is a different and relatively impoverished task.

My current distance from the classroom makes it hard to know what honesty there is in this account. My memory reminds me that sometimes I have cut corners and sometimes my readings have been moved only by the desire to avoid the embarrassment of facing the class the next hour with no papers to return.

It is even harder to know the impact that writing this essay will have on my future readings. Here I have done little more than hazard some observations on an only vaguely known process, but by so doing I have given my consciousness a more defined shape than it had previously. Articulating what we do changes what we do. Committing ourselves in public about what we do also challenges our own behavior. In teaching writing, I thought I was preaching what I practiced, but I found equally that I came to practice what I preached. We invent what we do and thereby construct an order in this protean world. To get the truth from Proteus, Menelaus must himself adopt the guise of a sea creature, catch the changing god in his lair at the verge of the sea, and hold on through the god's many transformations. Only then will the god assume a stable shape and reveal the way home across the sea.

13 On Writing Reading and Reading Writing

Lisa Ede
Oregon State University

"What does it mean and feel like to read student texts? What are the preconceptions, routines, constraints, and joys?" These questions, posed by the editors of this collection, first startled, and then intrigued, me. Like many teachers of composition, I suspect, I had not really thought much about how I read student essays—I just did it. Since the editors' guidelines encouraged "personal descriptions of and reflections on how [teachers] read student writing," I decided to keep a long-term journal where I would both describe and explore that previously unexamined experience.

I kept that journal during a term when I had two main teaching responsibilities: I taught a section of Oregon State University's required freshman composition class, and I supervised students working as writing assistants in the Writing Lab at Oregon State's Communication Skills Center, which I direct. Almost immediately, I realized that the experiences of reading the essays of the students in my composition class and my tutors' journals differed so significantly that it hardly seemed appropriate to use the same word to describe both activities. Investigating these differences has taught me a great deal about the complexity of my own reading processes and of my rhetorical situation as teacher. In the following, I would like to share the results of that investigation with you.

Reading Writing Assistants' Journals

This is fun. No matter how busy I am, I always look forward to reading my writing assistants' journals. Last quarter was a particularly frenetic term for me, yet I noted in my own journal near midterms that reading my thirteen writing assistants' journals over the weekend would be a reward for all I had been through (even though it would obviously take a substantial amount of time). I know most of the

147

writing assistants, who are undergraduates at Oregon State with quite a diverse range of majors, very well; some have tutored for two or three years. The center's Writing Lab Coordinator, Lex Runciman, and I encourage a jokey, collaborative, yet also committed, atmosphere in the Writing Lab, with few distinctions made between writing assistants and the professional staff. The informality and commitment carry over into the writing assistants' journals, which reflect their diversity, unpretentiousness, and enormous wisdom. Their journals always interest me, and they also help keep me informed about what is going on in the lab.

Both the writing assistants and I know that their journal is a relatively minor determinant of their grade for the course. If they are responsible, committed, and hard-working (and most are), they will get an A for the independent study course they enroll in. Despite this, the writing assistants take the journal seriously, perhaps because it allows them to disentangle some of the complexities and reflect on both the rewards and frustrations of tutoring, and also, possibly, because they simply enjoy writing. They tell me that they like the freedom the journal provides—a freedom that exists both because of the relatively minor role the journal plays in the grading for the course and (since there is, of course, no single correct way to write a journal) its genre. I provide the guidelines, such as the caution that the writing assistants should do more than just describe tutoring sessions, but encourage diversity and self-expression. The writing assistants seem to relax and enjoy their journals, and they know, I believe, that I enjoy reading them.

Though I always write marginal and final comments in my writing assistants' journals, just as I do in essays or in-class exams, I never think of or describe reading them as grading. The writing assistants will not be revising their journals—that goes against the essential nature of journal writing—so I feel the freedom to make my comments relaxed and spontaneous. I don't worry if I am giving just the right advice—I am not even giving advice, just responding. I write lots of questions, lots of personal responses like "how wonderful" or "what a perceptive observation." Few errors appear in their journals, other than the kinds of scribal errors that inevitably occur when you write quickly, so I don't need to split my attention between form and content to try to note them. And I never write comments only because I feel I ought to; I write simply what occurs to me as I read.

The experience of reading my writing assistants' journals feels very much like most of the reading that I voluntarily do for pleasure or for my research. I come to the text with a real reason for reading, and I anticipate either learning something I need to know or just enjoying myself. I read actively in the sense that I am always making predictions, asking questions, establishing connections, using a statement in the text to stimulate my own thoughts, thinking of times when I have thought or experienced something described in the text. But I know that my response can be holistic and synthetic. I do not need to push myself to provide a detailed analysis of the quality of the text or suggestions for revision. I can generally immerse myself in the very pleasurable act of reading.

Reading Freshman Composition Students' Essays

This is work. I learned it was work when I started graduate school and heard TAs and faculty members complain about the papers they had to grade over the weekend. The classroom was where you had fun; conferences with students were important and interesting; and they really could make a difference. But reading student essays—that, I learned via my acquisition of what Clifford Geertz would call the common sense culture of English departments, was work.

I still remember my first experience reading student essays. I was enrolled in a required course for new TAs, and we were given a set of four essays to grade as practice. (Why didn't the instructor have us write essays ourselves and respond to one another? Was it because of an implicit assumption that student texts are not real texts, that the interaction between text and grader—and it was clear that, in the practice session at least, our role was that of grader, not reader—was most crucial, not that between text, writer, and grader?) The prospect filled me with fear. Were my standards high enough? Would I write the right comments? I knew that I was supposed to balance criticism with praise, but in attempting to do this I was guided less, I believe, by the essays before me than by some platonic notion of the appropriate number and kinds of comments to be made. The instructor gathered our sets of graded essays, sharing effectively or ineffectively graded essays with the class. I can still see the red face and discomfort of one student whose comments were deemed too generous, too "touchy feely."

I began this discussion of my reading of my freshman composition students' essays with my own academic training, rather than with the class itself, because one of the things I learned, through reflecting about the process of reading my writing assistants' and composition students' journals and essays, was what a powerful influence that training still exerts on my reading of student essays, especially those written by beginning writers. My expectations, my sense of conflicting allegiances (to my students and to the standards of the profession), the way I talk about reading these essays with my husband, friends, and colleagues, all have been subtly affected by this earlier acculturation.

The realities of my classroom situation also encouraged my conviction—one repeated with discouraging frequency in my journal—that reading my students' essays felt more like work than anything else. I had an overenrolled class of twenty-eight students, so that the simple number of essays to read required time and energies that were in short supply. The following journal entry gives a good sense of the pressures I felt and how they affected my reading:

Tuesday, December 2

> I can't help it: reading student essays is work. At least that's how it feels right now. I worked almost every moment over Thanksgiving, and still I wasn't able to get my students' essays read. So it's Tuesday night and I've got 28 essays I have to read by Thursday. The only problem is that I also have to prepare for class, get ready for my trip on Thursday (I'll be heading to the airport with, of course, another set of student essays to grade on the plane and in motel rooms) and handle the usual administrative stuff at the center. This is not the ideal situation/frame of mind to have when reading student essays. I feel like I've got to hunker down, whip through these essays as quickly as possible, hold myself back, be efficient. As I read their essays—trying to become their ideal reader?!—I'll be thinking as much of me (my time, my life, my tiredness, all I have to do) as of them.

Why had I not simply read my students' essays at the start of the Thanksgiving vacation? Partly because, like my student writers, I tend to procrastinate. But also, I believe, my common-sense understanding of the culture of English departments reminded me that reading student essays ought to come after my "real" work—the work that figures most strongly in our reward system—scholarship. So I wrote a conference paper first, and then began reading my students' essays.

Another obvious influence on my reading of my students' essays was the make-up (twenty-three men and five women) and nature of the class. These students were taking the class because they were required to, and even though all but two were first-quarter freshmen, they seemed already to have heard both how hard and yet how irrelevant it was. (The male students, in particular, appeared reluctant, bored. Almost all pre-engineering, science, or business students, they seemed to reinforce one another's sense that caring about writing just wasn't cool.) My students' first in-class essay revealed their lack of confidence, equation of good writing with correct writing, and perception that writing requires the mastery of an arcane series of interconnecting rules, which somehow they never "got." It also revealed them to be the weakest group of writers I had encountered since I had begun teaching at Oregon State.

Once, when thinking in a different context about the teacher's role as reader of student essays, I tried to imagine how beginning writers struggling to pass their college or university's required freshman composition course view their teachers. Reaching into my Catholic past, I wrote the following litany, murmured (in my imagination) by countless students to their teachers:

> Oh invisible representative of the
> universal audience,
> grant me knowledge of your ways.
>
> O chalice bearer of culture, let me
> not offend your
> refined sensibilties.
>
> Oh gate-keeper of class and
> social success, look not
> too closely at my error.
>
> O font of knowledge and prince of
> logic, have mercy
> on me in my inexperience.
>
> Oh final arbiter, whose world is not
> my world, whose
> reason passes understanding,
> Grant me peace.

(Ede 1980, 8)

I worked constantly in my class to change that image, trying to be encouraging and collaborative, emphasizing to my students how much they already knew about language and writing, trying to get them to trust their own and their peers' responses to their writing. When I received their first set of essays I felt a sense of oppression and conflict, even before I read them. I knew that my comments, no matter how carefully worded, would discourage many. Writing in my journal after class on the day I returned these first essays I described my students' "silence, terrible silence." Looking back, I see that in a way my own sense of self was as much on the line as theirs. I wanted the class to go well: I wanted my students not only to improve as writers but to like the class. My comments on their essays would, I feared, break the upward momentum—the increased self-confidence, optimism, and enthusiasm—I had struggled to generate in my students. As I read their first essays, then, I found myself worrying about their response to my responses, even before I had written them.

Although I read my students' essays out of class, then, I cannot isolate that reading from classroom dynamics or deny the impact of those dynamics on my reading. Individual relationships with students also influence my reading. There is an entry in my journal, for instance, describing my anxiety as I prepared to read a particular student's fourth essay. His first two had been quite weak, perfect examples of theme writing, but suddenly with the third everything clicked—we celebrated together in my office as I read the rough draft. What if the third essay were a fluke? What if the fourth were just like the first two? I read his essay nervously, hoping it would be successful, a predisposition that I am afraid I didn't bring to the essays of all my students, like the two who sat in the back of the class laughing and passing notes like ninth graders or the one who missed two weeks of class so he could play golf.

I note often in my journal how physically tiring it is to read my freshman composition students' essays because I must concentrate so intensely and balance so many competing roles and obligations—I must try to respond/critique/motivate/evaluate, and sometimes even counsel, all at once. I also have to restrain my impulse simply to edit their essays. Throughout, even if I am skimming an essay to form a general impression before reading again and commenting, a practice I often follow, I am always reading with an eye toward what comments I will write in response. My reading of their essays is, in a sense, contaminated with or directed by the writing I will do in response, even before I begin writing. In responding, I in a sense appropriate my students' texts with my comments, so that when I read a revision I am reading to see how *we* have done. And when *we* fail to improve an essay I fail along with the student—unless, of course, it is clear to me that he or she is not motivated, is not really trying to improve as a writer. (Another kind of failure for me.) When I read revisions, then, I am always in part reading to determine not only my students' ability to revise successfully but my own effectiveness as a teacher as well.

I am aware of having implicit standards as I read: the genre we call the essay allows both my students and me less freedom than does the journal. Although I try to respond freely as a reader, with comments similar to those made in response to my writing assistants' journals, I am more constrained. There are certain macro- and micro-problems I must note if they occur, if only with a check. I am, after all, teaching a class that is part of that amorphous thing called a writing program. I have an obligation to my colleagues to follow our shared practices and standards, however loosely defined. Because I do not give letter grades on essays, I must be sure that my comments clearly indicate an essay's strengths and weaknesses. I am also aware that I tend to overcomment, so I am always asking myself as I read if I really need to make this or that point. I am aware of a tension between wanting to push myself to reach closure—to make the kind of judgment about an essay that will direct the rest of my reading and guide my comments—and maintain an open perspective.

One indication of the inextricable way in which *reading* my students' essays and *evaluating* them are connected in my experience was my startled realization, as I sat writing in my journal one day, that I always refer to reading essays from any composition class, beginning or advanced, as grading—even though I have not put individual letter grades on student essays for at least ten years. (I use a variation of portfolio grading.) So embedded was this connection that I never perceived any contradiction or dissonance in my continued use of this term.

If I have given the impression that reading my freshman composition students' essays is a constant agony for me, that I never lose myself with delight in their writing, that is, of course, quite wrong. I would not continue teaching composition if that were the case. But when I consider the experience generally—when I recall what it feels like to read a set of twenty-eight essays, some very weak, some competent, and some very good, every other week or so, with ten to fifteen revisions appearing every week—my overall impression still is that it feels like work.

On Writing Reading and Reading Writing

What does it mean to say that reading my freshman composition students' essays feels like work, while reading my writing assistants' journals does not?[1] It is possible, of course, to interpret this statement politically. Instructors who teach four sections of composition each term (as, I am sorry to say, instructors in my department do) *know* that reading students' essays is work. (Few have the luxury of assigning journals, given the number of papers they must read, although some do.) They know, too, that they form a pool of cheap labor used to "process" students who must complete one or more required courses. And their own reading of student writing is inevitably influenced by the sheer number of essays, research papers, and technical reports *they* must process in a given evening or weekend.

Thanks (?) to my numerous administrative duties and chairperson's good will, I generally teach a single composition class each term. For me, then, reading my freshman composition students' essays is work in a different sense: it is work (exertion, effort, frustration, sometimes reward) in the same way that most of my own writing is work. In fact, I realized one late night, after reading a set of essays, that in many respects reading my freshman composition students' essays feels more like writing than reading.

I can perhaps best explain what I mean in this ambiguous statement by referring to Jim Raymond's wonderfully titled textbook, *Writing (Is an Unnatural Act)* (1980). For me, writing (other than list-making, some routine tasks, and most personal letters) is in many senses unnatural. When I write I become overly self-conscious, and sometimes overly conscious of my readers. I worry about my ideas and fret over sentences and paragraphs. I struggle to balance a complex, interconnected series of processes and roles as I simultaneously plan, draft, and revise. I become acutely aware of my body—I am tired, hungry—and of time. I become intensely involved with my writing: so much is at stake. It is the unnaturalness of this intensity, its differentness from much of my daily life, that makes writing both so hard and so rewarding. Even when my writing goes well as, luckily, it sometimes does, the pleasure I feel—like that of a dancer or musician performing well—is also in a sense unnatural.

My experience of reading is usually not characterized by the same intensity, self-consciousness, or struggle. It is a more even, balanced experience, one where, even if I am reading a difficult work under time pressure, I somehow relax into my reading. Furthermore, since my reading process is hidden from me in a way that my writing process is not, reading does not present the same self-challenges. Though my reading always, of course, tests my ability to analyze, synthesize, and interpret, I do not confront my success or failure as directly as I do when I write. My process of reading seems to share more of the rhythms of my daily life.

Given these admittedly subjective descriptions of my "normal" reading and writing processes, it is clearer, I hope, why reading my freshman composition students' essays actually does feel more like writing reading than reading writing. There is the same self-conscious-ness, the same tension, intensity, and multiple conflicting roles. Because I cannot separate reading my students' essays from responding in writing to them and also evaluating them, I must push myself to define my ideas, to achieve closure, to test myself, even before I write my comments. I cannot just read or respond holistically; I must be analytical. But my commitment is not just to the accurate analysis of an essay's strengths and weaknesses; it is to the very real student who wrote it. In trying to balance these commitments—and those to my colleagues, the writing program, and the other students in my class— I am constantly, if generally unconsciously, walking a tightrope of conflicting demands.

I hope that my contrast between these two reading experiences and my assertion that reading my freshman composition students' essays feels more like writing than reading is not interpreted as an attempt to reintroduce the outdated view of writing as active and reading as passive. For a variety of reasons, writing generally does feel more active to me than reading, but, as researchers in reading have demonstrated, that is primarily because of differences in the way each is performed. Both reading and writing involve the active creation of meaning, in different but complementary ways.

No, the importance of this observation lies, I believe, in my long overdue recognition of the critical role that social, political, and ideological forces play in my reading. In a general theoretical sense, I had already recognized this, of course, as would anyone who had kept up with current literary and rhetorical theory. But I had conveniently bracketed the experience of reading my students' essays from that understanding. I don't think I have been alone in performing this interesting bracketing operation. Although researchers in a variety of related fields have been calling for a greater attention to the psychological and, especially, to the social and ideological dimensions of writing and reading, those of us in composition studies have, with the exception of some ethnographic researchers, generally tended to bracket the reading we do as teachers from that exploration. The effect of erasing those brackets is to make an activity that seemed natural, inevitable, and commonsensical suddenly difficult and problematical. Which, of course, it has been all along.

My reflections on my experience of reading my writing assistants' journals and students' essays leads me, then, to urge us all to pay greater attention to the ways in which psychological, sociological, and ideological dynamics influence the reading and writing we do as teachers. And although I have been focusing on my experience as a writing teacher here, I do not think the implications of my analysis are necessarily limited to composition studies. What is the difference, for instance, between reading a novel for pleasure and as preparation for a class? And what happens when a teacher reluctantly but determinedly reads a favorite classic novel for the seventeenth time so he or she will be prepared for class discussion? Could that experience of self-required rereading feel as much like work for that teacher as reading my freshman composition students' essays does for me at times?

Because those in our profession are highly trained readers, we have, I believe, come to see ourselves as more or less exempt from the forces that we know influence the reading of others, much as some doctors detach themselves from the world of the ill and the dying. And just as doctors' training has (at least until recently) encouraged this withdrawal from the world of illness and death, so too has our training (at least until recently?) encouraged us to see ourselves as ideal readers. Even before keeping a journal on my reading of student texts last term, for instance, I was aware that my own psychological, and even physical, state (how happy I am, how my research is going, how rested and healthy I feel) affected my reading of student essays, as did my personal response to them as individuals. But I implicitly saw these as lapses to be remedied rather than as an inevitable, though still problematical, part of my reading process.

What happens when we cannot ignore the psychological, sociological, or ideological forces at play in the reading we do as teachers or professionals in our field? Such situations occur, for instance, when as reviewers or members of editorial boards we read manuscripts for journals like *PMLA* or *College English*. Our response, of course, has been to assure anonymity through blind readings, as though reviewers cannot identify most authors through self-citation references or at least determine what "camp" they are in by analyzing the essay's strategies and arguments. A similar, though somewhat different, process occurs if we participate in holistic readings of exit exams or statewide competency tests. We may not know students' names, but their essays include social and class-related traces that inevitably influence our reading and responses. Nor can renorming our exhortations from table leaders necessarily erase the consequences of physical fatigue or psychological ennui.

As I indicated earlier, my reflections on my reading of my writing assistants' journals and freshman composition students' essays have caused me to perceive an activity that once seemed somehow natural, inevitable, and commonsensical as suddenly both complex and problematical. I am, I must admit, both startled and dismayed by my previous naiveté. Why could I not see all this before? But then I remember Clifford Geertz's reminder in "Common Sense as a Cultural System" (1983) that there is always "something . . . of the purloined-letter effect in common sense; it lies so artlessly before our eyes it is almost impossible to see" (92). Paradoxically, the act of withdrawing into myself and using my journal as a means of introspection has helped me to see a network of sociological, political, and ideological connections and influences that has been there, purloined-letter-like, all along.[2]

Notes

1. If my own experience is typical, many students enter graduate programs in English studies because of a deep love of reading. "What an ideal profession," we think. "My job won't be work at all, but pleasure." Even those of us who enjoy our work, as I do, recognize the naiveté in this view. Its lingering effects account, I believe, for at least some of my surprise at discovering that reading my freshman composition students' essays feels like work. It *is* work, after all.

2. This last statement is at least in part an untruth. For although my original observations about my reading of student texts did occur in isolation mediated only by my journal, I talked with several colleagues as I worked on this essay. Particularly helpful to my understanding of the implications of my observations were discussions with my colleague Susan Merritt, whose contributions I would like to acknowledge here. Thanks, Susan.

Works Cited

Ede, Lisa. "Audiences, Paradigms, Role Playing, and Evaluation: Some Implications." *Kansas English*, 65 (1980): 8–10.

Geertz, Clifford. *Local Knowledge: Further Essays in Interpretive Anthropology*. New York: Basic Books, 1983.

Raymond, James. *Writing (Is an Unnatural Act)*. New York: Harper and Row, 1980.

14 Reading a Text: Does the Author Make a Difference?

Stephen B. Kucer
University of Southern California–Los Angeles

Several years ago, I had a rather heated discussion with a colleague of mine about the appropriate manner in which student papers were to be read. During our discussion, my colleague proceeded to emphasize the importance of responding to surface structure errors so that students would become aware of the conventions which they were violating. As a faculty member in a reading program, my thinking on this issue had been greatly influenced by psychological and reader-response theories of text processing as well as by the research on the cognitive similarities between reading and writing.

Drawing upon my understanding of text processing, I suggested that a focus on the surface structure did not reflect effective and efficient reading behavior. The work of a number of researchers (Smith 1982; Goodman 1985a, 1985b; Rumelhart 1985; Kohlers 1972) has clearly documented that readers focus on meaning when interacting with print and rely as much as possible on nonvisual information when engaged in this interaction. The use of nonvisual information, or conceptual and linguistic background knowledge, allows the reader to judiciously select or sample only a minimal amount of visual information. In fact, it is this reliance on nonvisual information which allows readers to process print as quickly as they do.

I then suggested that my colleague was engaged in aberrant reading behavior when she focused to such a degree on the surface structure. She was, in a sense, reading student papers differently than other texts which she encountered in the world. At the same time, this type of reading behavior encouraged students to write in an aberrant manner. When responses to student papers consist primarily of the marking of errors, students quickly come to believe that it is a flawless surface structure which is of prime importance. The result is students who lose sight of the communicative and exploratory nature of written language.

All this is not to deny that there are dimensions in my reading of student papers which do not exist when I read other types of texts. However, these dimensions are rarely surface structure in nature. Instead, they involve my responsibility as the course instructor for the insights and knowledge which the papers display. In many ways, student papers represent my success or failure as a teacher as much as they represent what the students have learned about the topic, for it is my course which provides the framework for student thinking and writing. It is in this sense that my reading of, or perhaps I should say my responding to, student papers is unique.

It is just these similarities and differences in reading student and nonstudent papers that I explore in this essay. I begin with a discussion of some of the invariant processes which cognitive psychologists have suggested are involved in all acts of reading and how I make known these processes to my students. Cognitively speaking, I discuss how reading is reading, regardless of who the writer happens to be. Additionally, I discuss the unique dimensions of responding to student papers and how my responses are frequently addressed more to myself as teacher then they are to my students as writers. Affectively speaking, I discuss how, when the author is my student, it does make a difference in my reading.

Reading Is Reading

In one sense, the fact that the author happens to be a student is of little significance to me. Generating and responding to meaning is always my first priority. Regardless of who may have written the text, as a reader I am engaged in a process of building a world of meaning, or text world, for myself. The building of this world always entails the employment and orchestration of certain invariant cognitive processes. I use the visual information or textual cues which the text provides and the nonvisual information or background knowledge which these cues evoke. Based on this interaction between visual and nonvisual information, I predict upcoming meanings and integrate them with those previously constructed.

As I build these textual meanings, I find myself reacting to or dialoguing with the author. I agree, question, and argue; I litter the columns of each page with written comments. I suppose at heart that I am a responder to whatever I read. Surface-level features are rarely an issue with me except when they interfere with meaning. The fact that a student might have authored the text makes little difference in my reading or responding.

Paradoxically, I find that this construction of, and responding to, meaning is as much a process of taking apart as it is a process of putting together. When I put eye to paper, I rarely find a straightforward production of meaning. What usually occurs is the generation of thought which soon gets revised or even rejected. Reading is a recursive process, and the meanings which I generate are continually shaped and reshaped. Revision and a dynamic world of meaning are central to all of my encounters with written language.

A driving counterforce behind my reading, however, is the building of continuity or consistency among the meanings which I am constructing. Much like a tailor attempting to produce a seamless garment, my goal is to build a unified world of meaning, a world without disruptions or perturbations. These two counterforces produce a tension throughout my reading, a tension between an ever-transforming meaning world and my desire to control or impose order on it.

In my attempts to maintain continuity, I find that I engage in a number of strategic reading behaviors. First, I shuttle back and forth between past and present meanings. As new meanings are evolved, they frequently produce a shift in my perspective and a corresponding change in the significance of previous meanings. I must constantly appraise the acceptability of previous ideas from new vantage points and in response to an ever-changing context. In effect, I must always test hypothesized meanings against new information. Continuity building also requires that I look ahead. All of my reading is goal driven and involves the anticipation of future or potential ideas to be encountered, at least in a general form. Not only must previous and evolving meanings be continuous with one another, but they must also offer potential links to meanings yet to come. The existing text world constitutes the environment for a set of subsequent predictions (Halliday and Hasan 1980) and at the same time is constrained in its development by anticipated meanings. As meanings are evolved, I must judge them in light of the future.

In summary, what I face when reading a text by any author is the building and maintaining of continuity of these worlds of meaning. As I have illustrated in figure 1, there are those meanings which have been confirmed or judged as acceptable, if only temporarily. There are also those meanings at the point of utterance, meanings being formulated at many points in time during text processing. Finally, there is the world of meaning which I only anticipate. Because there is a symbiotic relationship among these three worlds of meaning, the development of a continuous text world demands that I "look ahead" as well as "back" when engaged in the process of reading.

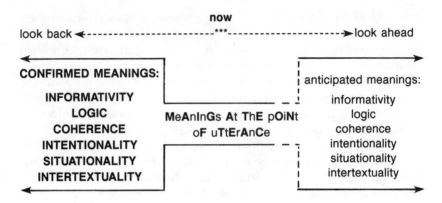

Fig. 1. Continuity building in reading and writing.

The notion of a continuous text, however, needs to be more fully defined if it is to provide insights into my reading behavior in general, and my responses to student papers in particular. In reflecting upon my reading behavior and coming to define the characteristics of a continuous text, I have drawn from the writings of Robert de Beaugrande (1980, 1984), a theoretician in the area of text processing. These characteristics, which are also listed in figure 1, serve as a framework for both my reading and my responding.

The first two characteristics which I use when assessing continuity are informativity and logic. The propositions presented must convey understandable or comprehensible information. They must be meaningful in and of themselves. In addition, ideas must be logical or reasonable; the ideas presented must conform or correspond to what I know about the world in general and about the topic in particular. In judging informativity and logic, I rely on my external source, my background knowledge. Meanings must also be internally coherent on both a global and local level (van Dijk 1980; van Dijk and Kintsch 1983). Each idea should be conceptually linked to those around it and also relate, at least indirectly, to all other meanings in the text. The meanings which I create when reading a text must form a unified and noncontradictory whole.

Intentionality is the fourth characteristic by which I judge continuity. Reading is a functional process; it is used to accomplish "acts" in the world. As such, my reading is always goal- and plan-oriented (Bruce 1980; Meyer 1982; Pratt 1977). If I am to accept the meanings which I encounter, they must reflect the purpose which drives me to read the text.

Directly related to the characteristic of intentionality is that of situationality. My goals and plans do not emerge in a vacuum but rather are situationally based. It is a communicative context which first provides the impetus for me to engage in the reading act. In fact, Halliday (1974, 1978; Halliday and Hasan 1980) has proposed that the meanings in any text always contain elements of the context from which they were generated; the context is embodied in the discourse produced. Therefore, the meanings must be relevant to the current or a recoverable situation.

Finally, I judge the continuity of the text world in terms of its intertextuality. Just as the meanings which I create must relate to a relevant situation, so too must they relate to previously encountered texts. No world of meaning stands alone and both its content and form will display features found in other texts. The text world must be linked to an existing text type, such as narration or exposition. In addition, it must reflect an organizational pattern, such as time-order, antecedent/consequent, or comparison/contrast, which is acceptable within a particular text type (Meyer 1982).

Being an instructor of literacy theory, I am conscious of the active role which I play in this process of meaning making and continuity building. When I encounter disruptions to continuity I will initially accept responsibility and attempt a repair. I will reread or rethink and seek to make the meanings more continuous. Only as a last resort will I blame the author. It is usually at this point in the process of reading that surface structure violations come into play. At times, violations to the surface structure, especially in terms of syntax, may interfere with my generation of thought. For surface violations which block meaning, I hold the author responsible.

Because I use this framework when I read nonstudent texts, and because I want my students to write nonstudent-like texts, I also use this framework when responding to their papers. I evaluate each paper for the comprehensibility and reasonableness of the information presented. Fortunately, because student papers are related to subtopics of my course, I usually have the necessary background knowledge upon which to draw. Even when students read particular articles with which I am not familiar, I find that I know enough about the topic to make sense of their points and to judge the basic logic of their arguments.

I also seek to find coherence among the ideas presented and clues as to what intentions should drive my reading of the paper. In a general sense, my intentions are always governed by the assignment which served as the source for student writing. When students are asked to address certain issues or to synthesize information from a number of sources, it guides my reading of their papers. However, each student will have unique ways in which these intentions are realized, and I try to be sensitive to the fact. In addition, because it is my class which serves as the communicative context for the writing assignment, I expect to see elements of the class within student papers. I look for links among the assigned readings, lectures, and class activities. Finally, the meanings in student papers should reflect an organizational pattern or form which is appropriate for the assignment.

This framework is particularly useful because, as indicated in figure 1, the characteristics of a continuous text apply not only to readers, but to writers as well. As the writer builds a text world and transforms it into print, his or her meaning making is also governed by a search for continuity. Similar to the characteristics which I look for as I read, the author will seek to make the text informative, logical, and coherent. The author will also want the text to reflect his or her intentions, to relate to the situation from which it emerged, and to display a conventional organizational form. Through the use of this framework, I find that my comments help students to focus on the critical elements involved in the composing process.

Responding to Texts: Readers and Writers

During the last several years I have developed a procedure which allows me to share with students my responses to their writing. As I have already mentioned, when responding to most texts I usually scribble my comments in the columns; initially I did this with student papers. However, I found that a lack of space, as well as atrocious penmanship, was limiting the usefulness of my comments. Therefore, with the help of a personal computer—though this may also be done with a typewriter or by hand—I have devised a procedure which allows me to more effectively communicate my responses to my students.

As I read each student's paper and encounter points where I want to respond to continuity, I place a numeral in the column, beginning with one. On the computer I then type the same numeral and write a response to the student concerning those characteristics of continuity which I have observed. These responses may focus solely on the text itself or may involve extensions or references to sources beyond the text; they may be positive or critical, questions or comments. After I have read and responded to each paper, I print a copy of my responses and give them to the student along with his or her paper. A few examples taken from a number of student papers will help clarify how this procedure works.

This past semester I taught a doctoral seminar on beginning reading and writing development. In one writing assignment, I asked the students to investigate an individual who had made a significant contribution to our understanding of early literacy development. In their papers the students were to give a historical overview of the individual's work as well as to synthesize and critique his or her key contributions.

Following are a number of responses which I wrote to several students. While my comments frequently address several characteristics of text continuity, for ease of presentation I have categorized each response in terms of its predominate focus. Also, because space does not allow for excerpts from the student papers, I have tried to select responses which are easily interpretable.

Informativity. The first response focuses on the lack of specifics and details in a particular study on which the writer was reporting. I understand what is written, but need a richer and more detailed discussion. In contrast, the second response reflects my inability to understand a particular concept and to relate it to subsequent concepts which the writer presents. In the third response, I understand the author's point, there is a rich discussion, and I simply extend the discussion through my comments.

- Because you don't tell the reader what the results of this study were, only what the study was about, it is difficult to evaluate the significance of the research. You need to give a detailed presentation of the findings.

- What do you mean by "prior knowledge" and how is it utilized during perception, prediction, and comprehension?

- These ideas are new to me, though they are certainly in line with Vygotsky and a semiotic perspective, that is, that all thought is mediated through the use of signs.

Logic. In the following response, I am able to understand the writer's point, but it does not make sense given what I know about the topic.

- You are confusing literacy processing with literacy development. The study of reading or writing processing focuses on those mental activities an individual uses when interacting with print. The study of the development of reading or writing focuses on what and how cognitive behaviors are developed over time which allow the individual to effectively interact with print.

Coherence. In the first response I comment on the strength of the paper's coherence; in the second I react to the lack of coherence.

- Nice introduction. You give a general overview of the issues and tell the reader which particular issues will be addressed. The rest of your paper then follows the format presented. This made it easy for me to understand how all of the ideas discussed fit together.

- You somewhat jump from point to point and then back again. It would help coherence if you discussed each idea more fully before moving on to the next one.

Intentionality. In the first response I react to the writer's inability to fulfill his stated intentions; in the second I note the lack of correspondence between the paper and the assignment.

- Given your stated focus of this paper, I'm starting to get a bit lost. I thought your intent was to discuss those cognitive strategies which are transferable from one language to another. I don't see this in the paper.

- You did a nice job of reporting on the work of a number of researchers. However, there was little synthesis or analysis, which was a basic part of the assignment.

Situationality. In the first response, I link the writer's point to relevant class readings, lectures, or discussions. The second response discusses the fact that the student's paper fails to adequately address Freire's contributions to literacy development in Latin America.

- Frank Smith's notion of risk-taking, as discussed in class and in the readings, would be relevant here.

- Given that this is a class on literacy development, I expected to see a focus on some aspect of learning to read or write. While it is important to embed Freire's work within a larger social-political context, a more extensive discussion of literacy would have been more appropriate.

Intertextuality. In the following response I comment on the lack of an organizational framework in the paper.

- There are too many lengthy quotations through your paper. Rather than discuss the research, you give the reader a list of quotes. Given these lists and the lack of elaboration, I had difficulty understanding the basic structure of your paper.

In order to help students fully incorporate the characteristics of continuity into their own interactions with written language, I also have them use the characteristics as a guide when they read class assignments. Each student keeps a reader-response notebook in which reactions to class readings are written. Similar to the procedure which

I use when reading their papers, as the student reads a particular article and encounters a point to which he or she wants to respond, a numeral is put in the column, beginning with one. In the notebook, the student writes the same numeral, the author's last name, and the page number on which the numeral is found. The student then writes his or her reaction. During the last portion of each class session, students are given the opportunity to share and discuss their responses. By having students engage in this counterpart reading activity, I can more effectively bridge the gap between readers and writers and help students see the supportive and reciprocal relationship between the two processes.

When the Author Does Make a Difference

There is a sense, however, in which it is significant that a student has written the text which I am reading. Because student papers emerge from a situation which I have largely created—my course—a special love-hate relationship exists between reader and writer. Student papers always tell me the degree to which I have been able to convey certain understandings and insights to the class. Their papers tell me where my lectures or explanations have been fuzzy or particularly insightful, or where class readings have been appropriate or in need of further clarification.

Given this relationship between text and context, I see my reflection in their papers and my ego becomes involved. I am unable to be the objective, detached observer; I love their papers where I look good and hate them where I do not. As I read their papers, my evaluation of the author as student becomes an evaluation of myself as teacher. While the basic cognitive processes remain the same, student texts highlight the affective dimension of reading.

Just as I hope that my responses will help students to grow in their own thinking and writing, I use my responses to grow in my own thinking and writing as well. In particular, I use the responses to make revisions in my courses. I find that student papers provide windows into my class which are more valuable than end of the semester course evaluations. Using student papers and my responses as a guide, I look for topics or issues in the course which are in need of modification. I will expand certain lectures, add new topics, or change course readings. I will look for activities which help clarify particularly abstract concepts. I will, in effect, seek to make the course more continuous.

In concluding, I must note that I am always puzzled and slightly impressed with those instructors who are able to distance themselves from the student texts which they read. Their ability to critically evaluate these papers without seeing it as an evaluation of themselves or their courses is something which I am seldom able to do. Student papers tell me as much about myself as they do about the students.

Works Cited

Bruce, Bertram. "Plans and Social Action." In *Theoretical Issues in Reading Comprehension*, edited by Rand Spiro, Bertram Bruce, and William Brewer, 367–84. Hillsdale: Erlbaum, 1980.

de Beaugrande, Robert. *Text, Discourse, and Process.* Norwood, N.J.: Ablex, 1980.

———. *Text Production: Toward a Science of Composition.* Norwood, N.J.: Ablex, 1984.

Goodman, Kenneth. "A Linguistic Study of Cues and Miscues in Reading." In *Theoretical Models and Processes of Reading*, edited by Harry Singer and Robert Ruddell, 129–34. Newark: International Reading Association, 1985a.

———. "Unity in Reading." In *Theoretical Models and Processes of Reading*, edited by Harry Singer and Robert Ruddell, 813–40. Newark: International Reading Association, 1985b.

Halliday, Michael. *Language and Social Man.* London: Edward Arnold, 1974.

———. *Language as a Social Semiotic.* London: Edward Arnold, 1978.

Halliday, Michael, and Ruqaiya Hasan. *Text and Context.* Tokyo: Sophia University Press, 1980.

Kohlers, Paul. "Reading Is Only Incidentally Visual." In *Psycholinguistics and the Teaching of Reading*, edited by Kenneth Goodman and James Fleming, 8–16. Newark: International Reading Association, 1972.

Meyer, Bonnie. "Reading Research and the Composition Teacher: The Importance of Plans." *College Composition and Communication* 33 (1982): 37–49.

Pratt, Mary. *Toward a Speech Act Theory of Literacy Discourse.* Bloomington: Indiana University Press, 1977.

Rumelhart, David. "Toward an Interactive Model of Reading." In *Theoretical Models and Processes of Reading*, edited by Harry Singer and Robert Ruddell, 722–50. Newark: International Reading Association, 1985.

Smith, Frank. *Understanding Reading.* New York: Holt, Rinehart and Winston, 1982.

van Dijk, Teun. *Macrostructures.* Hillsdale: Erlbaum, 1980. van Dijk, Teun, and Walter Kintsch. *Strategies in Discourse Comprehension.* New York: Academic Press, 1983.

IV Encountering Responses to Student Texts

The chapters of this final section ask us to take a step back from the student paper itself, from an analysis of how we read a student paper to a consideration of the interpretive overlays we apply to it. Underlying these essays is the assumption that our formal responses to a student text—our comments in the margins of and at the end of a paper, as well as our oral critiques—add a layer of meaning and complexity to the original text. Thus, these commentaries, too, must become the object of interpretive analysis. The five authors in this section—James S. Baumlin and Tita French Baumlin, Richard Beach, Anthony Petrosky, and Lee Odell—hold the view that writing instructors must develop a critical posture in relation not only to student writing, but also to their own evaluative responses to that writing.

By examining written evaluations through the frame of classical oration, James and Tita Baumlin help us to consider our responses as complex texts in their own right and to recognize the sophisticated rhetorical "work" they actually do. They consider the comments we often dash off in late-night grading sessions as acts of forensic, epideictic, and deliberative rhetoric which serve to defamiliarize a task that easily becomes reductive and formulaic. The Baumlins challenge us to consider our goals in our responses to students. More than an intriguing way of interpreting our readings of student work, the essay urges greater critical self-awareness on the instructor's part, leading to "a truly collaborative, negotiative rhetoric of response."

Such self-awareness presupposes a sensitivity to the rhetorical effect of our written evaluations. In the second essay, Richard Beach analyzes students' responses to his comments on their journals. His study convinces him that, by discovering ways his students are interpreting his comments, he can be a more influential reader and thus help students to develop into "deep" or "elaborative" thinkers and writers. Beach suggests that by sharpening our own interpretive skills through listening to critiques of our readings of student papers and, in turn, by developing an intrepretive awareness in our students, we may guide them to become "reflective practitioners."

Of course, being in touch with what our comments are "doing" does not provide us with an agenda for what we wish to accomplish with our commentary. While the Baumlins and Beach foreground the negotiative process that occurs between teacher and student to develop "elaborative" thinking, Anthony Petrosky makes use of Hegelian terminology to conceptualize another view of the function of interpretations and their relation to the original student texts. Using instances of student poetry, as well as essays, Petrosky demonstrates how his readings are intended as part of a dialectic. The student paper functions as a thesis that, countered by a deliberately antithetical reading, a "pushing against the grain," is then forced to a new and richer text. His reading focuses on the "particulars" of the writing, pressing for development of detail that will generate involvement, authority, and voice.

Lee Odell's chapter, with its focus on the challenge of making students more sophisticated interpreters, appropriately concludes the volume. His assumption, articulated or implied by many of the contributors to this collection, is that as students become more astute critics of others' writing, as well as their own, they invariably become better writers. The fundamental quality of interpretation that Odell seeks to develop—and which was most often absent in the student-readers/evaluators he studied—is the ability to recognize meaning as contextual. To be good critics and good writers, he contends, students must learn to live with uncertainty, recognizing that information can be viewed from multiple perpectives.

These essays, then, affirm what we already value in good writing and delight to find in our students' papers: genuine insight, concreteness, strong and individual voice, and sophistication of thought. They also suggest, however, that our interpretive responses to student texts can act powerfully to encourage those qualities, rather than merely to defend a grade, and that the students' experiences of becoming critical interpreters simultaneously involve a desirable expansion and deepening of their powers of written expression.

15 Paper Grading and the Rhetorical Stance

James S. Baumlin
Southwest Missouri State University

Tita French Baumlin
Southwest Missouri State University

The composition teacher is never more fully the rhetorician than she is come grading time. Trained to instruct students in the accommodation of audience and occasion, the writing teacher will herself—one would think—carefully exploit her own rhetorical situation when grading. The speeches will be brief, of course: one must address each student individually. Yet the marginal comments will institute a dialogue with the student's own writing, a questioning and cross-examining of the student's text, while the terminal comments, though again necessarily brief, will constitute an oration in miniature, a summation, a passing of judgment whose final word is in fact a letter, a letter grade. The teacher's terminal comments may indeed observe parts of the classical oration. The commentary may begin, for example, on a note of praise, an *exordium* to gain the audience's good will. It may attempt, in a miniature *confirmatio*, to drive its own argument home, to prove its own position (its own position, that is, with respect to the student's performance). It may end with a brief *peroratio*, an exhortation to work harder, to take more risks with language, to "keep up the good work." And alas, like the historic fate of the classical oration in the hands of academicians—in the rhetorical schools, say, of the ancient Sophists or of imperial Rome—the terminal comments are likely to fall into flat formulae and set speeches. After seemingly countless ceremonial repetitions and performances, the writing teacher's comments run the risk of becoming, like the Sophist's commonplaces, little more than elegant variations on the same (worn) themes, showing small awareness of aim, occasion, or audience.

How, then, can we as writing teachers, and, perhaps most importantly, as evaluators of our students' own worlds of discourse, best avoid the dangers inherent in our grading processes? Perhaps an initial step is to understand more fully some of the tendencies in our rhetorics of evaluation: all of us, given the paper load and the necessity to keep commentary at a minimum, are capable of reliance upon stock phrases and predetermined sets of criteria, and few of us have the time or the occasion to study our *own* comments as carefully as we study other texts. In order to gain some insight into the hermeneutics of paper grading, then, we conducted an experiment with a piece of student writing one of us received as a first assignment in a freshman composition class.

This initial assignment asked students to write in vivid language a narrative exploring some person or object whose meaning had changed in that student's life. We chose Linda Britton's essay (used with permission) precisely because we ourselves feel such a wide range of emotional *and* technical responses to her piece, and we saw in it a fertile ground for evaluative commentary. Here are some excerpts from her remarkable essay:

From Fear to Courage

He was tall, thin and wiry, his shoulders stooped from meny years of hard toil. His hands were leathery tough yet gentle, the color of the rich soil that he loved so. He smelled of the earth, sweat and the undertones of clean sope. His speech slow and contemplation, the tone of his voice was warm, arich and deep, yet quit. His eyes as cristel clear as a Colorado day. I remember how they expressed his very soul, how you could see the laughter twinkeling in his eyes, befor the first deep rumbel could be hurd. The sorrow and loneliness of a gentle man who lost his beloved wife. [. . .] As a child I was fearful and painfully shy, grandpa and I had a special bond, we both knew loneliness. When I stubbornly follow him into the filds. He would pause take my hand in his, give it a squeeze and ask "child why are you not playing with the other childron." I never could anser him, my shyness was so great. He would smile, his blue eyes full of love and understanding. [. . .] As we spent the days among his love for the earth, he talked of many things, I spoke vert little. He showed me how to touch the plants, how to wakd with a sure yet soft foot. He taught me to recognize the snakes to kill and the ones to let live. We had battles with the crows, coons, a fox or two and once a weazel. I will never forget the first panther that crossed out land and the fear that was instilled in my young mind. ran up my spine makening me shiver when it screamed out in the dark moonless night. I was outside that spring night, I heard the horses first, then the cows became excited. Dads hunting dogs snarling, tence, ready to do battle, pulling their chances taught, in thier effort to bust loose. Our pet dogs wimpering, tails tucked, barking only after they reached the safty from under the house. Just as I asked grandpa what was wrong, the first scream echoed thrueout the woods. Swiftly and with out a word grandpa picked me up and in one smooth stride, I found out that night just how silent he could move, as a shadow. And never would you hear the snap of a twig or the crunch of a leaf. The second sream sounded as if a demon was on our heels. He shoved my face into his shoulder, sternly but softly said quiet child. He paused and listened intently, ahead of us the house stood in darkness. Grandpa called out quitly to my dad, "Bill" dads voice almost a wisper came from dark shadows "Im here gor Linda? "Yep! was grandpa only reply. Silently with breath taken speed we crossed the open space between us and the housej. He set me down on the porch and said "move quickly child." The fear was so strong you could feel it creep across your skin, taste the metal in your mouth, that was so dry you could not swallow. My legs shook so violently I could barley move them. I was torn between the sanctuary of our home, or the safty of grandpas arms. Bur when grand pa says move quickly you know to do so, I chose the safty of our home.

Mom was in the kitchen all lights out, peering out into the darkness. My brothers and sister setting at the table, quit as mice. That itself was imperssive all seven of us not saying a word. Again we hurd the cat scream out, sounding as if it was the devil himself straight from Hell! The shot rang out almost simultaneously, then deathly silence came, no animal, no human, not a breath of sound. Then mom jumped back and gasped for grandpa was so quit he was on top of her befor she could hear or see him. He asked softly "where is Bill" moms reply revealed the fear in her voice. "He is not with you"?"no that damn devil doublrd back on me, cut me off and I lost Bill in the ravine back of the barn." He looked at my brother Sam, "you take this shot gun Sam and do not open the door unless you are tols." Leonora get your gun and come with me! Mom did what she was told she was raised a trappers daughter in the Rocky mountains. Sam took up where she left off. As we sat in total silence praying to hear our folks voices, I knew I had to be brave! I looked at Sam his shadow standing at attention, listening to the deathly quit around us. I must be brave!

Then we hurd moms voice first, then dads, we all jumped and talking at the same time. Soon after, grandpa come in saying the cat had moved on for now. He sat down at the tabel with coffee cup in hand, slowly sipping at the hot black liqued I love to smeal but was bitter to my young taste. He caught my look and gave me that special wink, smiled and asked "you okay girl?" I remember sitting up very straight, my reply was one of a brave little girl, though we both knew I shook so hard I could barely stand on my owen two feet. "Yep! I wasent afraid honest!" I looked at grandpa "was you scared? I asked. You bet I was Linda, a cat that size you best respect! and know he can have you just that quick! As he snaped his finger to emphasize how quick.The next mornen I went with him to check on the live stock, we found one young heifer down. She had deep gashes on her flanks, her throat was ripped open, the dark red blook upon the brite green of the new spring grass. Gradpa looked up from his squating position, "See girl what a cat that size can do" My brown eyes big in fear, that same mind griping fear of the night befor, creeping over my skin inducing gooce bumps, I shuddered and trembled as if a cold North wind blew in. [. . .] As we walked back to the house, grandpa looked down at me, took my hand in his and gave it a warm loven squeeze. "Girl you tried very hard to be brave last night. You did good, Im very proud of you. My hear swelled up with pride and my first tast of confidence was sweet!. [. . .] Now as an adult I can understand what grandpa ment when he told me back then. "To be brave just takes good common sense" You come from good hardie stock Linda, when the chips are down you will come thrue just fine. I have found thrueout the years his is very true, I do come thrue! So be it a panther or demons of other dimensions we all have our fears to conquer. My grandfather is no longer with us, my childering now look into the same loving blue eyes. My Mothers, How very much like grandpa she is. She never paused for one second to take up her gun and go with him. And I know I come from good hardie stock!

The End

With Linda's permission, we gave freshman writing students a copy of her essay, requesting their written responses; much class discussion had previously centered on "showing and not telling," and we felt that this essay could provide students with some fine examples of "showing," but we also wanted to gain some insight into the students' own understanding of evaluation. Students were to offer written comments and responses directly *to* this student and to assign a grade to the piece; we made it clear that the students were free to choose any grade they thought appropriate. The range of comments and grades was wide indeed: 90 percent of the students ranked this paper in the C to F range, while two students ranked it as high as an A. The following, with their infelicities of spelling and grammar, are some representative commentaries of the lower ranking:

> I feel that your original idea was relatively good, if it is the same one you had in mind. However, you ramble aimlessly throughout most of your essay and concentrate mostly on the panther. Try to avoid doing this next time. In addition, try using an outline to help you organize your thoughts. Your title suggests one idea and the essay presents another.

> You need to get more to the point in the intro. You need to work on your spelling and grammer. Spelling can be a major part of your paper, if someone really enjoy's the paper and is thrown off by spelling, it can ruin a whole paper. You need to spend more

> time reading your paper and read other's paper's to get idea's. . . . I really liked the topic. It needs more work. Trying to get more personal might help. Work more towards this type of writing.

> I have never seen so many spelling and punctuation errors in a paper until yours. Your sentence structure is terrible. You have a few run-on sentences and many sentence that could have been arranged in a better order to make them clearer to the reader. For your punctuation, I recommend that you work heavily on the use of commas.

Another student apparently felt the inevitable stress of assigning a punitive grade for mechanics while also greatly enjoying the paper; he solved his dilemma by offering an A for originality and a C for "grammer":

> The originality and the way you expressed yourself was very good. Only you can capture your own feelings and put them on paper and I fell you expressed yourself very well. Now your grammer has a little to be desired. You need to work on spelling. That is your weekest point. Really concentrate on this.

The two students who ranked the paper an A (one had even written A+ and then scratched it out) were also (coincidentally?) the two best writers in their class. The most intriguing commentary offered this:

> I can't truly determine of the misspellings are intentional to show the way in which people from these parts of the country talk. I would believe or would rather go with the intention of misspelling the words for it gives a personal touch to the work. It shows the way a person really talks that has been raised like Linda in this story. The misspelling of the words and the sentence structures gave a relaxed feeling. It wasn't as if the paper was the middleman trying to be proper and somewhat dulling, but it was like having the person there, Linda, actually talking to the reader, me. I feel that if a writing can make me feel what this reader felt, it has accomplished its goal.

Clearly these students' responses imply a wide realm of personal experience, some students apparently combining the punitive language of blame with the authoritarianism they associate with the teacher's role, others granting the writer, as a fellow adventurer in language, the *donnée* of using every possible technique for its effect upon the reader. In the discussion following their written responses, one of the students who ranked the paper C− asked the instructor if the paper was a published story that had been "ruined" just to confuse their grading project. Other students remarked that if the instructor had read this paper aloud, they would undoubtedly have ranked it an A, and, furthermore, if the errors were simply corrected, this piece could be published immediately. There was no consensus of opinion on the written piece itself, however, for the students clearly chose to emphasize radically differing aspects of the essay in evaluation.

How do our students learn such widely divergent ways of responding to texts—one choosing to speak only of the spelling, another commenting only upon the effect on the reader? The answer, of course, is obvious: they learn to evaluate by reading *our* comments upon *their* papers. Our next experiment, offering Linda's essay to a group of university writing teachers for grading and commentary, corroborated this notion, for the commentaries by teachers were, though perhaps more eloquent, no less varied and problematic. Like the student responses, the professional evaluations showed an equally wide range of grades. Moreover, the commentaries implied specific areas of emphasis which we now wish to clarify by comparing them to the three modes of classical rhetoric: forensic rhetoric, the rhetoric of accusation and defense (the rhetoric of law courts); epideixis, the rhetoric of praise (the rhetoric of celebratory address); and deliberative rhetoric, the rhetoric of persuasion and change (the rhetoric of political assembly). These three forms of rhetoric, systematized by Aristotle and subsequent theorists, have specific aims, applications, and occasions. All three are always available, however, to the rhetor and may be used in combination in the same discourse; most situations indeed demand a mixture of rhetorics—of praise, say, and persuasion, or of defense and praise. But, as the student imitations of the teacherly role pointed out, some teachers apparently become trapped within one particular mode of rhetoric, usually the forensic (though sometimes the epideictic). Teachers' written comments, when this happens, will seek always either to *justify a grade by* forensically accusing the "guilty text," or else to *praise a text* by epideictically pointing out what he or she "liked about this paper."

Again, it is our position that the truly useful response to a student's writing will include some aspects of all three rhetorics; as the teachers' responses to Linda's essay reminded us, however, many of us unfortunately often become trapped in one rhetoric or mode of response. Take, for example, the forensic grader. It is not simply our need to manufacture a quota of high, middle, and low grades that inspires a forensic rhetoric when grading: for some of us the forensic is a choice of personality or the consequence of our own education. The forensic grader, however created, will always call the student's text to the witness stand to be examined, cross-examined, and ultimately judged. The student's text, simultaneously the scene and perpetration of its own crime, becomes an object or event frozen both in time and in its present shape: for forensic rhetoric studies only *what has happened in the past*, showing little or no interest in the growth of this text or the possibility of future change—that is, textually speaking, in the possibility of *revision*. The text is something to be *judged*, after all, and not reformed. It is to be judged, moreover, solely as *product*. And in a gross perversion of due process, the student's text is necessarily *guilty until proven innocent*. No text, by the way, can be fully free of accusation if a grader is trapped completely within a forensic mode: the very slightest miscues in grammar or style will be duly ticked off and cumulatively weighed. The forensic grader, in this extreme form, will always judge by the strict letter of the law as well: successes in one aspect of composition will never fully compensate for a text's errors. Errors, the crimes of the writer, are indeed the forensic grader's sole focus, for this kind of grader either does not know what to look for otherwise or may be choosing the speediest and easiest method of evaluation. The fewer errors that are uncovered, the more fully the student's text is exonerated (and the higher its grade); this response is typically what we would call a "readerly" response—one which focuses upon those aspects which are (in this case) distracting to the reader. Consider, for example, the following instructor's response to Linda's essay:

> The language in this essay is definitely vivid, and in that sense it fulfills the assignment. However, the essay only describes an event as viewed from many years later; it does not indicate how the event has changed in meaning for the writer. It needs rigorous editing! I would assign the paper an evaluative marking of check-minus [D-F range] on a scale of check-plus [A-B range] and [C]. I haven't seen anything close to this level of grammatical errors in a college student's paper.

Although this teacher's commentary is more eloquent, it is actually not far removed from the student who wrote, "I have never seen so many spelling and punctuation errors in a paper until yours. Your sentence structure is terrible." Both responses focus upon accusation to produce guilt for errors; both speak of the text as an event in the *past*. How, then, is the student writer to think of her work as anything *but* proof of her incompetence? How, then, is she even to *look* at this text again in order to work with it, revise it (as it clearly deserves)? Although the teacher here refused to offer a letter grade, the translation of the check-system accomplishes no less a slamming of the door on this work (even perhaps on the student's own self-esteem) than another teacher's response: "I enjoyed this paper very much, but I think you can see from the numerous errors I marked at the beginning that you have a basic literacy problem. I didn't mark all the mistakes because I don't know that it would do you much good. I must give this paper an F." We noticed, in fact, that among the D and F rankings, the phrases "I must give this paper a/an . . ." and "I'm afraid this paper is a/an . . ." were quite prevalent, an apparent attempt to induce sympathy in the "offending" student, who should thereby realize that the teacher is *forced* ("must") or *fearful* ("I'm afraid")—in short, *helpless*—as a result of her poor performance.

On the other hand, many teachers among us find it a blessing to be able to bless the student who has touched us as readers and to celebrate that student's success. *Everyone* engaged in a new or stressful task needs some stroking, some "positive reinforcement"; B. F. Skinner was right in this. Even the most dismal failures, then, can be praised for *something*. Mina Shaughnessy, in all seriousness, revolutionized the teaching of basic writers through her recognition that *the weakest, too, need praise*. May we always, therefore, devote part of our commentaries to the kind of rhetoric that will make students feel good about themselves as writers, that will help "keep the door open" on a piece of writing. A problem arises, though, when we become inclined only to praise, or when our praise seems to undercut criticism or preclude further exploration and revision. How often have we praised a student's papers at the beginning of a semester, only to feel "locked in" to that same rhetoric when that student's early successes become formulaic, repetitive performances? And how often have we, as the teacher in the following response, used commentary simply to *rewrite* with delight the student's own piece?

> Linda, what I like most about this piece is that I forget I'm reading it. After the first page I'm caught up in your fear and in the excitement of the hunt. I'm looking for the cat with you. The "crack of the gunshot" and "the firstscream" begin building the suspense. It is vividly clear that your grandfather represents safety to you in the midst of terror: "I was torn between the sanctuary of out home, or the safety of grandpa's arms" [*notice here this teacher's standardization of Linda's spelling*]. Your characterization of your grandfather is very convincing and exciting because you've provided details and actions that support each other. . . . But the point of all this is that a traumatic experience in your childhood has changed you. You've made it clear to us that it isn't really the cat or the fear or the danger, it's your grandfather. You've shown how his humanity and his protection allowed you to learn courage. . . .

Like the student who found value even in the misspellings, this teacher clearly produces a tone of respect for the writer and her techniques. One problem, however, with this exuberant exegesis of Linda's essay may be that, like the forensic model, it fixes the essay as an event without a future. Even more noticeable is the fact that this teacher did *not* assign a grade of any sort to the paper, as she indicated in her note to us, because she would not grade papers until after revisions had taken place; and would not this response, functioning more to *explain* her own essay to Linda than to offer advice for revision, maintain the essay in its present shape, unchangeable though moving? Also a "readerly" response, this comment focuses only upon the joy which the reader found in *this* reading of the essay. Can we assume, then, that this teacher, when it is time to assign a grade, would react with the same exuberance if Linda were to turn in the same essay, unrevised, as this teacher's commentary implicitly advises?

Of the three rhetorics, perhaps the deliberative is most crucial to the reader and grader. By the term *deliberative* we do not mean a rhetoric of persuasion or emotional engagement; we mean, rather, a rhetoric focused on change, one that looks toward the future of a present discourse, one that can foresee new shapes and emphases in writing and can make recommendations on the basis of this foresight (a future-oriented vision, in short, which stimulates *re*vision). The forensic and epideictic, once again, consider only the past and present— consider the student's text, therefore, to be a completed product, an object fully existent and fixed in time. Deliberative rhetoric alone looks toward the future—considers, in short, what a text *could be*. A problem remains, however, even with the deliberative model, and it is a problem inherent in all the traditional rhetorics: all are fundamentally authoritarian. The forensic is obviously the most authoritarian, yet even the deliberative tends to impose the teacher's version of the text upon the student writer. Too often, even in facilitative commentary, we simply tell the student what to do to "improve" her paper; there really is no negotiation with the student, no attempt to leave the best and final choices of revision up to her. We *expect* the student to follow the agenda we establish for her paper, and to that extent we really do use a rhetoric of persuasion: for we need, after all, to convince the student that we are right in our evaluation of her writing and in the particular advice we give. Note, for example, the authoritarian language (the imperatives and repetitions of "you need to") in this teacher's response:

> For a revision you need to focus on your numerous and distracting mechanical errors. Run-on sentences, sentence fragments and spelling errors almost ruin the effectiveness of this piece. . . . Also you need to work on your description. You've overburdened this

> with adjectives. Let your wonderful narrative speak for itself at
> times. A third aspect you might work on is the development of
> your mother's character. Make it clear to us that this is her father,
> and perhaps take the time to draw comparisons.

One of the curious aspects of the deliberative mode of response is
that in the teacher's zeal to direct, the teacher inevitably relies upon
his or her own tastes (Why are there "too many adjectives" here?
Didn't the assignment call for vivid description?) or upon phrases
which have meaning for the teacher but for no one else (What does
it mean to "let the wonderful narrative speak for itself at times?" Isn't
that the defining quality of a narrative?). Surely we have all had
students disagree with our suggestions for revision. Could such a
refusal signal merely an inability to understand our directives? Or
could it signal a *refusal to give up control* of what is after all their own
discourse, a refusal to allow an alien authority to become, if vicariously,
the *author* of their discourse?

Thus, even the deliberative can become coercive; such are the
limitations of our traditional rhetorics of response to student writing.
Perhaps the task, then, is to go beyond the three rhetorics, to discover
a *quaternium quid*: a truly collaborative, *negotiative* rhetoric of response,
one that presents the critical judgments of a reader without assuming
an authoritative voice, without undermining the student's own authority. We might for a moment consider how our own responses to
insensitive or ineffective reviews from scholarly journals might reflect
the responses of students to our own commentary. The forensic reviewer
is in fact the most feared and obsecrated. Yet we respond with equal
dismay to the editor who accepts our essay while *imposing his own
schedule of revision* upon our writing, leaving little or no room for
negotiation, using his own authority to wrest the authorship from
us—to write our essay "his way." But we have all, hopefully, received
letters of provisional acceptance or even rejection that have truly tried
to help us extend our own authority over the writing, that have made
us feel good about ourselves as writers, that have made us want to
write further and revise. How rare and welcome such peer reviews
are! We wonder how rare, and welcome, they must be to our students.

Perhaps one method of generating a truly negotiative rhetoric in
paper grading might be to focus on heuristic, rather than analytic or
symptomatic, commentary. Here is one teacher's response to Linda's
essay which offers some alternatives to the previous extremes:

> You tell a good story! I'm impressed with the amount of detail
> you have here—and its effectiveness. I'm also impressed with
> how you handle what seems to be the main idea: learning how

to control fear. It seems to me, however, that you spend a lot of time on another idea: learning about nature from your grandfather. Perhaps one (the first I mentioned) is a part of the other? If so, that relationship is not made clear. In fact, as it stands, the paper breaks down into two parts that seem significantly different. One solution would be to drop the first part altogether, and focus on fear; another would be to try to integrate the two parts. If you chose to combine the two parts, some questions might be: why is the part about *nature* important? Is there some good reason for wanting it to stay in? By the way, the circled words are misspelled. Try to work on that.

While the presence of the three rhetorics here is evident, the most remarkable aspects of this response, we feel, are that this evaluator notices areas that lack clarity, asks questions about the writer's *intent* in those sections, and then—in a true "writerly" response—offers advice on various ways the student could revise, depending upon the effect that she herself wants to achieve. In this way, her freedom to maintain the text *as her own* is defended; the ways in which the essay misses the mark of this evaluator's highest standards are discussed, but the question and the *choices* offered to the student open the door to future exploration in language, either in this particular paper or in other assignments. The evaluator's *ethos* emerges not as the authoritarian red-pen wielder, but as a fellow writer who assumes that the writer *wanted* to achieve some effect(s) here and who, by virtue of his or her own experience as a writer, goes about discussing possible ways to sharpen those effects. And, aside from the psychological advantage of keeping this writer's self-esteem intact, this response also avoids the pitfalls of encouraging the "error-hunting" method of revision, implicitly insisting here that true revision involves re-visioning the piece at hand.

If we are to be truly *helpful* to our students in the words we give them, we must consider that this stance may necessitate sacrificing our own rhetoric, our own authority, to their needs for authorship and for creative control over their own discourse. To be sure, the appearance of the teacher, not as authoritarian but as fellow-writer, will usher in other complexities, for some of us in various institutions who deal with wide assortments of student personality types, ages, and maturities: it is difficult, frankly, to encourage creativity and individual expression while also maintaining high standards as well as demanding both productivity and discipline. It is clear, however, that a truly generative rhetoric of response—those commentaries which we must toss off so quickly at the bottoms of the hundreds of student essays we encounter—should somehow attempt to find the "writerly" responses which can preserve the integrity of the individual student's work, generate rethinking and re-visioning the piece at hand, and generate that student's own vision of herself as a writer at work, a writer in a dynamic state of *becoming*—as indeed we all are, student and teacher alike.

16 Evaluating Writing to Learn: Responding to Journals

Richard Beach
University of Minnesota

Despite the popular push for using more informal writing in the classroom—for example, journals, learning logs, and freewriting—to foster "writing to learn," little attention has been paid to effective techniques for responding to or evaluating more informal writing. I am concerned about this because I use journals in all of my courses. Unlike many writers' journals or journals used in counseling, the journals I use are for more academic purposes, as "assignment journals" designed to foster reflective, critical responses to the ideas and experiences in my course. Having students articulate their own ideas and opinions enhances their learning. And, having articulated their ideas, they have something to share in discussions.

Given the informal, exploratory nature of journals, I provide students with open-ended directions about what constitutes appropriate journal entries. They can respond to whatever readings or experiences "interest, excite, anger, or amuse" them. The lack of concrete directions tends to drive some dutiful, structure-bound students up the wall.

Because our format is informal and open-ended, I respond to journals in a different manner than I do to students' formal papers. In this chapter, I want to discuss certain factors influencing my written or taped comments to the journals. Then, based on a survey and interviews, I will discuss my students' perceptions of my responses.

Factors Influencing My Comments

Genre Expectations

In reading a text, I am constantly drawing on my knowledge of text structure conventions to make sense of that text. If I am reading a mystery, I draw on my knowledge of mystery genre conventions to predict potential outcomes and reduce uncertainty. However, as a different genre with its own expectations, journal writing often lacks and even defies the conventions of well-formed narrative or expository texts: overall coherence, logical progression of ideas, a clearly defined stance, focus on a topic, and so on. Based on a comparison of effective versus less effective journals, Toby Fulwiler (1988) argues that better journals are speculatory, tentative, exploratory, contradictory, emotional, and reflective, characteristics often assumed to detract from the quality of formal academic essays. Responding to journal writing therefore involves a different interpretative stance or way of reading than is the case with more formal, academic essays. In responding to informal journal writing, as I hope to demonstrate, I must shift from responding to organized "well-formed" texts to engaging in open-ended dialogue.

Descriptive "think-aloud" feedback that documents my comprehension processes may be quite appropriate for well-formed drafts which create and fulfill expectations. Well-formed texts invite me to read primarily for comprehension, creating an implied role of "comprehending reader." Informal writing invites me to read and reciprocate as a "dialogue participant," who behaves in an equally informal manner. In that role, I am less concerned about comprehending; rather, as in a conversation, I am more concerned about demonstrating to students that I am engaged by their journals and that I want to stimulate further exchange of ideas.

For example, as I am reading journal entries, I find myself abruptly leaping about from one idea to the next. A student is talking about an Updike story when she suddenly moves to cataloging gripes about another literature course, followed by some implications for teaching literature. If I were in my "comprehending reader" role, with expectations for coherence and unity, I would be primed to look for "intertextual" links across these disparate entries. However, as a "dialogue participant," I need to realize that I must suspend these expectations for coherence and react to the content of her entries.

Journals also invite dialogue. Students will frequently ask me for my opinion, inviting me to enter into a dialogue with them. In this role, I am able to pose questions or model responses that represent certain heuristic strategies for going beyond restating or reacting emotionally to experiences that reflect on the meanings of experiences. Leslie Williams's (1987) content analysis of preservice student teachers' journals found that three-fourths of the journals were devoted to factual restatement and emotional response, with one-fourth devoted to stating rationales or to critical analyses. One of my motives in responding to journals, as suggested by the extensive research on dialogue-journal writing (Staton, Shuy, Peyton, and Reed 1987), is to model certain heuristic strategies. By internalizing and anticipating those strategies, students learn to extend their thinking on their own. As these researchers found out, having participated in extended, year-long, dialogue-journal experiences, elementary students were increasingly more likely to elaborate on their entries, presumably because they internalized their teacher's questions, implying the need to elaborate. I have noticed, for example, that when I ask students to define their purposes for certain proposed teaching activities, in subsequent entries, they are more likely to consider their purposes.

Extended Monologue

One obvious difference between conversation and a journal is that in keeping their journals, students are engaged in monologues, which, in some cases, they may have difficulty sustaining in the absence of another's prompts. They may, then, only superficially reflect on a range of different meanings associated with a particular topic or experience.

Students are often more likely to sustain their thinking in entries when they are trying to define their own attitudes toward experience, as opposed to simply regurgitating information. For example, after having read the portraits of secondary writing teachers in Perl and Wilson's *Through Teachers' Eyes* (1987), students wrote extensively about their own attitudes toward teaching in order to clarify their beliefs about their roles as teachers. One student nicely described this process in attempting to define her attitudes towards her father: "a small moment in my memory was like a revelation, a dawning of understanding. I gained perspective, a move towards the adult world and a step further away from childhood. My father was no longer cast in stone; he was seen by me as a multifaceted individual."

A number of studies on journal writing suggest that if students perceive the journal as a means of defining their own attitudes and opinions, they may engage in more sustained, purposeful writing. Sternglass and Pugh (1987) found that graduate students preferred giving their own personal assessments of readings in their journals to simply summarizing those readings. Harste (1987) found that when his graduate students were encouraged to respond to a novel in terms of their attitudes and experiences, they devoted much of their journal response to relating prior experiences, attitudes/beliefs, and literary knowledge to the text. In my own analysis of students' literary responses in their journals, I found that students' abilities to express their attitudes about their experiences were related to the degree to which they were able to interpret texts.

In order to encourage students to express their own attitudes or beliefs, I try to reciprocate by expressing my own attitudes and beliefs about related experiences or ideas, which, in some cases, may differ from those of the students. For example, many of my students were astounded by the amount of work performed by the teachers portrayed in *Through Teachers' Eyes*. One student noted, "How can I spend time with both my relationships and my job. Are there more than twenty-four hours in a day?" My response to this was, "This does require a lot of work, but the teachers were spending a lot of 'working' in the classroom by responding to students' papers in the classroom rather than at home." Ideally, students may then reflect on my attitudes and beliefs in subsequent entries, resulting in further examination of their own assumptions. However, students rarely made explicit responses to my responses, something that I hope to encourage more of in future journals.

Considering My Students' Level of Development

In addition to these expectations about journals, my responses are also shaped by my students' level of development. My students are shifting developmentally from what Erickson (1968) defined as concern with "identity"—with one's own self in relationship to others—to a concern with "achievement"—with one's success as a professional teacher. Any developmental transition creates stress, requiring one to tap various sources of insight in order to carry oneself through the transition. In attempting to define their roles as teachers, my students frequently respond to descriptions of teachers teaching, as in *Through Teachers' Eyes*, as well as to negative experiences with some of their college instructors.

Based on their review of research on developmental levels and teacher education, Thies-Sprinthall and Sprinthall (1987) posit that preservice students fall into two levels of development, Mode A and Mode B. Mode A students prefer to learn in a factual, structured, defined mode; they are more compliant, "other-directed," social conformists; these students tend to believe that there is one "right way" of teaching. In contrast, Mode B students prefer to learn in a more abstract, unstructured, autonomous mode and are more comfortable with optional perspectives on teaching. In using a journal, Thies-Sprinthall and Sprinthall recommend that teachers provide Mode A students with more structured assignments and extensive, supportive feedback, and that they provide Mode B students with less structured assignments.

These two groups therefore have different preferred ways of or approaches to learning. In *The Experience of Learning,* Marton, Hounsell, and Entwistle (1984) define two basic approaches to learning—(1) an intention to *understand,* involving an internally-driven need to organize and critically evaluate information, and (2) an intention to *reproduce* information in compliance with externally imposed tasks. Mode A students are more likely to reproduce information while Mode B students are more likely to want to understand that information. In order to determine the preferred learning approaches for my students, I have given them the *Inventory of Learning Processes* (Schmeck, Ribich, and Ramanaiah 1977). This inventory provides information about students' propensity to be "deep" versus "shallow" thinkers, reflecting the distinction between understanding versus reproducing. The inventory also provides information on the degree of "elaborative processing"—students' propensity to apply new information to their own lives or to generate examples from their own experiences as opposed to simply reiterating information. Schmeck's research indicates that "deep/elaborative" learners deal more with the meanings of experience, translating information into their own conceptions, whereas "shallow/reiterative" learners simply repeat information in its original form.

I hope that using a journal will help students move from being "shallow/reiterative" learners to "deep/elaborative" learners. When I assign the journals, I tell students that they need not restate the information presented in the readings, but rather, that they should critically analyze and evaluate the readings and generate ideas for teaching—their thinking being essential to their becoming what Donald Schon (1987) calls the "reflective practitioner."

However, some of my students simply summarize the ideas presented without extending their thinking to their own experiences. In responding to these students, I pose questions designed to help them define their meanings. For example, if a student uses the concept "ownership," I may ask that student to define what he or she means by "ownership" or, if possible, to think of examples from his or her own writing experience.

Students' Perceptions of Journal Responses

We often have little sense of how students are reacting to our comments. But knowing how students perceive our comments may help us to better understand which kinds of comments are, in general, most or

least helpful for them. With this in mind, Judith Boyce (1987) interviewed sixth graders about her comments in their reading journals.
She found that students most preferred those comments that created
a personal dialogue with the student, "in which I was just another
human being rather than the teacher" (133). Similarly, Nancie Atwell
(1987) found that in exchanging letters with her eighth graders, the
most interesting letters occurred when she "responded as a curious
human being . . . when I leveled with readers about my own experiences, tastes, and opinions, sharing freely and frankly" (276).

Boyce also found that some of her students disliked her questions.
One student implied that the questions were not genuine because she
never answered them. Another student preferred comments "that add
to the idea" rather than questions that could imply criticism that a
student's entry was inconsistent with the teacher's expectations (133).
Based on these reactions, Boyce considered revising her questions to
"I wonder" statements so that her intentions would not be misinter-
preted. Moreover, Atwell found that "when I bombarded kids with
teacher questions, I turned the dialogue journal into a test" (276).
Boyce also noted that adopting a personal, conversational tone entailed
some risks. She wondered if, by opening herself up and expressing
her own personal opinions, she risked situations in which students
would not really care about her opinions or experience. At the same
time, she recognized that her students could assume the same attitude—
if they believed that she did not care about their experiences, they
would also be reluctant to risk exposing them.

Students' Reactions to My Comments

To determine students' reactions to my comments, I asked the students
in my composition methods class to quote specific comments that they
found to be "useful" or "not useful" and to give reasons for judging
them as one or the other.

Positive Comments

One of their most frequent reactions was that my comments were
only positive. Students also noted that I avoided direct criticism. As
one student noted, "By using, 'I missed' in 'I missed more specific
comments to some of the readings,' you avoided pointing the finger
at me, softening the criticism."

Descriptions of Strategies

Students also commented that my descriptions of their use of particular strategies—"listing," "mapping," "contrasting," and "citing evidence," for example—encouraged them to conceive of their own processes: "I went back and looked at my various strategies again." Others noted that knowing a repertoire of optional strategies helped them consider different ways of thinking about a topic. Similarly, based on his research on journal writing, Robert Wess (1987) found that by giving students a set of categories such as "restating," "recalling," "connecting," "synthesizing," and "interpreting" for categorizing their entries, he helped his students become more aware of optional ways of thinking.

Students' Perceptions of Myself

My queries about students' perceptions of my comments indicated that, as in any conversation, they were "reading" my comments to gain some sense of my interest in, engagement with, or attitudes toward their entries. For example, some students were simply seeking some reassurance about the appropriateness of their entries. Other students were put off by what they perceived to be routine, formal, evaluative comments that conveyed little interest in, or engagement with, their entries. In essence, they were saying, "We're willing to let our hair down—to be spontaneous, informal, and engaged, but you're not—you're still in the formal mode." Often, students interpret some of my self-disclosures about related experiences or ideas as an indirect signal that I am engaged with their entries—implying that I am willing to be a partner in the conversation, not a detached "evaluator."

Students also indicated that when I cite my experiences, it helps them link their ideas to a "real-world" context. For example, if they proposed a technique for teaching poetry, I noted that I used that technique with some success. They could then assess whether their ideas had any practical potential.

Questions

I found, much as Boyce did, that students judged my questions according to what they perceived to be my underlying intentions. They responded positively to questions that served to "engage me in written conversation" or that conveyed an interest in the student's topic. They were more critical of questions such as "What are some other related experiences?", which they thought implied that they had failed to meet my expectations.

Comments Linking Entries to Papers or Teaching

Students cited as useful the comments I made which suggested ways to use their journals to develop ideas for their papers. For example, in response to my comment that "this is something to think about for Paper II," a student noted, "A student might be very confused and flustered about an upcoming assignment, and a comment like this may help them out." Students also noted instances in which I connected or asked them to connect their ideas to teaching suggestions: "[you] took my experience and showed me how I can use it in the classroom." Many students wanted even more evaluative commentary about whether their teaching ideas would work in the classroom, in some cases, inviting a dialogue with questions such as "Are these going to work?" "Why or why not?" "What do you suggest?" "What kinds might they like or dislike?"

Comments Perceived as Unhelpful

Students were critical of my attempts to restate or paraphrase their entries, noting that they "already knew that." Similarly, they noted that comments such as "good criticism" or "good idea" "really didn't mean anything" because they "didn't give reasons and criteria for saying [what is] 'good.'" For example, in response to my comment that conferences can be time-consuming, that "this can be a real problem," a student asked, "Why does it cause problems? What problems? Can they be avoided?" And, as in Boyce's study, students had difficulty interpreting what they perceived to be ambiguous comments. For example, in response to the question, "You are constantly redefining purpose," a student noted that "I didn't know if my doing this was good or bad."

Responding to Individual Differences in Journal Writing

While there were some common threads in these reactions, many of the students' responses reflected their unique purposes, needs, attitudes, and preferred approach to learning. Some students are much more "writer-based," employing their private shorthand that borders on incomprehensibility. On the opposite end of the pole are students who are quite concerned with carefully following what they assume "I want" in the journal.

For each of these students, I vary my responses according to my perceptions of their purposes for their journal writing. They may want to define their own beliefs about teaching, keep a record of teaching ideas, analyze their own writing, complain about a class, or keep field notes. In this way, I avoid letting my responses be dictated by my beliefs about what the students' purposes *should be*. Rather than reading my comments in terms of whether their entries conform to my expectations, students may then intuit from my comments that I am sensitive to their individual purposes. Thus my comments may serve in encouraging students to use their journals for their own purposes, rather than simply for fulfilling an assignment.

I also try to intuit certain needs, needs that often concern the desire for self-assurance rather than the desire for autonomy. Some students, particularly Mode A students, need a lot of positive reassurance because they are concerned about whether they are "doing it right" or "being on the right track." In contrast, other students, who are not in the least concerned about "doing it right," treasure their journals as "their own," and view my evaluative comments as unnecessary and even somewhat hollow.

Illustrations of Individual Students' Purposes and Needs

The following are some illustrations of my individual college students' purposes and needs. In order to provide some understanding of the differences in these students' orientation towards thinking and learning, I will cite their scores on three scales from the Schmeck *Inventory of Learning Processes*: "deep," "shallow" and "elaborative" thinking, scores from "1" (low) to "10" (high).

Laura's journal contains entry responses to most all of the readings. She consistently noted that she "liked" a reading, then summarized it. As she read, she noted that she "liked" the reading and often cited some related experiences or teaching implications, with few self-sponsored entries about other matters. For example, she responds to Donald Murray's book, *A Writer Teaches Writing* (1984), with the following entries:

> I liked his explanation of genre and the "form lies within the material"; that it is the form that is the meaning and that it is important to look, reorder, etc. that form by looking through "different lenses."

> I also liked the importance Murray placed on leads. I think that just working on leads/titles in the beginning would build confi-

dence in the students because it gives them something to work
from—some concrete basis.

The fact that she consistently stuck to this assigned pattern or
structure reflects the orientation of a highly conscientious Mode A
student, who is concerned about fulfilling the assignment in the
appropriate manner. Her score on the "deep" scale, "7," was average,
but her score of "10" on the "shallow" scale was the highest possible.
She also had a relatively low score, "3," on the "elaborative" scale.
Her attitude toward the journal was very positive. In her own journal
she notes that "an enormous amount of learning occurs in journal
writing—thoughts flow easier; there's no pressure; experimentation
can occur." In her interview, she defined her primary purpose as
"keeping a record of thoughts or activities; Murray had some interesting
activities; I really liked writing about them because I wanted to make
sure I would remember them." However, one problem with her entries
was that they became overly dependent on the readings "to make
sense out of teaching writing," at the expense of articulating her own
original ideas. When, in the interview, I asked her to define her own
strategies for dealing with issues such as grading or "classroom control,"
she was often not sure what to do. She also "didn't like writing about
my own writing processes—that was more analytical; I had to dig
inside and come up with some things that made some sense." Her
dependency on external structures is evident in her belief that students
"need a real structure in order to get anything done" or that "a teacher
needs a structure for what we're going to cover."

Given her dependency on external structures, she was consistently
concerned about whether she was "doing the right thing" or was "on
the right track." "When I started writing, I had a hard time knowing
what exactly you wanted in the journal." She therefore valued my
comments as "helping me think that I was on the right line." She
notes that my comment, "These are key points," "made me think that
I'm getting the right concepts." However, while "the feedback did
help, it still didn't tell me exactly what you were looking for." When
asked how she would grade a journal, she noted, "I do think that
[students] should be held accountable for the criteria," and that "if a
kid was 'off-track,' it would help if I said you could so some of this."
Given Laura's learning approach, my comments serve primarily as
reassurance. However, her interview comments suggest that she is
gaining increased confidence in using writing to express her own
thoughts, but remains uneasy about asserting her own unique ideas:
"whatever comes out is a reflection of my own creativity—that has

me scared." "With the creative—you can do whatever you want—and that makes it harder."

Knowing what I know now from my interview with her, if I were responding to her journal in the future, I would pose more directive questions that would challenge her to define her original thoughts, in order to nudge her toward recognizing her creative inner resources. What this suggests is that, prior to responding to the journal, I should hold conferences with my students about their journals to get a clearer sense of their purposes and attitudes.

In contrast to Laura, Lori is a highly individualistic Mode B student who values her autonomy. Her score of "6" on the "deep" scale was similar to Laura's score, but, in contrast to Laura's high score of "10" on the "shallow" scale, she had a "2," and, in contrast to Laura's "3" on the "elaborative" scale, she had a score of "10."

She placed a high priority on fulfilling her own goals; without a strong sense of purpose, she had little interest in writing. In my interview with her, she noted that she was least enthusiastic about what Laura most preferred doing—responding to the readings. She viewed her responses to the readings as simply "reading checks," "exercises" devoid of any purpose. In contrast to Laura, she viewed my positive comments about these responses to the readings as a superfluous part of a teacher/student evaluative ritual, rather than as a genuine conversation. Moreover, she was disappointed that I failed to sense her lack of interest.

To alleviate the "in one ear and out the other" syndrome, she decided to experiment by adopting different roles and was pleased that her role-playing invited more of the personal involvement and self-disclosure of mine that she valued. She was keeping a journal in another one of my courses and used it in conjunction with a research project to keep field notes and daily comments about some of the students she was working with. Noting that she throws herself into her research projects, she discovered that the journal provides her with a more clearly defined purpose in that "the journal comes off the project," serving as a "life raft" to help her "keep track of my students and my feelings." In this situation, "my purpose is not your purpose"; her interest in the project shaped her field notes and reactions to related readings, rather than simply fulfilling a "dry assignment." Lori valued not only autonomy, but also intellectual intensity. She therefore sought signs of engagement or intensity in my comments that verified my sense of her engagement. She became irked when I failed to perceive her boredom and sought to provoke more engagement on my part. All of this suggests that, rather than assuming that students like Lori do not need much feedback, I need to share some of my own intensity.

In contrast to Laura, Tom has a low score on the "shallow" thinking scale ("3") but the highest score possible on the "elaborative" scale, a "10." He was particularly interested in applying his ideas to a range of different experiences, reflecting his high "elaborative" score. Rather than being concerned with "being on track," he enjoyed "going off on a tangent," and particularly liked the fact that in the journal he could leap around readily because he "didn't have to make transitions." Tom's journal illustrated a consistent concern with the value of self-expression as related to defining his own attitudes and beliefs about experience, a search for meaning. As a high "elaborative" thinker, he uses his entries to roam about, seeking ideas from a range of experiences. As he notes, "If I haven't spent enough time gathering information, then it is difficult for me to write. I am always amazed when people sit down to the typewriter with nothing in front of them."

Tom was one of the few students who responded to a number of the published autobiographical narratives written in my composition methods class, using his responses to further define and clarify his own attitudes toward growth and change. For example, in response to a portrait of a son choosing a different career from that of his father, he noted that "Don's piece helped me keep in perspective how I can carry forth from my father even if I don't do so in his footsteps." In response to a student's description of her failure to make a cheerleading team, Tom found that he admired her "honesty,": "She truly believed that becoming a cheerleader would indeed make all of the difference in the world," concluding that "she changes and that is the essence—the Deon in the beginning of that story was not the same as the one who ended it."

His interest in autobiography stemmed from his need to define his own role or self-concept. He noted that in coming from a family of scientists, he had had to legitimatize his own career choice of becoming an English teacher. He recounted an incident in another class in which the teacher began class by sitting in the back of the room and saying nothing. As the class finally initiated their own discussion, he assumed a leadership role: "I liked it because as 'the leader' the students directed their comments to me. And I, in turn, tried to keep the discussion moving along." He also noted that "there are numerous levels of selves within literature as well as different ways our selves react to that literature. I am not going to argue the orthodox line that there are no selves (only imaginary ones), but I am amazed when people argue that there is only one true self."

Given his interest in defining attitudes and self-concept, I felt a strong need to reciprocate because I grew up with a well-known professor/father and identified with his need to acquire one's own voice as distinct from that of one's father or family. Thus, in response to his comment about multiple selves, I noted, "I believe that we develop 'selves' through our articulation with others and that our conceptions of selves are constantly changing."

However, in contrast to Lori, Tom perceived my self-disclosure and involvement as an intrusion into his autonomous, private search for meaning. When I asked him about engaging in a dialogue with his own students, he argued that "injecting personal thoughts" into a journal may result in "their journal looking like my thoughts," a concern consistent with the value he placed on self-expression. While he liked some of the evaluative comments, in contrast to Lori, he seemed quite satisfied with the somewhat minimal responses I provided.

Consistent with their own preferred approaches to learning, each of these students therefore had different purposes and each valued different kinds and degrees of responses. Laura, dutifully following the assignment, used the journal to keep a record of teaching ideas, while Lori used it to generate ideas for her paper, and Tom used it to explore experiences related to defining self-concept. While Laura and Tom valued my evaluative comments, Lori viewed them as unnecessary. While Lori wanted more self-disclosing dialogue, Tom resisted dialogue as an intrusion.

What I Learned from My Students' Reactions

In thinking about my students' reactions to my comments, I recognize several ways in which I could improve my responses:

Improving My Ability to Intuit Differences in Approaches to Learning and Purpose

I need to attend more carefully to individual differences in students' approaches to learning and purpose. Once I am able to perceive a student's particular approach or purpose, I can respond accordingly. As I noted previously, I may want to hold conferences with my students to help them to define or clarify their purposes or needs. Or I may ask students, within the journal, to define their purposes or needs.

It is also the case that helping students to clarify their purposes may shift their concerns away from using journals simply to fulfill an assignment to using the journals for their own needs. Students who had some sense of why they were using the journal seemed to be more intellectually engaged with their journals than those who were simply completing my assignment. Because Lori knew that she needed "to keep track of my students," her field-note entries had some purpose.

Encouraging More Deep/Elaborative Thinking

While I certainly want to accommodate individual differences, I also want to try to continue to push students like Laura toward more deep/elaborative thinking. If my students are to become "reflective practitioners," to use Schon's term, they need to do more than collect or generate activities; they need to reflect on the purpose, value, and consequences of those activities.

In order to foster this reflective stance and to maintain some dialogue with my students, I would try to model how I define the purpose, value, and consequences of the activities I am using in the classroom. For example, if a student notes that "freewriting sounds like a good idea," I would note that, "When we did the freewriting the other day about 'judging others,' I wanted to generate some feelings about the difficulty of judging others' writing, which we could share in discussion."

However, as I have argued in regard to the use of modeling in conferences, unless students can reciprocate in subsequent entries, I have no idea as to whether my modeling has any influence on the students. I therefore plan to encourage students, in the spirit of establishing more of a conversation, to respond to my comments. Furthermore, I clearly recognize the need to continue to break out of a detached, evaluative stance and share my own related ideas and experiences. My students may be more likely to reciprocate or reply to my ideas and experiences than to a comment such as "interesting ideas." In reading about my frustrations with trying to motivate students, they may, in sensing my willingness to admit problems, want to share some of their own problems.

Encouraging Perspective-taking

One reason for the lack of engagement in many journals is that, although students are expressing their opinions, they are not playing those opinions off against other, opposing opinions or examining those opinions from different perspectives. For example, in responding to a short story, they may too readily adopt the perspective of one character without considering other characters' perspectives.

To encourage more perspective-taking, I will ask students to create inner-dialogues or debates, then have them address or debate authors, cited authorities, or myself. Students could also adopt a range of different roles or personae in their journals, shifting from one perspective to the next. All of these strategies may result in more engaging journals, which would enhance my own engagement with their work and increase the potential for interchange and dissonance that is the essence of learning.

Works Cited

Atwell, Nancie. *In the Middle: Writing, Reading, and Learning with Adolescents.* Upper Montclair, N.J.: Boynton/Cook, 1987.

Beach, Richard. "Applying Life to Literature: Readers' Use of Autobiographical Experiences to Interpret Literature." Paper presented at the Annual Meeting of the National Council of Teachers of English, Los Angeles, California. November 22, 1987.

———. "Demonstrating Techniques for Assessing Writing in the Writing Conference." *College Composition and Communication* 37 (1986): 56–65.

Boyce, Judith. "Visions of Communication: The Use of Commonplace Books in the English Class." In *Seeing for Ourselves: Case-Study Research by Teachers of Writing,* edited by Glenda Bissex and Richard Bullock, 127–38. Portsmouth, N.H.: Heinemann, 1987.

Erickson, Erik. *Identity: Youth and Crisis.* New York: Norton, 1968.

Fulwiler, Toby. "Responding to Students' Journals." In *Writing and Response: Theory, Practice, and Research,* edited by Chris Anson, 149–73. Urbana: NCTE, 1988.

Harste, Jerome. "What It Means to Be Strategic: Good Readers as Informants." Paper presented at the Annual Meeting of the National Reading Conference, Austin, Texas. December 2, 1987.

Marton, Frederick, D. J. Hounsell, and Noel Entwistle. *The Experience of Learning.* Edinburgh: Scottish Academic Press, 1984.

Murray, Donald M. *A Writer Teaches Writing.* 2nd ed. Boston: Houghton Mifflin, 1984.

Perl, Sondra, and Nancy Wilson. *Through Teachers' Eyes.* Portsmouth, N.H.: Heinemann, 1987.

Schmeck, Ronald, Fred Ribich, and Nerella Ramanaiah. "Development of a Self-Report Inventory for Assessing Individual Differences in Learning Processes." *Applied Psychological Measurement* I (1977): 413–31.

Schon, Donald. *Educating the Reflective Practitioner.* San Francisco: Jossey-Bass, 1987.

Staton, Jana, Roger Shuy, Joy Kreeft Peyton, and Leslee Reed. *Interactive Writing in Dialogue Journals.* Norwood, N.J.: Ablex, 1987.

Sternglass, Marilyn, and Sharon Pugh. "Retrospective Accounts of Language and Learning Processes." *Written Communication* 3 (1987): 297–323.

Thies-Sprinthall, Lois, and Norman Sprinthall. "Preservice Teachers as Adult Learners: A New Framework for Teacher Education." In *Advances in Teacher*

Education, Vol. 3, edited by Martin Haberman and Julie Backus, 35–56. Norwood, N.J.: Ablex, 1987.

Wess, Robert. "Journal Writing and Student Learning." Paper presented at the Annual Meeting of the Conference on College Composition and Communication, Atlanta, Georgia. March 19, 1987.

Williams, Leslie. "Relations Between Supervisor/Teacher Intersections in Reflective Journals and Improvement in Practice." Paper presented at the Annual Meeting of the American Educational Research Association, Washington, D.C. April 20, 1987.

17 Imagining the Past and Teaching Essay and Poetry Writing

Anthony Petrosky
University of Pittsburgh

> I wish to make clear that the self I am speaking of here, and the one with which we will be concerned in the classroom, is a literary self, not a mock or false self, but a stylistic self, the self construable from the way words fall on a page. The other self, the identity of a student, is something with which I as a teacher can have nothing to do, not if I intend to remain a teacher. That there is a relation between these two selves, between writing and thinking, intellect and being, a confusing, complicated, and involving relation indeed—this is undeniable. . . . But the nature of this relation, that of the self to the roles or styles in which it finds expression and through which it grows, is one that only an individual writer or thinker has the right to work out. . . . Ideally, hopefully, primarily, our concern is with words: not with thinking, but with a language about thinking: not with people or selves but with languages about people and selves.
>
> William E. Coles, Jr., *The Plural I*[1]

Before going on to discuss my responses to students' essays and poems, I should say something about the way my classes are designed and (mostly) conducted. No matter what I teach—composition, poetry writing, or a graduate seminar in response theory—I establish my classes as workshops, as places where students do the work of readers and writers by entering into ongoing conversations about each other's writings and readings. I duplicate papers (students, my own, other writers) or passages from them, ask questions that invite conversations about what students think the writing has to say, and encourage critical comments, partly through my questions and partly through my own talk. Often I will establish a dialectic—an occasion in a class discussion for opening up a particular passage or moment in a piece of writing— by posing questions that allow students to discuss the passage under consideration by pushing against its grain, in a manner of speaking, by polarizing it so it might appear not as the necessary or right or only thing to say, but as one of many possible things to say within the polarities or context made possible by the passage itself. In one of the papers I will discuss later, for example, a student develops his interpretation of his past high school graduation by portraying it as a time of high anxiety and fear, a time to suddenly realize that his future would be his, not his parents', to control. He says, "I was getting scared and insecure knowing I was to be on my own." To push against his comment, one that speaks, I think, from a generalized sense of a past event rather than from a particular moment, I might ask the class, as a part of our discussion of this paper, if they believe, from the paper, that graduation is all fear and anxiety. Where does the fear and anxiety come from in the story he's telling? Are there other emotions, perhaps joy or celebration, represented in the paper? (And there were.) How, then, might graduation be presented as more than fear and anxiety without writing out the fear and anxiety? And, too, without allowing the fear and anxiety to close it down, to make it only that?

By pushing against passages, especially the over-generalized ones that Coles refers to as "theme writing," I hope to help students move away from theme writing and to see multiple perspectives, more often than not ones that they offer themselves in their papers, and to take a critical stance towards their own writing—a stance that inevitably asks them to see the past, whether it is distant or only moments ago, through the particulars that might represent it, and to then imagine experiences (including readings) as complicated, messy things that defy quick and easy representations. I should say too that this does not happen easily, as easily as, perhaps, it sounds. My students are usually novices at presenting their "readings" of experiences and texts, and they feel uncomfortable "making up things," or imagining what they don't know for "a fact," as one sophomore said during a class discussion where I was pressing her to formulate alternative "readings" of breakdancing as a cultural ritual. And there is the sense, too, in which writers generally become something like novices in the face of beginnings that ask for an imagining or reconstructing of the past, whether that particular instance of the past is represented by events and people or ideas formulated in response to readings. Reconstructing and imagining are difficult work, and it is, I think, much easier to make sweeping general gestures from the past than it is to ground writing and talk in specific moments. Part of learning to ground writing in particulars has to do with learning to talk about writing, to talk about what has fallen on the page, and there is a discipline to pointing to specific passages or moments in a paper and commenting about those, not about some generalized response that might have to do with the author's intention or a generous reading of that. By establishing a conversation and pushing some (or a lot) against the grain, it is possible (but certainly not necessarily the case) that reseeing papers and passages will become more than adding or subtracting sentences to elaborate or clarify what is already there. A conversation that takes as its habit the ground of a paper, the particulars and their relationships and extensions, and what is on the page (the grain) as one of the possibilities of what might be there, as presented by the dialectic it establishes, offers, I think, opportunities for students to imagine writing as an ongoing tangling and untangling and tangling. And it is possible in this context to then imagine papers and passages (and poems) as moments in that tangling and untangling, moments that are more plastic and open to play than set and locked, as they often say, in words. Within a dialectic (and there are problems, to be sure, in posing a dialectic in polarities, but it has been for me a useful place to begin) students at least have the opportunity of learning that what is on the page is one possibility among others. And through workshop discussions, through conversations where they speak with each other, they can hear and comment on other comments, and they can learn how to ask questions of writing, questions that point to passages and moments in texts—whether they are students' texts or professionals'.

I think, too, that when there are numerous people involved in a conversation about a piece of writing, it is possible for imitation to play a subtle but important role. With multiple comments and questions, everyone participating in the conversation has the opportunity to imitate, to step into and assume those readings and critical frames that seem interesting or smart to them. The multiplicity of play in conversations allows space for various takes on pieces of writing, and in this space the opportunity exists for people to try on, so to speak, the various frames, and this imitation seems as important to me as the kind of imitation that comes into play when we try on the perspectives or voices or styles of other writers. I understand imitation in the contexts of its consequences in conversation, and in the possibilities inherent in putting before students compelling, challenging, and quirky examples of writing—examples that, in other words, might make it possible for them to learn something that someone else does or desires to do. I know that attention to imitation, like attention to particulars (or, in another language, "details") is not now a very popular way to talk about writing, and partly, I think, this is the result of a history where both were used didactically as the points of lessons and drills, but those excesses do not have to enter into occasions where students are presented with examples surrounded by critical conversations about them. Once again the context makes all the difference, and it is quite a different kind of learning that goes on when students have conversations, for instance, about particulars in specific pieces of writing, than when they are simply told to put more details in a paragraph or, worse yet, given sentences to which they must add details. Imitation, whether it has to do with subjects, or voices, or styles, or particulars, can be taught in a much more subtle way, through conversations that ask for shifting attentions. And the affects are often visible (at least as I have seen them), then, in bits and pieces in writing and in the kinds of talk, including the kinds of questions, students bring to essays and poems.

Out of habit and a compulsion to write while I read, I write comments on students' essays and poems. They almost always take on a life of their own. I ask questions, and I speak back, sometimes pushing against a passage, sometimes summarizing what I make of a passage and asking if that is what the writer makes of it, and sometimes praising strong readings or arguments or images. At times I ask students to revise papers (or poems) and other times I simply speak back and let the students do what they want. There are no grades given for individual papers or poems (all my evaluation is done using the students' complete portfolios of writing at the end of the semester), and I hold individual thirty-minute conferences at least twice a semester and more if I can. I always feel more in touch with students' writing during these conferences than I do writing comments on papers. Even when my questions and comments are elaborate and try to explain themselves by pointing to passages in a text, I feel less certain about their effects than I do when I raise them in conferences where conversations are possible, but it is simply not possible for me to hold conferences more than a few times each semester, and there are too many advantages to workshops, to those larger conversations, to even allow me to imagine my wanting to proceed only through conferences.

It has also always been difficult for me to predict how involved my students might become with an individual essay assignment or poem. This uncertainty, among other things, has led me to avoid discrete assignments and to turn instead to semester-long assignment sequences that pose problems for students, problems that they "work" through their reading and writing. I think students can be more involved with sequenced assignments than with discrete, unconnected tasks because sequences can compel them to make commitments to extended academic projects, like, for example, "Growth and Change in Adolescence"[2] (the one used in our Basic Reading and Writing courses at Pittsburgh) that involve numerous reading and writing tasks designed to build on and spiral off of each other. The Basic Reading and Writing (BRW) set of assignments invites students to use reading, writing, and class discussions in an ongoing study of adolescence, a study that is conducted through their writing about themselves and about the adolescents they encounter in books such as *Catcher in the Rye* and the theories of adolescence they study in books such as *Coming of Age in Samoa*.[3] Sequences like the one we use in our BRW classes encourage students to develop their own "readings" and points of view in concert with those of the professionals who wrote the essays and stories they are reading and in concert with their classmates.

I do not use assignments in my poetry writing classes, at least not the way I do in my composition courses, but I have imagined semester-long projects for my students, and these projects then guide the kinds of poems and tasks I put before them. When I teach the Introduction to Poetry Writing course, for example, I think of my students as novices (and most of them are), who write a poetry equivalent to an over-generalized essay, not because they want to or have learned to, but usually because they have allowed themselves to be seduced by big subjects like love or death or world peace (as is usually the case for novices, I think, and as we will see examples of later), and they do not know much about modern poetry, because they have not read much of it. When I set a project for these writers, I think about helping them learn to tell stories in poems and to ground those stories in images and particulars that allow them to invest their emotions in what they are writing. I put examples before them that I think they can speak to with interest and commitment, and I may ask them to write particular kinds of poems, poems that, say, pay attention to the details of landscape or faces, as a part of their work on this larger project of telling stories in poems. And, of course, we use our class time for conversations about the examples I bring before them and about their own work. For a more advanced group of students, perhaps an intermediate group writing poems that are almost exclusively stories lush with particulars, I would set the semester's project around more experimental writing that speaks through lyrics or meditations, and those would be the kinds of examples that I would bring to them and the kinds of poems I would ask them to write. And although my sense of projects for my students in the poetry writing courses is not guided by sequences of specific assignments, the projects proceed around central concerns and I see my responsibilities, then, in much the same way as I see them for my composition courses, and a large part of those have to do with the examples and readings that I bring to my students and the ways I ask for their attention and imitation in conversations and in writing.

Now let me turn to some examples of students' compositions. Here is the first draft of an essay by Robin, a college freshman, written in response to the first assignment in that BRW sequence. The assignment asks for an essay about a significant experience that happened in the last two years, an experience "that has changed the way you are or the way you think about things." It goes on to invite a description of the experience and an explanation of "why and how this experience was a significant one."

> The most significant thing that happened to me in the last few years was when my father had a nervous breakdown. It changed my whole world, my family came apart, the man I loved and depended on for our food and clothes and shelter was sick. The most important man in the world to me was sick, crazy I thought. My father stands six feet three inches, his skin shines like black fresh coal, his eyes so loving and strong are a pretty brown, his hair is natural curly, his feet a size 15 to the whole big structure. My father looks good for his 48 years, borne on Dec 30, 1937 by Mrs. _____ and father by Judge _____. He came home late on saturday night drained and tired. He works at a GE plant day after day doing the same old job for the past 15 years of his life. Working all day long on a garbage truck to help give us brats the extra things we wanted but didn't need. We have a nice house in a nice neighborhood. My father is looked up to by all the neighbors because he works so hard for us. Last year he saved up enough money to send my mother and sister to California. I worked and paid my own way, first class flight. He had alumunum siding put on the house while we were gone for a special surprise for my mother. He had given us so much and worked so hard I guess it just got to him. Always giving and never receiving, he had to know we loved him and loved everything he did for us. He became depressed, lost and lonely and afraid. We all helped nurse him back to health with the doctor help. And now I know how to share and appreciate this wonderful man more. Understand his faults and know that he's not perfect. I love this man with his faults and all I know that all people have problems big and small and that you have to deal with it.

This paper by another student, Chris, is also from Robin's class. It was written in response to the same assignment.

> In the past three years especially significant experiences have happened to me. I think life is full of experiences all to aid ones personal outlook, personality and judgment. As I said I've had numerous experiences and it all started when we moved from Long Island to PA. All these experiences helped to broaden the outlook for an angered and confused teenager Me. An experience that scared me the most which I chose to explain was my graduation.

It all started in Jan when everyone was saying things like; "I can't wait to get out of this hole," or "I can't wait to get out of this jail." But I was getting scared and insecure knowing I was to be on my own. Eventually many others like I'd say a majority felt that way by may and june. Its funny all you life your parents have been saying don't prescrastinate or do homework etc. Your parents were always there with a home, food and clothing no danger except boo boos. Now you realize your out of school playtime, party life and its time to put out. You ask yourself questions like; what am I going to do? What do I want to do? Will I pump gas until I'm sixty five? or will I be a bum? What real headbenders to think about for sure.

This was a significant experience in that I was forced to choose between wasting time and looking for oneself. After all what is success but finding happiness which is finding yourself.

I cannot help but admire Robin's draft for the risks it takes, risks that were very apparent in class discussions of drafts of this assignment from other students who, like Chris, chose to write about more commonplace experiences like graduation or balancing a budget or doing laundry for the first time. I like the way, too, that Robin's draft brings forward the particulars about her father. By writing about his physical stature, his responsibilities, his job, and his generosity, she offers the possibility of a strong, authoritative reading of him and his nervous breakdown. She says that "the most important man in the world to me was sick, crazy I thought," and this, along with the descriptions she brings forward and her insistence that "He had given so much and worked so hard I guess it just got to him," makes his giving (and, perhaps, as she suggests, his never receiving) a key element in her attempt to represent what happened to him. When I commented on this paper, I pointed to the particulars and to her highlighting of her father's generosity, and I raised questions about where she might go from here with the essay. Did she want to say more about how her father changed? Where could she place herself and her feelings in this experience so her writing about it might show us what happened to turn this powerful man into one that was "sick, crazy I thought"? Did she want to say more about how she nursed him back to health? And what about the faults? She did not bring them forward, yet they seem to want to take a place, but it is difficult for me to make the connections. What might they be? How might she discuss her feelings about them? How are they connected to his strengths? Does a more elaborate discussion of this belong in this paper? My comments to Robin played off of moments she offers in the paper, and I tried to stay close to those that I thought were key, and during the class discussion, other students noticed, in particular, her mention of her father's change, her nursing him back to health, and her thinking that he was perhaps crazy. They wanted to know more, so the discussion turned to a conversation to get Robin to say more, and as she did, students told her that much of what she was saying could go into the paper. Robin's draft gave them a lot to work with.

Unlike Chris's draft, Robin's opens up her subject. She has a certain kind of authority over it, an authority that derives from her willingness to speak for herself and to use writing to bring forward particulars to push at a subject about which she is uncertain, a subject in which she had a significant emotional investment even though she had not worked it out or tied it up in a neat package. Chris's draft, on the other hand, closes down his subject; it does not pay attention to particulars the way Robin's does and, instead, it presents graduation as a cute but frightening experience (although the paper does not do much specific work to bring forward anything frightening about it, except the questions it raised), an experience that can be easily reduced to sayings like "I can't wait to get out of this hole," and then to something that causes "real headbenders to think about for sure." Robin's opening up of her subject, an opening that proceeds in part through the particulars she brings forward (however incomplete they are) and in part through the insistent and frightened, caring voice, signals her involvement in this essay. Chris's lack of particulars and his quick reduction of graduation to cute quotes and questions signal his marginal involvement in the essay. This is not to say that he was not involved in graduation or that it did not affect him; it is to say, though, that when I read these paragraphs as writing, as "language about thinking" or "languages about people and selves," Chris's language, his writing as writing, does not offer a "reading" of an experience the way Robin's does, and it proceeds in a manner that shuts down his subject, that reduces it to commonplace generalizations put forward in a cavalier voice, a voice that represents him as Mr. Cool, Mr. Funny-about-what-might-have-been-a-frightening-experi-ence. When I commented on Chris's draft, I told him that I thought he had reduced his graduation to a quick commonplace, and I pointed to his switch from first person in the second sentence of his second paragraph to his use of second person "you" as a signal that he wasn't writing about himself any longer and that he had "written away" his experience by generalizing about this "you." What particulars, what "little stories," could he bring forward to present the way he felt during the time graduation was on his mind? Was it all fear and anxiety? How might the anger and confusion mentioned at the end of the first paragraph enter into the discussion?

In a way Chris needs to begin again, to see that his writing is not saying much that anyone else couldn't say about graduation, and to decide, then, whether or not he wants to continue writing about graduation; and if he does, he needs to put some time into writing about the particulars that he hints at that could bring his experience forward as his. During the class discussion, almost all of the students' comments asked Chris to write about why he was angry and confused and to tell a story or tell of times when he realized things were changing. The class was saying, I think, that he needed to locate those moments he might write from, those moments when he felt angry or confused or suddenly aware that things were changing. Robin needs to do some locating too, but hers has more to do with where she wants to place herself in this piece (for example, on the outside narrating it or on the inside unfolding it as it happens) and what, then, she wants to elaborate and comment on.

Both papers, in their first attempts to say why and how their subjects were significant experiences, reduce their conclusions to aphorisms. Robin says that "I love this man with all his faults and all I know that all people have problems big and small and that you have to deal with it." Chris says, "I was forced to choose between wasting time and looking for oneself. After all what is success but finding happiness which is finding yourself." Although the assignment might be said to beg these kinds of closures, especially, from novices, by asking writers to go on and draw conclusions about why and how the experiences they wrote about were significant, it can also be said that it puts students in the position of having to present conclusions, and that students have little experience drawing conclusions from the particulars of their writing. The aphorism or platitude is, then, a seductive way out of a difficult situation. That both Robin and Chris take it is not surprising, even though Robin has presented particulars about her father's breakdown from which she might work towards a conclusion derived from her paper rather than from some generic statement about "all people." And again, my responses to these conclusions try to push against what the students wrote. I asked Robin, for example, why she ended by presenting a sentence on "all people." Where is Robin? Where is her father? How might what is significant to them be different from what is significant to "all people"? How could she present those differences? How could she connect them to the particular things she says about herself and her father? And, again, what about the faults? What makes the faults so significant? What do the strengths have to do with the faults? Chris's conclusion is more problematic since he does not have particulars to work from the way Robin does, and I asked him to put it aside until he did another draft of the essay.

In presenting my responses to these two papers, I hope to demonstrate, in part, the importance of treating writing as writing, of responding to what students have written and to focus, then, on the evolution of a piece of writing not as a human relations problem—not, that is, as an occasion for me to question or discuss their relationships with the people or ideas represented in the essays—but as the work of an author using language to open up and discuss a subject.[4] It is also easy to read into papers, to attribute specific readings in an act of generosity where the writing only presents generalized or received comments. It would have been easy to do this with Chris's paper. He offers anxiety over graduation as the occasion for his paper, but he does not provide a compelling account of that anxiety or his experiences from which it grew, and it would have been easy to read into his writing, to invent it for him, to say, "sure, I can see the anxiety," because it is hinted at and revealed in a general way. Instead of reading into Chris's paper or writing it for him, I pushed against his writing by pointing to and questioning the easy generalizations and quick closing down of his subject, and by asking him, then, what he might do to open it up, to present the particulars, the stories, that could represent it as he claims it was—fearful and anxious.

I also chose to present these two drafts because they demonstrate things I spend a considerable amount of time discussing in composition and writing classes—students' involvement with their writing, the authority their writing derives from its use of particulars, and the voice their writing presents. All three of these—involvement, authority, and voice—have something to do with the particulars a piece of writing (whether it is an essay, a poem, or a story) offers as its ground, as the characteristics that make it one writer's piece and not another's. All three seem intertwined, but it is possible to comment on them individually, I think, by pointing to sentences and passages in papers. I look for signals, but I also let the writing tell me its story. Robin's paper demonstrates, as I have said, that she is prepared to open up a discussion of her father's breakdown. Chris's demonstrates that he has not yet opened up his subject, that he is still willing to represent graduation as cute sayings and easy generalizations. Chris's voice—that which carries sentiments and attitudes—develops as off-the-cuff and cavalier, and I imagined that he could continue to play with that if he grounded his writing in key moments.

I want to turn now to three poems by students. I want to do this before going on to propose general comments about my responses to students' writing, because, as I have already suggested, there are ways in which my responses to students' essays and poems share a common landscape, and I am not sure I like this (and I want to think about it more) because it clearly points to how I imagine good writing. There are differences too, of course, if only because poems are not usually written in response to an assignment the way essays are (although as I mentioned earlier, they might well come from writers "working" on projects). And the grammar or surface of the forms works by different rules, and writers' and readers' expectations are usually different for poems than they are for essays. But poems and essays as writing also exist, for me, in a common landscape marked by writers' involvement with what they are writing, with their attention to voice, and with their development of a certain kind of authority that comes, in part, from taking a stand, from saying, in effect, "this is what I think or see and here is how I ground it." And, of course, this is what I think good writing is—writing that takes a stand or offers a stance with a sense of involvement (or emotional commitment), writing that is grounded in particulars, that notices its rhythms and voices. These elements (as I have been calling them)—involvment, voice, and authority—proceed, I think, from writers' attention (not necessarily conscious either) to particulars, to where they locate themselves in their writing and to what they bring forward to represent or ground the subjects or things they're writing about.

Here are three drafts of poems by students. They were written by English majors at Pittsburgh. The first was written by Nancy, a sophomore, and the last two were written by Gregg, a junior.

THE NORMAL THING TO BE

I'm like people,
and people are like me,
yet somehow I am different.
Abnormal they call me.

If they call me abnormal,
and I am like them,
and they are like me,
then doesn't that make them abnormal?

If they are abnormal,
and if they are like me,
then wouldn't I be abnormal?

If I am abnormal,
and they are abnormal,
then we all are abnormal,
so wouldn't that make us all normal?

If we are all normal,
then why do people call me abnormal?

If I am not abnormal,
am I still different?

If I am different,
how can I be like people,
and how can people be like me?

Is this abnormal, or is this different?

There is an immediate problem that comes into play when I discuss students' poems and it has to do with what they read, the problem of what they know about poetry from their reading, and even though the same problem comes into play when I discuss students' essays, it seems to be more prominent when I consider poems. It is the question of context, or to put it the way my students put it, it is the question of knowing where the writer is coming from in terms of what the writer knows about poems (or essays) from reading poems (or essays). Students who read modern poetry (and there is a wide range of it) write differently than students who do not. Students who read modern poetry learn the language, subjects, and postures of the community of poets they come to admire, and they write, then, in imitation (at least as a beginning) of what they read. Students who are unfamiliar with modern poetry and study, say, only contemporary British or American poetry have very different models in their heads of what poems are, and they also have very different senses of how to use language. The same is true, I think, of students who read essays in magazines and journals—they write differently from those who do not, especially from those who read only or mostly textbooks. One of the enormous problems of schooling has to do with the inadequate (and often terrible) examples of essays and poems set before students in high school and college textbooks.

So one of the first things I think of when I read students' poems (and it is puzzling to me that I do not do this when I read essays) is where the poems locate them in a possible universe of poetry. Nancy is, I think, a real novice. The poem tells me, because of its subject and language, that she has not read much modern poetry outside, perhaps, of poems like this one. She is caught in discursiveness, and while this does not have to be a problem for poets who can use it effectively along with images and invention, she is also caught in big, ungraspable subjects like "normality" and "abnormality." There are no images in this poem, and she does not tell a particular story; instead, she tries to discuss herself as an example of these big subjects. It does not work, mostly because she does not have particulars to hang on to, to ground her talk in. The lack of details and images makes it difficult for this poem to convince me that it knows what it is talking about, that the writer has some authority over her subject, although it is clear, I think, that she is involved enough to be worrying over it. But it is only a draft, and the poem points to a number of ways she might go with this piece.

She could, of course, begin again and write about something else, something she knows about or feels closer to, but I think the worrying here points to what she wants to do. She is concerned with being abnormal and the set of questions surrounding that seems to intrigue her. That is obvious enough, but how can she get from her concerns to a compelling poem? I suggested she begin by bringing forward those moments that might stand for or represent what she thinks makes her abnormal. If it turns out that she is not concerned with being abnormal, but with being different from others, she might again try to bring forward those images or stories that make her different from specific people, people she could represent with particular images or stories. Or she might, if it turns out that she is concerned with how she can be like people and how they can be like her, begin by writing about particular times with particular images and stories that could show how she is like specific people. A turn this way to particulars would give her something to speak from, something to think about and play with, and she could strengthen the timid voice trying to confront these gigantic subjects by making them manageable and, then, opening them up, so she might demonstrate some involvement with her subject. Nancy, as it turned out, did not want to give this poem the time it would have taken to ground it, to rethink it, and her response to my suggestions and questions was that she just did not want to work on it anymore.

This next poem of Gregg's strikes me as very similar to Nancy's and very similar, in a way, to Chris's paper.

> i get glimpses of many things.
> i figured out a cafe in Albuquerque
> what is man
> i have solved the energy crisis
> upteenth times
> world peace—poverty—ignorance—
> urban blight, you name it i've solved it

it is not uncommon for me to understand
very sublime things such as the existence
and essence of God and the universe
but the problem is this. . . .
iforgetthemveryquickly
and that reminds me

Like Nancy's poem and Chris's essay, there is not much to hold on
to here. After mentioning glimpses of things and locating himself in
an Albuquerque cafe, Gregg goes on to close down his subject by
cataloging generalizations and settling for a clever ending that invokes
forgetfulness. To push against his tendency to take the easy way out
of his announced ends—that is, of telling us the particulars or stories
of what he does glimpse—I responded by pointing to the first two
lines as a statement of what he might offer in the poem, and then
questioned his telling us he has solved the energy, peace, poverty,
ignorance, urban blight, and God problems. What is a reader supposed
to think these problelms are? What kind of writing gives me a list of
such gigantic "problems" and asks me to believe its author has solved
them? How might I get a glimpse of what was glimpsed in that cafe?
What stories or particulars could be brought forward to stand for or
present some aspect of one or two of these problems? Who, finally,
speaks like this? God? Someone trying to be clever or ironic?

My point here is to turn Gregg to his writing and away from his
intentions or what he has in his head, to ask him questions that might
push against the quick, unearned list of generalizations his poem offers
as what he glimpses. I want to let him know what the writing on the
page presents and how, as a reader and writer, I react to it.

Here is another poem Gregg wrote after spending a part of a
semester reading modern poetry. Like Nancy, he was a novice and
had not read much beyond contemporary American and British poetry
he had studied in a college course.

The city streets were barren as i walked without
a sound toward the cold steel of the skyscrapers
i inhaled my surroundings:
a noiseless taxi drove from my sight
leaving—stillness;
a couple in their fashionable winter coats carried
luggage into the bus station and departed Pittsburgh
and me without saying a word.
A man and i traveled the city streets together
locked in a mission to successfully exist in the same
space—his world never crossed mine—worlds apart.
He talked to me
i smiled and watched the clouds above the Steel Building

drift over our heads
i wondered where these clouds were going—knowing how
like attracts like perhaps i would meet them some day,
i fancied, near a bus station in Seattle with the young
couple arriving as well in fulfillment of the scriptures.
i didn't know
as i looked into my companions eyes i could see the
flashing *walk*sign
he looked at me as if to say "well?"
and i stood still as the world filtered through me.

This poem offers particular images and details to give its abstract, meditative stance a context. The world filters through the writer, he wants to tell us about it, about the tempered existence of people in the same space. Instead of simply saying that the world filters through him or that he inhales his surroundings, he points to and names a few things that define the sensations he is interested in presenting, so that when he gets to the last line, it is believable. Through its images, through the particulars of its story, the poem demonstrates its authority to invoke the stillness, isolation, and elusiveness, and it allows its author that certain kind of authority that says, in effect, "this is what I see, here are the particulars by which I define these peculiar sensations."

As I read this poem, I thought immediately that Gregg learned something about the weaving together of images and discursiveness from his readings in modern poetry. I still had questions about the poem I wanted to raise. I pointed to the particulars and mentioned how they gave the poem a kind of authority and very laid-back voice, a voice of wonderment located in specific details, and I asked whether or not it might be possible to say more about the surroundings, to dig even deeper into that moment and try, then, to define it not only by the departing taxi and fashionable winter coats, but by other sights or sounds. Was the stillness essential? If so, how could it be kept intact and the surroundings intensified? I was puzzled by the young couple "arriving as well in fulfillment of the scriptures" and asked how the poem might be made to help me understand this. How might this reference be anchored in an image or explained without becoming overextending? I also wanted to know about the lines. Is every line broken where it is for a reason? How do the line breaks contribute to the voice? The longer lines play to the laid-back voice and the shorter ones create counterbalancing tensions. Was this intentional? Would it be possible for the poem's lines to highlight images and the voice of wonderment without chopping up its laid-back quality?

It is obvious that my responses to this poem (and to the others) privilege images and details and "little stories," the particulars I have been referring to, but it is not a question of poems (or essays, for that matter) simply unfolding as a series of images. Discursiveness—those statements about images and sensations—carry poems along too. The poems I chose to discuss here present students' writing that leans too heavily on discursiveness without attention to particulars, but the opposite has often happened in my classes. It is not unusual for students to write poems that are catalogues of images, that read like image-stamping machines. I do not want to give the impression that these examples are anything more than examples, but I think it is also accurate to say that novice poets get caught in the easy quickness of discursiveness in much the same way novice essayists get caught in theme language and received generalizations. Pushing against these is difficult for students, especially if they are not involved in the assignment they have to write, but it is something they can learn to do as a part of learning how to talk about writing.

My responses also privilege questions over directions. If I give students ways to revise, or if I tell them how I might revise a particular moment in an essay or poem, they almost always follow my directions and then the revision is mine not theirs. I stay away from directions (at least with these students); instead, my responses take the form of questions (sometimes with little summaries). I question specific passages or moments that strike me as significant or telling. This occurs, as I said earlier, in the context of a workshop where students are asked to comment on each other's writing before I do. Questioning, though, whether it is done in a class discussion or as written comments on students' papers, can be just as overwhelming as giving directions, so I try to focus on two or three moments in the essay or poem that might get the writer thinking about revision as something more than just tinkering with lines or phrases.

It should be clear, too, by now that my responses to essays and poems do not differ that much. I work with the writing on the page and begin by looking for a sense of authority and involvement and voice. There is also a theoretical argument (a suspect one, I should say) that has allowed me to think about why and how my responses to poems and essays are similar, and it has to do with the nature of poems and essays. M. M. Bakhtin claims that poems are authorial monologues (expressions of "authorial individuality"),[5] single voices trying to rise from and above their sources (like angels perhaps), and against poetry he places the novel, the best of which dissolve the singular voices of the authors to reveal a "vast plenitude" of voices, the voices of the characters which take over. Multivoiced novels and stories are dialogic, while poems are monologic. Even though single writers create novels, they create them with many voices speaking in dialogue with each other, and it is these multiple voices, this dialogue, that makes it possible for readers to privilege one voice (and its perspective) or some voices (and their perspectives) over others in their readings. Poetry, even if it includes such things as quotes or multiple perspectives, speaks to us as an authorial monologue. Bakhtin claims that "no matter how many contradictions and insoluble conflicts the poet develops within it, it is always illumined by one unitary and indisputable discourse." "In poetry," he says, "even discourse about doubts must be cast into a discourse that cannot be doubted."[6] He is saying, I think, that poetry speaks in a unitary voice with a certain kind of authority, and that it is impossible, then, for a poet to set up voices to speak against his or her voice, because even if he or she did, they would be only sources for the poet's "monologic steadfastness."[7] Bakhtin claims that "the language of the poem is his language, he is utterly immersed in it, inseparable from it, he makes use of each form, each word, each expression according to its unmediated power to assign meaning (as it were, "without quotation marks"), that is, as pure and direct expression of his own intention."[8] Everything a poet uses for a source—including others' language, descriptions, or retold stories—is, as an "indispensable" prerequisite "of poetic style,"[9] shaped into the poet's language, the poet's characteristic voice which is struggling to present its point of view. I think the same things can be said of essays. They can be thought of, like poems, as authorial monologues that struggle to rise from their sources. They speak through their writing with voices that represent literary selves; their similarity to poems can be attributed to what Bakhtin refers to as "the language of poetic genres." An essay, like a poem, develops a specific, singular point of view; it speaks with one monologic voice. This is not to say that poems and essays might be identical, but that they are, extending Bakhtin's thinking, similar in how they make use of their sources to present unitary voices.

Bakhtin's notions (as he reimagines stylistics away from formalism) about the differences between poetry and novels derive from the idea that language takes its meaning from dialogue which is grounded in particular social contexts that reveal everyday life, class conflicts, and the construction of communities. Clearly, he privileges the novel with its multiplicity of voices speaking to each other and, then, the author's interior voice which is in constant dialogue with the outside world. And as seductive as this general equation (novel = multiplicity of voices; poem = a monologic voice) is, there are some interesting problems here. I am particularly taken with Bakhtin's swift and elegant dismissal of poetry (and, I think, essays) as a kind of Newtonian art with its assumptions, as he sees it, of the separation of inner and outer life, and its language of the monologue, and because he offers me a way of thinking about poetry and essays—as monologues trying to rise from their sources—that blurs some of the old genre distinctions and helps me pose the similarities of my responses to essays and poems as another problem.

But before going on to this problem, I would like to play for a minute with another that Bakhtin offers, and this has to do with how we might understand that move from an inner voice in constant dialogue with the outside world (for presumably poets and essayists share the inner voice with novelists) to monologic writing. What then turns the interior dialogue into a monologue for poets and essayists? And what are "pure" and "direct" expressions of intention? Dialogues transformed to monologues? The myth of a singular language postured by a writer? The form of the poem (or essay)? The creation of a self, a "literary self," as Bill Coles calls it, a stylistic self, that seems to be singular throughout poems (and essays); that seems, that is, to at least be read that way by readers? Derrida points out that there are no logocentric texts, only logocentric readings, and in this sense, I think the question is more directly the last one I posed about singular literary selves. That is, is it my assumptions about what the text (in this case the fact of the poem or essay) is—a monologue—that accounts for my reading of it as such, or is it the text with its apparent absence of multiple voices? Or both? Bakhtin would say, I think, although I am far from sure, that it is the intention to speak with a singular voice that transforms the interior dialogue (of the self with the world) into a monologue, but does this mean then that monologues, because they are intentionally singular, are consistently one-voiced in the sense that they represent one, unified self? Can't monologues be schizophrenic? And aren't monologues at least in dialogue with their readers?

I want to raise these questions to muddy the waters a little, because as helpful as Bakhtin has been in my thinking about the similarities of poems and essays, his ideas frame a larger and more intriguing problem that has to do with my expectations about "literary selves" (and how they might be said to be grounded in writing) and the singularity of those selves or voices in essays and poems. It is a commonplace of poetry workshops to speak of a writer's voice, of a writer finding his or her voice, and it is often the case that when critics study a writer's works, they will speak in terms of recurring themes and a consistent voice that represents that particular writer and his or her posture towards subjects, audience, and self. Much the same thing happens with essayists (and novelists for that matter), and I can imagine responses to students' work in the context of these same expectations. But, then, is this a question of writers working within an inevitable monologic voice, or is this a question of readers' expectations, expectations that point writers in the direction of logocentric discourse instead of, say, a schizo-discourse—a writing of multiplicities, of multiple voices not necessarily trying to make a point, as we say, but to offer instead intersections of voices and ideas, places to continually return to because they are elusive or suggestive and they are not leading to one thing? This is an interesting idea to me, because the possibilities of multiple voices in single essays and poems plays against logocentric discourse and its expectations, expectations which, I think, frame my responses to students' essays and poems. The question of where to go from here if I am willing to allow my students' multiple voices in their writings is another essay, at least, but I can imagine that initially it would involve bringing before them examples of writers writing against the monologue with multiple voices or multiple texts running on the same pages, and that this alone would be an interesting beginning in another conversation about writing. And I can imagine assignments that invite this kind of writing from students, but I am having a difficult time imagining my expectations for reading and responding to such writing, and that is what makes me suspect that this might be much more intriguing than what I am already doing.

Bakhtin, to shift spheres for a final concluding moment, thinks that "the language of poetic genres, when they approach their stylistic limit, often becomes authoritarian, dogmatic and conservative, sealing itself off from the influence of extraliterary social dialects."[10] And I would think too, to return for a moment to my students' concluding moves that shut down their subjects, that the language of overgeneralizations, of received aphorisms such as "what is success but finding happiness which is finding yourself" and "I'm like people/people are like me . . . ," approaches a stylistic limit by assuming final authority to seal off subjects from other influences, including further readings and thinking, and they are, in my experience, enormously seductive for students, whether they are writing essays or poems. But there is also another way to think about the language of poetic genres approaching stylistic limits, and that has to do with what I might call the predictability of the genres, or perhaps it is the predictability of my expectations of them as a reader. Maybe my responses to students' essays and poems are similar because their writing (and mine) is inscribed in the expectations of logocentric discourse and the notion of singular, consistent selves—"literary selves" (and personal selves) that are grounded in the particulars of the past. And maybe the compelling story here is that my predictability and my expectations, as I have related them through my responses to students' essays and poems, are like stylistic limits that act to seal off my students' writing, to keep it within the boundaries of academic expectations, rather than to open it up to the play of multiple voices and selves.[11]

Notes

1. William E. Coles, Jr., *The Plural I: The Teaching of Writing* (New York: Holt, Rinehart and Winston, 1978), 12–13.

2. David Bartholomae and Anthony Petrosky, *Facts, Artifacts and Counterfacts: Theory and Method for a Reading and Writing Course* (Upper Montclair, New Jersey: Boynton/Cook Publishers). Our book presents the materials, including the sequenced assignments, for this semester-long college course that we developed at the University of Pittsburgh. Examples of other sequenced reading and writing assignments can be found in Bartholomae and Petrosky's *Ways of Reading: An Anthology for Writers* (New York: A Bedford Book of St. Martin's Press, 1987).

3. The following books are required for the BRW course: *I Know Why the Caged Bird Sings*, by Maya Angelou; *The Catcher in the Rye*, by J. D. Salinger; *Hunger of Memory*, by Richard Rodriguez; *Passages*, by Gail Sheehy; *The Vanishing Adolescent*, by Edgar Friedenberg; and *Coming of Age in Samoa*, by Margaret Mead.

4. See Coles's discussions of students' papers in *The Plural I*. He insists on treating students' writings as writing, not as statements about their personality or their relationships with others, and he focuses on the way students use "Themewriting" to close down subjects, to offer received generalizations that tell rather than show. Writing represents its author and that author's attitude or posture toward a subject, an audience, and toward a self. Representations can be changed, and readers' comments on students' writing can put students in a position to see how they represent themselves, their subjects, and audiences.

5. M. M. Bakhtin, *The Dialogic Imagination: Four Essays*, edited by Michael Holquist and translated by Caryl Emerson and Michael Holquist (Austin: University of Texas Press, 1981), 267. Bakhtin uses this distinction between the "authorial individuality" of poetic genres and the multiple voices of novels to both criticize stylistics—as it has tried to imagine the novel in terms of poetic genres—and to propose a way of discussing the novel that breaks it free of traditional stylistic definitions. Bakhtin proposes to define novels as dialogues among multiple voices and not, as traditional stylistics does, as unitary monologues.

6. Bakhtin, 286.

7. Bakhtin, 286.

8. Bakhtin, 285.

9. Bakhtin, 264.

10. Bakhtin, 287.

11. I am grateful to the members of my winter 1987 graduate seminar who read and commented on an earlier draft of this paper. I am especially grateful to Ellen Bishop, who read and commented on every draft of this paper and whose suggestions helped me resee its direction.

18 Responding to Responses: Good News, Bad News, and Unanswered Questions

Lee Odell
Rensselaer Polytechnic Institute

As do many other teachers of composition, I make a practice of scheduling individual conferences with my students. In one of these conferences, a student came to a passage in which I had, simply as an aid to my memory, underlined what struck me as the key points in his argument. In response to my underlinings, the student launched into an elaborate explanation of all the things he had done wrong. It took me a minute to realize what was going on and a couple more minutes to reassure him and explain what the underlining meant. Eventually he calmed down and then remarked: "It's just that whenever I see a mark on my paper, I panic."

In considering my student's comment, I began to rethink my interest in the problem of responding to students' writing. As do other contributors to this volume, I want to discuss both a procedure for providing students with responses to their writing and also some of the assumptions underlying that procedure. But these discussions simply provide a basis for my central concern in this essay: an examination of ways in which student writers assess comments on their writing. In addition to asking what kind(s) of response should student writers be given, I want to raise this question: How do student writers respond to their readers' responses? This latter question seems especially important for composition teachers who are interested in ways responses to early drafts can help shape both the form and content of a final draft. Because of this interest, many teachers are trying to provide more and more occasions for writers to receive responses to their drafts, responses not just from the teacher but from other students as well.

Two Sets of Assumptions

This practice is justified by assumptions that seem so compelling that it is hard to imagine a set of assumptions that would argue against

221

providing a variety of responses to students' writing. Yet these other assumptions do exist. Consider the following comments made by a student while we were having a conference about an early draft of his essay. At several points during the conference, this student asked me whether he was "on the right track" with his essay. Near the end of the conference, he told me that he had come to value the chance to hear his teacher's opinion of an early draft of his writing:

> I had a teacher in high school that did that [reviewed early drafts]. Yeah, a 10th grade teacher. If the paper was due on Tuesday, you could bring it on Monday . . . and she'd look it over and tell you what was wrong. 'Cause basically she graded on grammar. She didn't really grade on content. And so she circled the mistakes and let you take it away and correct it. And if she didn't catch a mistake [in the early draft] and you could show her the old copy and your new copy where it was the same mistake, she'd say "Okay, you got me. It was my fault. I didn't show you the mistake."

From the perspective of many teachers, this way of dealing with student writing may seem questionable. But from a different perspective—one I suspect that many students may share—there may be several reasons for seeing the teacher's reported actions as understandable, even desirable. For one thing, the teacher's manner of providing a response would appear to simplify and clarify the writer's task. This sort of response requires the student to worry about the judgments of only one other person, the teacher. In addition, the student can assume that the teacher's comments are highly authoritative, reflecting a level of knowledge and expertise that does not allow substantial disagreement. Thus the student does not have to grapple with the uncertainty that is inevitable if there can be legitimately conflicting judgments about the form or content of the student's text.

Beyond providing the appearance of simplicity and clarity, the teacher's way of responding could be seen as having two additional virtues. For one thing, it is likely that this sort of response will seem very familiar to students. Despite current theory and research in composition, many students still find their teachers adopting the role of "teacher as examiner" and, consequently, evaluating students' writing by comparing the knowledge and conclusions of the student with knowledge and conclusions which the teacher developed prior to reading the student's work. Furthermore, this type of response may be quite acceptable to students; it may parallel their assumptions about knowledge and the role of teachers. A rather extreme form of these assumptions appears in an anecdote told by a colleague who was teaching an undergraduate composition course at the university where I teach. One of his students sought out my colleague during office hours and asked exactly what he would have to do in order to make A's on the essays that would be assigned during the remainder of the semester. When my colleague tried to indicate the difficulty of providing a succinct yet comprehensive answer to this question, the student was distressed: "He looked at me as though I was either a fool or a knave—a fool because I couldn't answer a basic question about my subject matter or, even worse, a knave because I knew the answer and wouldn't tell him."

My colleague's experience parallels William Perry's (1970) finding that undergraduates at Harvard were likely to begin their college careers with relatively little tolerance for uncertainty or ambiguity. They tended to make several related assumptions: that it was possible to know with certainty what was true or real, at least in an academic subject; that their teachers' primary responsibility was to impart this knowledge; and that a student's role was to acquire this knowledge. Early in their college careers, Perry reports, students might come to see that some teachers were not living up to their responsibility. But even when they encountered uncertainty or ambiguity in their college courses, students were likely to attribute those experiences to a teacher's ineptitude or a teacher's attempt to help students learn to "find the right answer on our own" (69). It was relatively late in their college careers when students came to think that reasonable people might legitimately have conflicting views of an experience and that knowledge was limited and subject to continual revision.

In trying to explain the attractiveness of the tenth-grade teacher's way of responding to students' writing, I have not been trying to justify it. But I have been trying to make sure we do not dismiss this teacher as a straw figure. I disagree with the teacher's practice and the assumptions that appear to underlie that practice. But I have to acknowledge that this practice and these assumptions constitute forces to be reckoned with. The experience reported by my composition student may epitomize a significant portion of students' prior experiences in writing; it may constitute a familiar, attractive set of rules by which the game is played.

In an effort to change the rules that most of my undergraduate students seem to be accustomed to, I have drawn upon assumptions that are widely discussed in the field of composition studies but that contradict views implicit in the student anecdote I have been discussing. One basic assumption is that knowledge—a teacher's as well as a student's—is more contingent and uncertain than the student's anecdote suggests. As scholars in a number of fields have argued, our knowledge is constrained by the perspectives from which we examine any body of information. Our process of observing or reading is not simply a passive recording of what is "out there," but, rather, is a complex interpretive process that is profoundly influenced by our values, needs, past experiences, and even, as Stanley Fish (1980) has pointed out, our membership in a particular social group. Furthermore, our knowledge is subject to continual analysis and change. This change may entail a relatively limited revision of existing knowledge or it may entail the profound revolution that Thomas Kuhn (1962) has referred to as a paradigm shift.

A second assumption is that the process of writing is often a social process, especially when that process involves examining information and formulating assertions. One part of this social process is identifying and trying to accommodate the needs and interests of the person or group of people that comprise a writer's audience. As rhetoricians have long argued, the effort to understand one's audience and to determine the ethos one wishes to present to that audience can shape the style, organization, and content of one's writing. Other parts of the social process may or may not include the readers for whom a document is primarily intended. But they do require writers to engage in a variety of social interactions—ranging from informal conversations to formal document reviews—that accomplish one or both of the following goals: informing writers' conceptions of their audiences and shaping both the form and substance of their writing. Thus texts do not evolve in a vacuum. And if writers are to understand what they want to say and what their texts mean, they need to understand how others respond to those texts. This process of social meaning-making is especially important given the preceding assumption about the limitations of our knowledge. As we understand how others perceive our texts or the subjects we are writing about, we may not arrive at conclusions that are absolute and unchangeable. But we can expand and refine our perspectives, ultimately increasing the explanatory power of our ideas.

Procedures for Providing and Assessing Responses

On the basis of the preceding assumptions about the limitations of our knowledge and about the social aspects of the composing process, I design my undergraduate composition courses so that students, usually working in groups of two to four persons, regularly review early drafts of their classmates' papers. In an assignment near the end of the semester, the draft/response process is tied in with work on oral presentations. For this assignment, students are to do the following: (1) identify a campus problem that is significant and challenging without being so complex as to defy solution; (2) identify a person on campus who is in a position to make changes that would help solve the problem; (3) try to convince this person that the problem is, in fact, worthy of some action; and (4) pose a practical solution to the problem. Prior to writing their final drafts, students discuss early drafts in small groups and then make formal oral presentations to the class. At all points in the composing process, but particularly during the oral presentations, the class is asked to try to raise the questions or objections that would likely be raised by the writers' intended readers.

In having students do this work, I hope to accomplish two goals that derive from the basic assumptions mentioned earlier. Assuming that knowledge is tentative and limited, I want students to demonstrate some responsible ways of dealing with uncertainty. More specifically, I want them to display strategies that enable them to assess critics' comments without comparing either their work or critics' comments with some absolutely reliable body of knowledge that is assumed to exist independently of writer and critic. On the assumption that writing is a social process, I want students to consider others' perspectives on their work and also to make decisions on the basis of the ethos they wish to project and the characteristics of the audience they are addressing.

Near the end of a recent semester, I attempted to find out whether these objectives were being met and to answer the central question of this article: How do student writers respond to responses from their peers? More specifically, I wanted to know: How do students assess peer responses that may reflect varying degrees of authority and perceptiveness? Are they willing to use these responses as a basis for revising their writing? Do their assessments reflect reasoning that is consistent with my goals in asking students to respond to each other's writing?

As a means of answering these questions, I asked students to allow me to tape-record individual conferences in which students assessed their critics' comments prior to writing their final drafts. Before coming to these conferences, students were to categorize those comments, identifying three or four that seemed especially helpful and another three or four that seemed especially unhelpful. During the conference, students explained to me why they found specific comments helpful or unhelpful. In all cases, I tried hard not to express or imply my own judgments about a given comment but rather to encourage students to explain the reasoning that underlay their judgments about each command.

In analyzing interview transcripts, I found that students often spent a good bit of time doing such things as providing background information about their topic or explaining the substance of a classmate's comment. Thus I analyzed only those passages in which students directly addressed this question: Why did you think X's comment was helpful or unhelpful? There were ninety-one such passages, each concerned with a different response from a reader of the essay. Of those passages, eighty are subsumed by the five categories mentioned in the text of this essay. Five passages referred to issues that seemed completely idiosyncratic; each of them was made by only one student, and none of these issues seemed related to issues raised by any other student.

Responding to Responses

There were occasions when students went to extremes in responding to their classmates' comments. One student, for example, was a bit intransigent about one passage in his next-to-last draft: "The last time [on a previous draft] I said I'm really right and I *still* say I'm right." And another student seemed almost too willing to accept criticism of a particular passage: "I don't know where I fell down in that area, but it seems from their comments that I need to make [his argument] more clear." When I deliberately raised the possibility that his critics' comments might be "wrong," the student replied, "They could be, but I need to look at my paper and make sure [the comments are] wrong before I go away and throw them out as being no good." Such extremes as these, however, were quite rare. By and large students had rather carefully reasoned explanations as to whether or not they found a given comment helpful.

Strategies for Analyzing Criticism

As they discussed their classmates' criticisms of their writing, students seemed to be concerned with five basic issues:

- Whether the critic's (or the writer's) knowledge of the subject was factually *accurate and complete*;
- Whether a comment was *consistent with the writer's worldview,* that is, the writer's perception of how things ought to be;

- Whether a comment could be verified by the *writer's own re-reading* of his/her text;
- Whether a comment was *consistent with the writer's knowledge of him/herself*;
- Whether the comment seemed *appropriate*, given the ethos the writer wanted to create or the writer's understanding of his/her audience.

None of these issues was raised explicitly by the students. That is, for example, none of the students came right out and said, "Well, when you get a comment, you have to think about whether your statements are factually accurate and complete." Rather, the underlined phrases represent categories in which specific statements can be placed. Because these types of statements occurred repeatedly, I assume they represent strategies for assessing comments, procedures that can be repeated in a variety of contexts.

Accuracy and Completeness

Seven of the students were concerned with the accuracy and completeness of their own or a critic's information. For three of these students, this was a major concern; they raised this issue in at least one-third of their comments. Thus this issue appears in 15 percent of the total number of comments made by all students. This issue was particularly evident in students' willingness to defer to critics who raised factual questions for which the writers had no answers. In one case, such questions ("They really ragged on me, I mean, they ripped me to shreds [with] questions I couldn't answer. . . .") led a student to abandon one proposed solution, to which she had devoted a good bit of time and energy, and propose an entirely deferent solution. Other instances were less dramatic, leading only to changes in wording or to addition or deletion of information in specific passages.

Students were especially likely to reject classmates' comments when they could claim that those comments were based on faulty knowledge. For example, when one student proposed a solution to what she felt was an inequitable meal plan in one of the dormitories, a classmate had asked why a dissatisfied student could not simply move to another dormitory. The writer's comment to me was, "You can't do that because there is no space in the other dorms. [The critic] apparently lives off campus. . . ." Another writer proposed a procedure that would improve the campus mail room's delivery of express mail and packages. When a critic suggested that the problem might be found in the mail room's record-keeping procedures, the writer noted, "What this person didn't know is that we already . . . keep records of all the packages that come in, all the packages that [are picked up], and all the packages that stay in the mail room." In other words, the critic's suggestion simply duplicated a practice that, according to the writer, already existed.

Writers' Worldview

In the preceding section, claims about dormitory space or mail room record keeping might reflect a writer's personal knowledge. But at least they were assertions of fact that could be easily verified by another observer. Other assertions, however, were not nearly so verifiable. These assertions, made by thirteen students and accounting for 20 percent of the total number of comments, seemed to be based on writers' personal perceptions of how things should be. One student proposed a program that would lead to more regular maintenance and repair of the asphalt surface in a campus parking lot. When classmates suggested that it might be difficult to find additional personnel to carry out the maintenance and to provide these personnel with appropriate training and equipment, the writer dismissed their concern as "irrelevant." He contended that "the people I'm talking to, that's their *job*, maintenance and repair[ing] things. . . . The people that are there really know how to repair it and they do have the equipment, too. . . ." When pressed as to the basis for his certainty about the ability of maintenance to perform the solution he set up, he admitted having no direct information about the situation but reiterated that his solution was feasible because "that's their job," the clear assumption being that people who are assigned what the student saw as a straightforward, well-defined task should be able to perform it. A similar assumption appeared in the reasoning of the student who wanted to improve the campus mail room's delivery of packages. When someone objected to his proposal for having work-study students deliver packages, he dismissed the criticism: "Students delivering these packages, since they're working for the mail room, you assume they have some sort of a responsibility to do the job and not shirk off during their duty. So they wouldn't be stopping in the Union [or] dropping packages."

Both students' arguments are attractive. It would be nice to believe that things operated as they described. Further, one can think of instances that are consistent with the writer's assertions. There are times when the campus maintenance department has enough trained personnel and equipment to make exactly the repairs one hopes for, and there are student workers whose sense of responsibility lets one rely upon them absolutely. But the claims are troublesome for two reasons:

1. Although stated as assertions of fact, they are, instead, assertions of value; things ought to work as the students describe.
2. They reflect only students' perceptions of how things are/ought to be; students never raised the issue of whether the intended reader might share those perceptions.

Writers' Re-reading of Their Texts

In the preceding examples, writers assessed their classmates' criticisms by comparing those criticisms to the writers' knowledge and beliefs. In other cases, eleven students (in 20 percent of the total number of comments) evaluated critics' claims by comparing those claims against the writers' experience of re-reading their own texts. One student, for example, said he had come to agree with the claim that one passage was not as clear as it should have been: "Well, just going back and reading it after being away from it a while it just, it takes a couple of times [re-readings] before . . . the meaning that I wanted originally sinks in." Another student came to agree with his critics' view that his paper was disorganized: "Well, when I read the comment and then looked back at the paper . . . I saw how [two ideas] were separate [and how one idea] doesn't fit because it has no connection." In making such comments as these, students did not elaborate on the basis for their conclusion. Their tone of voice and their not volunteering elaboration suggested to me that their conclusions struck them as obvious. Assessing criticism of a passage is rather like the process of understanding a *New Yorker* cartoon: you look at it and either you get the point or you don't. Explanation is either tedious, unnecessary, or impossible.

Writers' Self-Knowledge

Another form of assessment, one that occurred rather infrequently, was a comparison of critics' statements to the writer's knowledge of him/herself. It appeared only once in the comments of each of four students. One student remarked that her classmates thought that her writing displayed an inappropriately angry and antagonistic persona. She acknowledged that "I kind of knew it . . . like, I had a feeling that [a more reasonable persona] wasn't going to come across." She confirmed this intuition in part by noting that several people had voiced the same criticism, and in part by acknowledging something that she felt was true of herself. After pointing out several passages where her persona seemed to change from dispassionate and reasonable to angry, she remarked, "I think it's the latter voice that is really me." She was, she remarked, genuinely upset about the situation she was writing about.

Two other students verified their critics' statements by referring to their knowledge of their personalties or to their tendencies as writers. One student accepted the criticism that his writing was disorganized: "When I was writing, I was sort of speaking it out in my head, and I have a tendency to wander [away from the point at hand]." Another student grudgingly accepted the claim that his writing seemed dogmatic: "It's one of the problems I have a lot. It's like I'm right and other people aren't. I try not to do that, and I really get upset with myself when I do." A fourth student accepted a critic's claim because it was consistent with his own prior experiences. Annoyed about the difficulty of finding campus laundry facilities where machines were in working order, the student at first ascribed the problem to inadequate maintenance. But classmates pointed out that a more likely cause was students' tampering with the machines so as to make them operate for free. The student said he thought this view was better than his original view because, he said, "A lot of people do that. . . . my brother does it. . . . I did it last year. For a while after I ran out of [laundry machine tokens]."

Appropriateness for Ethos and/or Audience

References to voice or audience appear in the comments of all but three students and appear in approximately one-half of the total number of all comments. Occasionally students referred solely to ethos. One student, for example, was unwilling to accept a suggestion from a classmate because he felt the suggestion would make her sound "whiny." Somewhat more frequently students referred to the audience's knowledge; they accepted a comment because they felt it pointed to relevant information that their audience might lack, or they rejected a comment because they felt it would lead them to refer unnecessarily to information their audience already possessed.

Most frequently, students referred to the response they anticipated from their audience. In some instances students wanted to preempt confusion or misinterpretation. For example, the student who was concerned about campus laundry facilities accepted a classmate's suggestion that he make one passage "more forceful." The student's reason was that, if he did not do so, the reader might "think I was just complaining, [that] it was just my problem" and not a problem that affected lots of students. In other instances, students seemed to feel that their intended audience deserved a certain amount of deference because of the audience's age and status. One student, for example, agreed with her classmates' view that she needed to tone down her anger a bit: "Well, if I go into the administrators and say 'I'm mad,' they're gonna say 'Too bad.'" Another student was not concerned with a critic's view that his voice sounded "too removed": "I don't think I should go overboard with being emotional about the problem, especially to a person who is director of security and transportation . . . because I think he would just dismiss it quickly. . . . He's just gonna say 'I don't want to deal with this.'" Similarly another student rejected a critic's suggestion to make his voice "more forceful" because "the audience might feel that I'm accusing them, that it's their fault that this is a problem and that they should be doing something that they aren't."

Much less frequently (in only two instances) students explicitly raised the issue of their status in relation to their audience's status. One student wanted his audience to realize that his work was "not just a paper I wrote for a class."

Another student was afraid that his status as a student might undercut his authority to make certain kinds of claims; he was afraid that his readers "might get a little offended. 'How do you know so much about our system? How do you know there's money we can move around [to support the student's proposed solution]? You sound very sure of yourself.'"

Good News, Bad News, and Unanswered Questions

This reference to feeling "sure of yourself" touches upon the successes of the course and also upon two apparent problems. To begin with good news, it became clear that most of the students in this class were able to function reasonably well when confronted with a wide range of responses to their writing. Students were able to identify points in their essays where classmates' comments led them to explore their topic more thoroughly or to modify their style so as to create a voice that would be appropriate for their intended reader. Furthermore, all but two of the twenty-two students demonstrated that their assessments were not completely idiosyncratic or random.[1] Rather, those assessments showed students making reasoned judgments by repeatedly making statements that focused on a limited number of issues. In effect, most of the students seemed to have strategies for assessing comments on their writing, strategies that students could conceivably rely upon in a variety of situations where they had to form conclusions about the validity and usefulness of diverse comments on their writing.

In one respect, students' use of these strategies pleases me a great deal. I like to think that my composition course allows students to make use of or to develop ways of thinking that have some applicability beyond my specific course. Unfortunately, these strategies imply a view of knowledge that is inconsistent with one of the basic assumptions of the course—the assumption that knowledge is contingent, that information can be viewed from multiple perspectives, each of which influences the "meaning" of that information. Deprived of the authority of a teacher, these students invoked the authority of their personal experiences, perceptions, and interpretations. They were willing to admit that they might have overlooked some factual detail. But they never indicated that reasonable people—either classmates or the intended reader—might have quite different interpretations of a given aspect of the subject they were dealing with.

A closely related problem is that although students referred to their audience's knowledge about a given subject, those references focused only on the extent to which the audience possessed or lacked information known to the writer. The students never mentioned the possibility that the audience might possess information that contradicted or outweighed the information presented by the student; nor did the students mention the possibility that the audience's perspective might lead to an interpretation of a fact that differed substantially from the student's interpretation.

Perhaps inevitably, this analysis of student performance raises more questions than it answers.

1. How do these students' strategies compare with the strategies of more experienced writers?

- It seems reasonable to assume that any writer might assess new information by comparing it with his or her existing personal knowledge. (See the discussion of this point in Young, Becker, and Pike 1970, 157–59). However, there is also reason to think that experienced writers may be very much aware of the perspectives of other people in the social or institutional context in which they write (for example, Odell 1985). Thus it seems important to find out the extent to which (and the circumstances in which) experienced writers assess comments by referring to something other than to their individual perceptions, etc. For instance, we need to know whether (and when) these writers refer to differing world-views or to knowledge that is consciously shared by other members of a social/institutional group.

2. To what extent can students' responses to responses reflect the instruction they received in the course?

• Early in the semester we spent some time examining data from different perspectives. Perhaps we should have done more of this work or perhaps I should have devised class activities that would ask students to adopt different perspectives in examining information pertaining to the problems they wished to solve. Would this sort of instruction have influenced the view of knowledge displayed in students' assessment of their classmates' responses? Indeed, is it possible for any single course to have much influence on students' view of knowledge?

3. To what extent do students' comments reflect their level of cognitive development?

• Most of these students were freshmen and sophomores. Is it likely that as seniors in an advanced writing course (for example, my university's Technical and Professional Writing course) these students would have had different ways of assessing their peers' criticisms?

4. In what ways is the work of these students' comparable to that of students in different types of schools?

• Students in my class were attending a fairly selective technological university at which approximately 70 percent of the undergraduates plan to be engineers. My work with these undergraduates over the past six years suggests to me that most of them accept the implications of the motto on the university seal: "Knowledge and thoroughness." In what ways are the strategies of these students similar to or different from strategies displayed by students in a liberal arts college, a state university, or a community college?

One might easily expand this list of questions to consider the ways subject matter, patterns of classroom interaction, or familiarity with audience might influence students' work. For those of us who are concerned with students' ways of responding to peer response, the important thing is to realize that these are the kinds of questions we need to be asking. The answers will help us continue to reform our own understanding of what is—and what should be—happening in our classrooms, as our students grow in their ability to deal responsibly with uncertainty.

Notes

1. One of these two students spent most of the conference talking about the difficulty of thinking of ways to revise his writing. The other student spent his conference time trying to think of ways to deal with a unique difficulty: approximately one week before his paper was to be completed, he discovered that someone else had solved the problem he was writing about.

Works Cited

Fish, Stanley. *Is There a Text in This Class?* Cambridge, Mass.: Harvard University Press, 1980.

Kuhn, Thomas S. *The Structure of Scientific Revolutions.* Chicago: University of Chicago Press, 1962.

Odell, Lee. "Beyond the Text: Relations between Writing and Social Context." In *Writing in Non-Academic Settings,* edited by Lee Odell and Dixie Goswami, 249–80. New York: Guilford, 1985.

Perry, William G. *Forms of Intellectual and Ethical Development in the College Years.* New York: Holt, Rinehart and Winston, 1970.

Young, Richard E., Alton Becker, and Kenneth L. Pike. *Rhetoric: Discovery and Change.* New York: Harcourt, Brace and World, 1970.

Appendix

Each contributor to this volume received the following guidelines explaining our purpose:

> We are soliciting a deliberately diverse set of accounts from experts about processes involved in reading student papers. These accounts will, we believe, move composition and literacy studies in new directions. In the last decade, teachers/theorists have discussed ways to evaluate and respond to student papers. Now the discussion, in the context of current theories of communication, leads us toward an awareness of the interpretive issues involved in reading student papers. The uniqueness of student writing as a text and the peculiar writer-reader-text relationship that arises from interaction with the student text are phenomena which deserve our critical attention.
>
> The objective of the volume is to present teachers' rigorous, personal descriptions of and reflections on how they *read* student writing. Therefore, a literal description of how a teacher decodes or grades/responds to student writing is of interest only as it is a part of the entire transaction of reading a student paper.
>
> Your own idea of what reading involves will guide you as you draft your essay. Consider the interpretive assumptions you bring to a piece of student writing—the technical and ethical tasks/complexities (perplexities!) associated with your reading, given the total hermeneutical situation, or conditions of interpretation. What does it mean and feel like to read student texts? What are the preconceptions, routines, constraints, and joys?
>
> Your account may be concurrent (you may want to write it as you are actually reading student papers), retrospective, or both. You may want to focus on a specific reading experience or refer to your habitual experiences, or both.
>
> While we expect to find diversity in accounts, we do ask that each of you do two things:
>
> 1. Deal in a concrete way with real student writing by reference, quotation, or excerpt.

2. Convey the conceptual framework that bears on your reading. If (as is suggested by a couple of abstracts we've received) you read student papers in workshop situations, still we ask that you begin by explaining the way in which you as an individual read, working outward from there.

A reader of the collection, whether a theorist or a writing teacher, should find in each essay both the description of the experience of reading student writing and reflections on that experience. Reflections on the volume itself will, we hope, open new areas for all of us to explore.

In order to ensure that many perspectives are represented, we anticipate that the average length of essays will be fifteen manuscript pages. NCTE requires the use of the *Chicago Manual of Style* format.

Editors

Bruce Lawson is assistant professor of English at the University of Texas at El Paso. He received his Ph.D. in rhetoric, literature, and linguistics from the University of Southern California. In addition to his involvement in the composition program at UTEP, Lawson teaches undergraduate and graduate courses in the English Renaissance. His special interest is the political rhetoric and iconography of the English Commonwealth.

Susan Sterr Ryan teaches composition, reading, and literature at Santa Monica College in Santa Monica, California. She studied rhetoric, literature, and linguistics at New Mexico State University and the University of Southern California, where she also served on the editorial board of *The Writing Instructor.* In twelve years of teaching high school and college, she has developed special interest in adult education and multicultural education.

W. Ross Winterowd founded and is currently director of the graduate program in rhetoric, linguistics, and literature at the University of Southern California at Los Angeles. His most recent books are *The Culture and Politics of Literacy* (Oxford University Press) and *The Rhetoric of the "Other" Literature* (Southern Illinois University Press). He is currently working on an epistemological history of composition/rhetoric, as one of the humanities, from the German idealists to the present.

Contributors

James S. Baumlin is associate professor of English at Southwest Missouri State University in Springfield, Missouri. He received his Ph.D. from Brown University, specializing in Renaissance literature and the history of rhetoric. His critical essays have appeared in such journals as *Texas Studies in Language and Literature, College Literature,* and*Explorations in Renaissance Culture.* Essays coauthored with Tita French Baumlin have appeared in *College English, CEA Critic,* and *Freshman English News;* he is currently coediting, with Tita French Baumlin and Winifred B. Horner, *Ethos: New Essays in Rhetorical and Literary Theory,* for Southern Methodist University Press.

Tita French Baumlin, assistant professor at Southwest Missouri State University in Springfield, Missouri, received her Ph.D. from Texas Christian University, specializing in both British Renaissance literature and rhetorical theory-composition. Her essays have appeared in such journals as *Studies in English Literature, Papers on Language and Literature, Renascence, Explorations in Renaissance Culture,* and *Rhetoric Review;* articles coauthored with James S. Baumlin have appeared in *College English, CEA Critic,* and *Freshman English News;* they are currently coediting, along with Winifred B. Horner, *Ethos: New Essays in Rhetorical and Literary Theory,* for Southern Methodist University Press.

Charles Bazerman is professor of English at Baruch College, CUNY. He earned a B.A. from Cornell University and an M.A. and Ph.D. from Brandeis University. He has chaired the Baruch composition committee since 1976 and acted as chair of the CUNY Association of Writing Supervisors. Recently, he spent a year at the National University of Singapore designing a writing program. In addition to publishing several composition textbooks and writing handbooks, Bazerman has extended his textual interests into the field of science in his book, *Shaping Written Knowledge: Studies in the Genre and Activity of the Experimental Article in Science,* and in his present research into scientific phenomena of the seventeenth and eighteenth centuries. He is particularly concerned with social forces in written language.

Richard Beach is professor of English education at the University of Minnesota, and has acted as chair of the NCTE Assembly on Research, and secretary of the Conference on English Education. He earned his B.A. at Wesleyan University, his M.A. at Trinity College, and the Ph.D. at the University of

Illinois. Beach is presently coediting *Becoming Readers and Writers during Adolescence and Adulthood* and coauthoring *Teaching Literature in the Secondary School*. He is interested in researching the uses of prior literary experiences and autobiographical responses in interpreting literary texts.

Jim W. Corder took the Ph.D. at the University of Oklahoma in 1958. He joined the faculty of Texas Christian University in the same year and has been there ever since. He was promoted to full professor in 1966. He has served as chairman of the Department of English, dean of the College of Arts and Sciences, and associate vice chancellor. He is the author of *Lost in West Texas* and *Chronicle of a Small Town,* as well as *Contemporary Writing* and other composition textbooks and various papers on rhetoric and composition.

Sharon Crowley, professor of English at Northern Arizona University, has made significant contributions to the fields of composition theory and the history of rhetoric through her many publications and participation on the board of *Pre-Text*. Currently Crowley is working on a book which tries to adapt post-modern theories of discourse to composition pedagogy. Also in the works are an introduction to deconstruction for teachers, and a textbook, *Reclaiming Authority: Classical Rhetoric and Contemporary Writers*.

Lisa S. Ede is associate professor of English and director of the Communication Skills Center at Oregon State University. She received her Ph.D. from Ohio State University. Ede has published widely in composition and rhetoric and collaborative writing and received many honors, including an NEH Fellowship and the MLA Mina P. Shaughnessey Prize (1985). She also finds time to serve on the editorial boards of *Pre-Text* and *The Journal of Basic Writing*.

Elizabeth A. Flynn is associate professor of reading and composition and director of the Institute for Research on Language and Learning at Michigan Technological University. She is particularly interested in feminist criticism and coedited *Gender and Reading: Essays on Readers, Texts, and Contexts*. Flynn has also published articles and chapters on rhetorical theory and interdisciplinary writing. She edits *Reader: Essays in Reader-Oriented Theory, Criticism, and Pedagogy,* and is currently doing a study of Virginia Woolf's reading process.

John F. Flynn received his Ph.D. from Ohio State University and was German Academic Exchange Fellow at the Universität Düsseldorf. He has a dual role at Michigan Technological University as assistant professor in the Humanities Department and as assistant professor of technical writing and speech in the Department of Chemical Engineering. Flynn is interested in western European intellectual history and particularly in the history of science and philosophy of technology.

Margaret Himley is assistant professor in the English Department and writing program at Syracuse University. She is presently involved in designing and institutionalizing a series of writing studies across all four years of undergraduate experience, which introduces students to the many literacy practices that constitute the academy in general and their majors in particular. Himley is also working on *Shared Territory*, a book-length project which explores the theoretical and methodological possibilities of a Bakhtinian or dialogic approach to early written language development.

Norm Katz earned his Ed.M. and Ed.D. from Harvard University, where he now teaches in the expository writing program. In addition to university teaching, he has, in his own words, "taught every grade between fourth and twelfth over a period of twenty years." Katz is currently interested in interdisciplinary writing, particularly in the field of economics, and has recently taught a successful experimental course in writing for economics students.

Stephen B. Kucer is assistant professor of curriculum, teaching, and special education at the University of Southern California at Los Angeles, where he also directs the reading and writing specialization in the Graduate School of Education. Recipient of the NCTE Promising Researcher Award, Kucer has published articles and chapters on reading and writing connections and integrated literacy curricula. He is currently interested in examining the parallel role of revision in reading and writing, and is doing classroom- based research on integrated literacy curricula.

Janice M. Lauer is professor of English and director of the graduate program in rhetoric and composition at Purdue University. She is coauthor of *Four Worlds of Writing* (2nd ed., 1985) with G. Montague, A. Lunsford, and J. Emig, and *Composition Research: Empirical Designs* (1988) with W. Asher. An active participant in the profession, she has chaired the College Section of NCTE and served on the board of directors of the Rhetoric Society of America, as well as on the executive committees of CCCC and of the MLA discussion group on the History and Theory of Rhetoric. For the past twelve years Lauer has directed the Purdue Summer Rhetoric Program.

Patricia Y. Murray is director of composition at De Paul University and teaches freshman writing, technical writing, advanced composition, and graduate courses in composition theory and stylistics. She received her Ph.D. in rhetoric, linguistics, and literature from the University of Southern California and is coauthor with W. Ross Winterowd of a textbook series, *English Language and Skills*, for secondary students. Currently, she is developing a Master's Degree program in composition which emphasizes writing in the professions. She has a particular interest in pedagogy that integrates reading, writing, and thinking at both high school and college levels.

Lee Odell is professor of English in the Department of Language, Literature and Communication at Rensselaer Polytechnic Institute. In addition to teaching at the university level, Odell has taught junior and senior high school, and his interests in writing across the curriculum extend from the elementary to the college classroom. He is particularly interested in the ways in which writing and thinking relate to the interpersonal contexts of the classroom and to the goals of teachers in different subject areas.

Anthony Petrosky, a professor at the University of Pittsburgh, holds a joint appointment in English and education. Along with David Bartholomae, he is the coauthor of *Facts, Artifacts, and Counterfacts* and *Ways of Reading.* Petrosky's first book of poems, *Jurgis Petraskas,* received the Walt Whitman Award from the Academy of American Poets and a Notable Book Award from the American Library Association. He has recently completed a second collection of poems, *The Man Who Looked Like My Father.*

Tilly Warnock is assistant professor of English at the University of Wyoming, where she has directed various activities, including the university's writing center, the statewide Humanities Leadership Project, the Wyoming Writing Project, and the Wyoming Conference on Rhetoric and Composition. At present, Warnock is writing a composition textbook for Scott-Foresman and a book-length study of Kenneth Burke's *Rhetoric of the Symbol.* In addition to all of these activities, she writes poetry and fiction.

James Thomas Zebroski is assistant professor of English and writing at Syracuse University. He has had a variety of teaching experiences at all levels, including public high school, freshman writing at Ohio State University, and undergraduate and graduate courses in writing and humanities at Saint Edward's University in Texas, and Slippery Rock University in Pennsylvania. Zebroski is particularly interested in the psychological theory of Lev Vygotsky and its connections to issues in writing development. He finds that Mikhail Bakhtin's work complements Vygotsky's and has important implications for all of us who teach composition.